Churning of the Heart: Volume One
Introduction to Spiritual Life

Also Available from Sadhana Books

Churning of the Heart: Volume Two
Memories of Maharajshri

Churning of the Heart: Volume Three
Union With the Infinite

Churning of the Heart: Volume One
Introduction to Spiritual Life

❀   ❀   ❀

By Swami Shivom Tirth

SADHANA BOOKS
An Imprint of Berkeley Hills Books
Berkeley, California

Published by Sadhana Books
An Imprint of Berkeley Hills Books
P. O. Box 9877
Berkeley, California 94709
www.berkeleyhills.com

This work was originally published in 1999 by the Devatma Shakti Society, Mumbai, India, in Hindi, with the title *Hriday Manthan*.
© Copyright 2002 Swami Shivom Tirth and Swami Shivmangal Tirth.
All rights reserved, including the right of reproduction, in whole or in part in any form.

Cover design by Elysium, San Francisco.
Cover photo of Swami Vishnu Tirth.
Printed in the United States of America.
Distributed by Publishers Group West.

1 3 5 7 9 10 8 6 4 2

Library of Congress Cataloging-in-Publication Data

(Available from the publisher)

DEDICATION

To the sincere, sadhan-loving, dutiful devotees and spiritual aspirants, gifted with profound sentiments, who have submitted themselves reverentially to their respective gurus.

— Shivom

Contents

Foreword		9
Introduction		11
1.	Arrival at Narayan Kuti: My First Lesson	24
2.	My Initiation and the Science of Shaktipat	31
3.	Sadhan and Sadhana	40
4.	What is Required for Sadhan?	43
5.	The Tea Predicament	64
6.	Guru-Shishya Relationship	69
7.	The Role of an Aspirant	78
8.	Sadhan and Social Conduct	90
9.	Seva Marg: The Path of Service	107
10.	Attachments and Aversions	111
11.	Sevak Dharma: The Essence of Service	117
12.	Controlling the Mind	123
13.	Maharajshri: A Unique Personality	125
14.	On Anger and Aversion	130
15.	A Writer's Pride	137
16.	Tolerance: The Means to Mental Peace	145
17.	On Cheating God	149
18.	Significance of Guru Purnima	152
19.	Lust, Anger and Greed: The Doors to Hell	154
20.	There Is Only One Dharma	156
21.	The Role of Kriyas	159

22. I Cannot Initiate You	161
23. Tolerance	164
24. Your True Self Has Awakened Now	168
25. Surrender to Kriya-Shakti	171
26. The Dilemma of Good and Bad	175
27. Why the Ashram is in Dewas	177
28. The Nature of a Saint	180
29. Maya	183
30. Service and Sadhana	187
31. The Supreme Personality of Maharajshri	188
32. Sadhan and Japa	193
33. The Problem of Maya	196
34. On Nonviolence and Human Birth	199
35. The Problem with Academic Knowledge	202
36. Householders, Aspirants and Sadhan	205
37. Miracles, Politics and Selfishness	208
38. The Stained Jug	214
39. The True Nature of Service	221
40. The Meaning of Sanyas	224
41. Nature as a Role Model	226
42. Shaktipat and Love	230
43. My Bramhacharya Initiation	233
Epilogue	238
Glossary of Terms	251
Index	260
About the Author	271

Foreword

The three-volume series, *Hriday Manthan,* was originally written in Hindi and thus its distribution has been restricted to readers of that language. Hindi readers have appreciated the trilogy greatly. Sadhana Books in Berkeley, California, USA, has accepted the responsibility of bringing the English translation of this series to readers under the title *Churning of the Heart,* for which I am grateful. I hope the English-reading audience will welcome this trilogy with the same enthusiasm and sentiment as the Hindi audience.

The three-part series is a compilation of the instructional speeches and spiritual activities of Swami Vishnu Tirth Maharaj, and the story of a disciple with a defective inner-self. On the one hand, the aspirant is troubled with the desire-filled nature of his heart; on the other, he draws inspiration from the compassionate words and actual incidents and experiences of Maharajshri. The heart of the disciple lies in between and, churned with the rod of instruction and sadhana, keeps rising and falling. The above-mentioned state of contemplation, or churning of the heart, is imperative for every novice sadhak. The series is a presentation of this state.

I hope the English reading audience will like this series and be inspired to churn their hearts through these sermons.

Shivom
Indore (M.P.), India
July 9, 2001

Introduction

I came to Narayan Kuti, in the town of Dewas, in September 1959. At that time Gurudev Swami Vishnu Tirthji Maharaj, now merged with the divine, had gone to Nepal. He returned at the end of November. In January 1961, he initiated me into bramhacharya. As a result, this book has been written with a focus on 1960.

Forty-year-old memories tend to become quite blurred, hence whatever surfaced on the stage of my heart has been compiled here. Maharajshri was a great man who had achieved freedom from attachments. Each and every word uttered by him was like the active form of Goddess Amba. He spoke with his heart and not with his mind or intellect. His speech was always filled with a desire for public welfare.

After such a long interval it is impossible to remember his exact words. Some I have been able to remember. In the case of others I have attempted to capture their essence in these writings to the best of my abilities. When Maharajshri spoke it was as if the words were blossoming in his heart and manifesting through his voice. It is not an easy task to capture in writing the voice of the heart after a gap of forty years. It is only by the grace of Maharajshri that I have been able to attempt this.

The sermons of Maharajshri in this book are basically the churning of my heart. The voice of Maharajshri compels the listener to churn his heart. On listening to Maharajshri's voice, I also was given an opportunity to peer inside my mind and see my faults. His speech had clarity and a feeling for public welfare at the same time, thus each and every word of his would touch the heart. I had very little opportunity to benefit from his sermons that took place in 1960. First and foremost I was unable to attend, and if I attended one, I would carry such a huge burden of ashram duties with me that I could not concentrate on the sermon. But I enjoyed his early morning walk conversations greatly. At that time I was the only person with Maharajshri, and he would also be in a more relaxed state of mind. As a result the spiritual discussions were very good and intense. This book is comprised mainly of Maharajshri's morning walk discourses.

Churning of the Heart has only two characters, Maharajshri and I. But this does not imply that there were no other important persons in the ashram at that time. Before me there were many people worthy of his grace who held important positions in the ashram. As far as initiation was concerned, I was a novice. In fact, not withstanding the grace Maharajshri showered on me, I was only a servant who was of no special importance to other people in the ashram. It was merely by chance that I was assigned the task of accompanying Maharajshri on his morning walks and thus had the opportunity to be in his company. I am writing this book on the basis of those conversations.

In reality this book is the churning of my heart — an opportunity to look within myself in the light of Maharajshri's nectar-filled words. I have written this book more for myself and less for others. The greatest advantage of writing this book was that, even after forty years, just the recollection of the times I spent with Maharajshri create a perennial feeling of being in front of him. Sometimes showering love, scolding at times or explaining something, sometimes serious and on other occasions laughing — in some form or the other he always remained in front of my eyes.

I have a strong desire to document all the memories of my association with Maharajshri. The first book about the memories of 1960 is already in your hands. In the second book I have compiled the memories from that point up until my Sanyas Diksha, my initiation into the life of a renunciate, which took place in 1965, along with the discourses and events of that time. The third volume will cover the events from that date until Maharajshri's union with the infinite in 1969. I am already seventy-six years old. Only Gurudev knows if I will ever complete this work of mine, considering my weak constitution and fading eyesight.

From my conversations with Maharajshri and his company, I became aware of the many difficulties on the path of spirituality and the need to develop a generous and tolerant mind. Swami Gangadhar Tirth Maharaj had made the task easy with the discovery of Shaktipat. But the easy part is restricted only to the awakening of the Shakti. The road ahead is still very arduous. In fact, it becomes more difficult because of the activity of the Shakti. The samskaras, the accumulated seeds of past actions, begin to emerge on the surface of the mind rapidly, thus the emotions and vibrations of the mind take root inside very quickly. The state of mind fluctuates rapidly. The rate at which destiny bears fruit increases at an intense pace. The spiritual aspirant must face the effect of these internal changes in the outside world.

The first difficulty before the spiritual aspirant is that of moving away from the material world. Not only is the world visible outside; it is also present inside in the form of desires arising out of accumulated impressions. We can refer to this as our internal world. Apart from making the being happy and sad, the external world strengthens the internal world. In reality, it is the internal world which makes the mind unstable, gives rise to desire-patterns, and hence is the cause of happiness and sorrow in the external world; it is the internal world, which extends outside. It is so deeply rooted inside in the form of accumulated seeds of one's past actions that it has no desire to leave. There is no freedom from the external world without the removal of this internal world. Frequently a human wrongly believes that he has advanced spiritually, but this illusion is destroyed when he falls down with a crash.

Even though it may seem that the problem is an effect of the outside world, actually it is due to the samskaras, the accumulated impressions, of the internal world, because the external world is simply a shadow of our accumulated impressions. These samskaras take the form of desires and are reflected in the external world. These inner samskaras are responsible for making a person unstable. Due to them the physical body of the individual begins to wander in this world. Attachment is not there in the world; it is in the mind. Our desires and defects, too, are in the mind. They give rise to different kinds of expectations. If we think in terms of such expectations, we ourselves are the problem and the difficulty lies within us. How can it be that the world holds us when it is we ourselves who do not want to let go of this world!

Giving up this world, in other words, sacrificing our attachments in this world, is not easy. This attachment is the root cause of all defects and is due to our ignorance. The issue of ignorance, illusion or a feeling of reality — whatever we may call it — will come to the forefront after we give up our attachments. Ignorance gives birth to ego and from ego arises our attachments. It is extremely difficult to come out of this complication of Maya, illusion. The harder a person tries to break away from it, the more he gets entangled in it. A person does not even realize he is entangled.

From this perspective, an individual becomes entangled in this world because of two things — ego and attachments. These two together create the internal world. These two alone are responsible for giving rise to all defects. An individual goes astray in this world because of these two. The path of spirituality cannot be lit without destroying these two. If this is clearly understood, the role of sadhan, spiritual practices, also becomes clear. But the first task is to destroy our attachments. To destroy attachments, first we have to get rid of our feeling of doership, thin out our destiny.

Once somebody asked Maharajshri the difference between pride and false pride. He replied, "If you have wealth and you are proud of it, then it is pride. But suppose you do not have wealth and are proud of someone else's wealth. That is false pride. If an individual doesn't have strength, but is proud of it, that also is false pride. Everything a human being has acquired in this world is not his, because it can be taken away from him at any time. In spite of this he takes pride in his belongings. This is false. A person has no strength, but he portrays himself as invincible. A person is not intelligent, but believes himself to be the most intelligent person in the world. Without possessing any qualities he behaves as if he is perfect. All this is false pride." Such was Maharajshri's style of thinking.

The chaitanya, the conscious-self, remains active on different planes through the mind and the senses but still remains separate and unaffected by the mind and the body. The body is simply a medium; there is no question of it being active because of its gross nature. It can be compared to a machine, which is the medium of work through which electricity operates. Due to his ego a living being becomes the doer, unable to experience the difference between the chaitanya, the conscious-self and the body. This is called the dormant state of the conscious-self. Even though it is functioning, the conscious-self gets pushed behind and life-force comes to the forefront. Awakening is the state where one begins to experience the separateness between the body and the conscious-self. Then the sense of doership begins to transform into the sense of an observer who sees the conscious-self function through the body and the mind. At this stage, a person's false pride begins to disappear.

In order to reach the awakened state, the soul of the spiritual aspirant may perform various kinds of penance and austerities and pray to God. He may attain different types of miraculous powers, but he will not thereby experience the awakened state. The living being is so strongly attracted to the external world that his mind, his tendencies and his life-force do not wish to become introverted at all. He may undertake many spiritual practices, many rituals and do introspection. But the desired goal is not achieved. How could it be? The impact of these practices is on the mind, which is trying to concentrate. Temporarily the mind does get focused, but restlessness soon overpowers it. Even within the circle of Maya, illusion, the spiritual aspirant rises at times, but eventually he gives up. The opportunity to experience the conscious-self does not arise.

The main reason for this is the inner world, the reservoir of samskaras, the accumulated seeds of past actions. These samskaras take the form of passions and are responsible for the rise of mental modifications according to their own nature. On an individual plane, consciousness flows downwards — in other words, in the direction of the world. The sense organs are always pouncing on worldly pleasures and their fruits. Inspired by the samskaras, the mind is always supporting them. As a result, neither does the world disappear from sight nor can the mind or sense organs become introverted. Even the life-force does not give up its relationship with the world and reverse its outward flow, towards the soul. Neither does the experience of the separateness of the body, mind and conscious-self begin.

The conscious-self is called "consciousness" when it begins to work through the sense organs. The beginning of the experience of the separateness of this consciousness from the body and the mind is an important turning point in sadhan. This is also the beginning of the dissolution of the ego.

The elemental [tattvic] knowledge and the direct experiential knowledge of consciousness, which is called science, is the door to the experience of the all-pervading conscious-self. Without this, neither is the path to destroy the samskaras illuminated, nor is the way to dissolve your ego.

Even after true awakening, the matter of prarabdha — fate or destiny — should be reviewed and understood because it still has to be endured. Although accumulated samskaras can be thinned out by performing actions with the sense of an observer, of non-doership, fate is not going to keep silent without bearing fruit. In Guru Maharajshri's opinion, the only solution to this is to bear the result of one's own actions with patience and happiness. Even without awakening, fate will still rise, but with awakening, this process will be faster. Fate will start yielding results quickly. Thus it is imperative that a sadhak, a spiritual aspirant, be very brave in facing his destiny.

Maharajshri's style of thinking and his explanations of every subject were based on the scriptures, but at the same time they were scientific, and based on personal experience. If he did not have any experience of a particular topic, he would without hesitation mention the scriptures on the basis of which he spoke. He would say that the people who deliver sermons often stretch the subject so much that they themselves get tangled and confused. It thus becomes more difficult for the listener to understand the essence of the sermon. The best way, he believed, is to present the moral of the subject in such a way that it directly enters the heart of the listener. He also used to say that people give fifteen to twenty different meanings of each stanza of the Ramayana and believe they are great intellectuals. However while writing the Ramayana, Tulsidasji had only one meaning and one emotion per stanza in his mind.

Until recently, we believed that the school of thought and principles of the Bhagavad Gita were totally different from Shaktipat. However, when we heard the commentary on the Gita from the divine lips of Guru Maharajshri, our misconception was cleared. Maharajshri used to say, "Not only the Gita, but all religious books have talked about Shaktipat. There is only a difference in words and style." He also considered the Bible to be among these books. It is not necessary that the word, "Shaktipat," be used. The word is not important; what matters are the lessons which are imparted.

It must not be construed from all this that Maharajshri was no more than a great man who spoke eloquently about spirituality and other important matters. Along with his knowledge of scriptures, of business, of day-to-day living and science, he was also well endowed with sadhan, spiritual practices. He had a strong grip on the workings of Shakti. He was capable of blessing and of interrupting its actions, but he never stopped the kriyas [automatic movements caused by Shakti] of any sadhak, even if he was very unhappy with him. He firmly believed that it was the Shakti's responsibility to punish. On the basis of Maharajshri's handwritten diary, I have written about his sadhan and his experiences in the book entitled *Sadhan Diary*.

I remember an incident where a particular gentleman was initiated; he must have been around seventy years of age. He was proficient in *japa*, chanting practices, and had practiced posture stability extensively. He would sit rigidly like a piece of wood and straight like a pole. Maharajshri explained to him that during sadhan the body should be loose, but the man was so habituated to sitting rigidly he was unable to relax. He kept 108 beads in a box. During meditation, he would take the box and place it in front of him. His mantra was quite long. One by one he would pick up the beads, read his mantra and set them down at his side. But his kriyas did not progress. Maharajshri explained to him a number of times that he should sit loosely or Shakti would itself loosen him up, but he did not give up his rigidity.

Three days passed without even the slightest sign of progress. When Maharajshri entered the cave, the man was sitting firmly, engrossed in picking up and setting down his beads. Standing there, Maharajshri watched him for a couple of seconds. At that instant, it seemed as if sparks were flying off Maharajshri's body. His face was serious but calm. He was charged with Shakti, and the moment he placed his hand over the gentleman's head the man screamed loudly. His legs unfolded and straightened out and he began to have intense kriyas. His beads were scattered throughout the cave by his kick and his stiffness was broken.

In the background of Maharajshri's talks there was always the strength of personal spiritual experiences. Every word that was uttered by his divine lips had blossomed in his heart and been purified by his discretion before taking the form of speech. Sweetness in his speech, determination in his mind, a feeling of well-being for the whole world in his heart, and an inquisitive mind, simple and sober, such was his personality. Be he in sadhan or in contact with the outside world, the rope of chaitanya never slipped his hands.

Let me narrate another of my experiences: When Maharajshri came to the Ujjain Mahakaleshwar Temple at four in the morning to attend the aarti, prayers, I was accompanying him. At the time of the aarti, it was blissful everywhere — chanting of mantras, decorations, the sounds of bells, cymbals and drums. There were ashes flying everywhere. I had shut my eyes and was trying to concentrate on Shankar [Lord Shiva]. Even after the prayer was finished my eyes were closed, and while I was still concentrating, I heard a voice from the idol of Shiva, "Why are you concentrating on me? I am leaving now." I opened my eyes and saw that Maharajshri was stepping out of the door.

The scriptures have acknowledged the Guru to be an incarnation of Shankar, but my mind had not reached such a state that it could see Shankar in the Guru. My heart was full of devotion for Guru Maharajji and I believed that he was endowed with all good qualities, but I hadn't yet developed the awareness of godliness in him. This experience, as it were, awoke me from a deep slumber. Various thoughts flashed across my mind like lightning. I decided to speak to Maharajshri about this.

The next day, during our morning walk, I mentioned our visit to the temple and narrated my experience to him. On hearing it, Maharajshri laughed loudly and said, "Our inner feelings, passions and samskaras are the basis of our memories, dreams and experiences. The feeling in your mind towards me has slowly gained strength internally and become ripe. You are totally unaware of these small changes taking place within you. When you found a conducive external environment — the Mahakaleshwar's aarti with its ashes — in that harmonious atmosphere, engrossed in meditation, those harmonious feelings took the form of an idol and manifested themselves in the form of this divine experience. The voice that you heard was also an effect of those emotions. Outside there was only pleasantness, everything else manifested within you.

"According to the scriptures, the Supreme Lord does reside in every being as the Supreme Self. In this way every being can be said to be its manifestation. But as it is hidden behind an illusion, neither can the being itself recognize it, nor can other people see it or its actual cosmic nature. If we think from this point of view, then not only I, but you and all other beings are God; so are the animals and birds. The doctrine of sadhan, spiritual practice, is to see God in ourselves and all other beings. But only he can see God in every being who has first identified him within. Only he who is established within the Supreme Self can see the Supreme Being inside someone else."

I asked Maharajshri, "An element of the Supreme Lord is

there in every being, but is the inert state something different?"

He replied, "The division of inert and conscious is also an illusion of the mind, because inertness is just a specific state of consciousness and hence an image of God. He who sees God in all beings notices the presence of conscious energy in mountains, trees, clouds, waves, etc. This is the ultimate goal of sadhan, which only a rare person can achieve. You experienced that I was God, but if you haven't experienced God within yourself until now, how can you see God within me? Hence your experience was a reflection of your emotion."

The above-mentioned incident has been given in the Introduction and not within the chapters of the book because it took place after 1960. Any other person in Maharajshri's place would have been flattered by this incident. Superficially he might say, "I am a common man. It is because of your devotion that you think I am God." However he would be pleased inside. But Maharajshri's greatness lies in the tactful way in which he explained the incident to me. I am not praising Maharajshri simply because he was my Guru. He was truly praiseworthy.

Maharajshri used to pay full attention to new initiates. He would ask whether they had had lunch, and what arrangements had been made for their lodging and sleeping. If they became sick, he inquired after their medical care. He would make every possible attempt to resolve their problems regarding sadhana with great accuracy and efficiency. He was so kind that he would listen to anyone's woes with tremendous patience and suggest the appropriate remedy. It was his belief that the whole world is troubled with different types of problems and worries. There is so much selfishness around that people want happiness only for themselves, and yet everyone is unhappy. A strange kind of turmoil surrounds us. No one wants to listen to the problems or worries of another. By talking to someone about your sorrows, the mind feels lighter. But who is there to listen? There is only the ascetic to whom you can go and cry. Even though we cannot do anything, the least we can do is listen.

I lived in close proximity to Maharajshri's feet for a continuous span of more than ten years. He gave me many opportunities to serve him and I derived joy from them. I also committed many mistakes because of my impure mind. But Maharajshri always showered love on me. Even his scolding permeated love. He scolded, but he also forgave. This wasn't just with me. Many disciples have enjoyed the love and grace of the Guru. Maharajshri had a very generous and magnanimous heart. Not only did good souls seek shelter in it; even sinners would find solace in it. He would say, "Do not hate sinners, they need your help and kindness. And who is totally free of sins and defects. Don't demoralize the downtrodden, help them rise."

As I said in the beginning, I intend to write a series of three books about Maharajshri. As of now only the year 1960 has come before me, which is presented to you in the form of this book. When the other two parts will be written, and if I will even be able to write them, I cannot say right now. Who knows when the messenger of death will come and grab me!

Today the physical form of Maharajshri is not present amongst us, but the Shakti keeps working directly and indirectly. Even today many sadhaks, spiritual aspirants, have experiences involving Maharajshri. His speech still echoes in many hearts. His sermons are still available for our guidance. Upon manifestation, the Guru-tattva, the power of the Guru, works from within and, when unmanifest, it works by establishing itself in the infinite cosmos.

Finally, with folded hands, I humbly pray at the lotus feet of the divine Guru to shower his grace on all living beings. May he give rise in them to love of God, sense of duty, generosity, forgiveness and tolerance. The beings in this world are extremely worried, tense and ignorant. They cannot be drawn to your lotus feet even if they so desire. They are repeatedly pulled towards the world. Hence, there is no other way for their salvation except by your divine grace. You are infinitely kind and very generous.

Pray forgive us all. Kindly forgive us.

Swami Shivom Tirth
Shri Vishnu Tirth Park
Valley Of Flowers
Pipaliya Rao, Indore (M.P.)

I. Arrival at Narayan Kuti: My First Lesson

The sun had already set by the time I reached the cottage, Narayan Kuti. From a distance, the cottage looked as if all the flowers of marigold and all the xenias of the world had been brought together there. On stepping inside the gates, I felt a divine power cast a spell over me. The sight of the cottage recalled images of the ashrams of the ancient rishis. As I moved ahead with a cloth bag on my shoulder and a wire-strapped tin can in my hand, I saw residents of the ashram. Introducing myself, I said, "I have come from Nangal [a town in the northwestern part of India]. Maharajshri wrote a letter to me, asking me to come here." The answer was, "But Maharajshri has gone to Nepal. He will return in a couple of months." I was slightly disturbed on hearing this.

The ashram was situated in a mountainous region, at the base of a hill. Terraces had been created by cutting into the slope. At the lowest level were a small kitchen and a well. On the level above was Maharajshri's residence. At the other end of that level was a small Shiva temple. On the level above this there was a partially built house. Everything else was flowers. I had a letter of introduction from a gentleman in Nangal and the letter I had received from Maharajshri. I showed them both letters. They read the letter of introduction, but were unable to read Maharajshri's letter as it was in Urdu and none of them read Urdu. But as the letter was written on Maharajshri's letterhead, there was no doubt that the letter was his.

I was asked to stay in the kitchen. At night, lying on my bed, I began to think, "Where have I come from and where have I arrived? Where is the Mandi district of Himachal Pradesh and where is the town of Dewas in Madhya Pradesh!" Then I recalled the people of Himachal Pradesh, their behavior, their eating and drinking habits, their customs, their language, the weather, the tall mountains and the deep valleys, the Sutlej River and the green pastures. "How I used to roam like a free bird. While coming here, I did not have anything with me. I accepted no money from anyone nor did I keep any with me. The train does not know whether a traveler is rich or poor. It treats everyone equally. Without the fare, there is no ticket and without a ticket, travel is not possible. I had finalized my itinerary but how was I to get to Dewas? I did not own the train. Without my saying a word, people gave me forty rupees for my travel expenses." (In those days, it was a large amount.) "In this way, I am sitting in Dewas right now."

When I woke up the next morning, an unexpected incident happened. I was undoubtedly a novice sadhak. The truth is I wasn't even a sadhak; I had a lot of pride. I would get upset with the smallest of things and failed to show the slightest sign of patience. Someone said something that hurt me. It wasn't such a big issue that it couldn't have been ignored, but I felt very angry inside. When such incidents happen, the mind alone knows what it starts thinking: "Have I come to the wrong place? If this continues how will I last until Maharajshri's return?" The place that I felt was divine until yesterday seemed so uncomfortable now. I felt like running away. But what about my initiation? With this thought in mind, I pacified myself.

The truth is this was my first lesson in the ashram: tolerance. I felt that Guru Maharajshri had already started his work as a Guru from Nepal. It was as if he were explaining to me, "You are stepping into the field of spirituality, so get one thing clear: every step is slippery. Every moment there is an obstacle. It is imperative that you tread very carefully. Only a small reason came in front of you and you stumbled." With such thoughts coming to mind, my enthusiasm was renewed and all my sorrows were gone. Once again, my face became cheerful.

Now I began to wonder, since Maharajshri was going to return after a couple of months, how I was going to spend my time until then. If there were a service I could render, then I would do so. When I asked one of the ashramites to give me some work to do, he said, "What work? Just do bhajans [sing devotional songs]." His advice did not appeal to me. Another bramhachari from Garwhal was living in the ashram, waiting for Maharajshri and for initiation. He had quite strong likes and dislikes. When I had a conversation with him, he provoked me. I realized that he would stop doing so only after destroying my mental poise. It was advisable to stay away from him. After that, I avoided conversation with him.

In front of the kitchen, there was a patch of land, unused and quite rocky. I began to remove the rocks by digging them up. After some days most of the rocks were removed and only soil was left behind. It still had rocks in it but it was good enough to grow vegetables. I asked someone to get some vegetable seeds. In a few days the vegetables were in full bloom.

Some people from Dewas had accompanied Maharajshri to Nepal. Maharajshri was going to visit a number of places during his return, but the other travelers from Dewas came home. A couple of them were residents of the ashram. Around the same time the person who was handling purchases for the ashram left for some reason and his responsibilities were passed on to me. I also helped in the cleaning of Maharajshri's cottage. In this way I was being evaluated as a potential ashram resident. After some days the cook also left. I did not know how to cook, but until some other arrangement was made, I was to cook whatever I was able to. A woman used to come to the ashram to clean the utensils. She was absent so often that most of the time, we had to clean the utensils ourselves.

In a way my ashram life had now begun. I had been in a

jungle in Himachal Pradesh, in a shelter with a roof of leaves, no walls, no possessions, one set of clothing on my body and another set being dried. Whenever the mind desired, I would go and sit on the banks of the Sutlej. I had no clear understanding of spiritual practices, and mostly chanted, read and sang devotional songs. I accepted nothing and owned nothing. Now there was a difference. Food was cooked twice a day; there was a house to live and sleep in; tea was served twice a day; there were people to talk to; prayers took place in the temple. My mind wished to fly back to Himachal Pradesh. Wherever even a few people come together, attachments and aversions invariably arise. Except for the constant rhythm of the Sutlej, there had been no one else in Himachal Pradesh with whom to have a conversation. A silent, calm atmosphere. But what about my initiation? My thoughts would stop at this point.

I continued to chant. There was a library, so I would study something or the other and I would also sing devotional songs. I would rarely go and sit with people, but people would come and sit beside me. I had no interest in their conversation but they wanted to talk. Often the subject would be likes and dislikes, or they would talk about themselves, or there would be discussions of politics, or they would start talking ill about someone. There were no polite and sincere spiritual discussions. I would mostly remain quiet and listen. The greatest attraction was the sound of kriyas coming from sadhaks sitting in the cave. There was so much joy in those kriyas and sounds, as if the sadhaks were sitting there not caring about the world. After experiencing such bliss, why did they get mired in the swamp of attachments and aversions upon coming out of the cave?

Finally the time came when Maharajshri was to arrive. With the news of his arrival, signs of change were clearly visible in the atmosphere. Just as a red tinge spreads everywhere in the sky before sunrise, similarly a harmonious atmosphere began to spread throughout the ashram. Spirituality, generosity and tolerance were noticeable in the conversation of people. The subject of attachments and aversions disappeared. Everyone's heart was filled with enthusiasm.

At last the day came when Maharajshri arrived at the ashram. A gentleman was with him to serve and accompany him. I had seen Maharajshri in Gaziabad earlier, and in Nangal I had been in his service for three days, thus he wasn't unknown to me. But on the very first day two incidents occurred that totally shook me up.

Maharajshri called me and asked, "Do you know how to weave a rosary?" On my saying, "Yes," he handed me a broken rosary of Rudraksha and said, "This broke during my travels." I counted the beads and they were all there. "Get a silk thread from the bazaar and repair it."

I took the rosary and tried to figure out a place to keep it safely, because I was sleeping in the kitchen. In one corner of the kitchen was a room occupied by one of the ashramites. I placed the rosary in a bowl at his place of worship in the room and I went to the bazaar to get the silk thread. When I came back the rosary had vanished. I searched everywhere but was unable to find it. This was the first task Maharajshri had assigned to me and I was afraid that I had fouled it up. Because of fear, I was unable to tell Maharajshri. Eventually I mustered up some courage and presented the facts to him. Maharajshri said, "What is there to fear if a rosary is lost? If it is lost so be it. I get a lot of rosaries."

The other incident is as follows: In the evening, the man who had accompanied Maharajshri to Dewas expressed a desire to stroll up the hillside. Maharajshri called me and told me to accompany him, to show him around and to return with him to the ashram. The man and I began to converse while walking and soon reached the hilltop. He asked whether I had any work pending in the ashram. I told him there was a lot of work to be done and I was responsible for some of the ashram chores. He told me to return to the ashram without any hesitation. He said that he would wait there for some time and then return.

When I returned to the ashram, Maharajshri was sitting in the courtyard. He said, "I asked you to bring him back with you. Why did you leave him and come back alone?" I explained that the gentleman had told me to return to the ashram if I had any chores to do and he would return in a short while.

Maharajshri sternly replied, "I told you to return with him. Why did you come back alone? Now go back up the hill and do not come back without him." I again climbed the hill. On reaching the top, the man was nowhere in sight. I thought perhaps he had gone back to the ashram, so I returned. On reaching the ashram, I found out that he wasn't there either. It was getting dark, the evening prayer was going on and Maharajshri was in the temple. When the prayer was over, Maharajshri inquired if the gentleman had returned. I replied that I couldn't find him anywhere on the hilltop. In a dejected tone Maharajshri told me, "You will have to climb the hill again and find him."

As I turned to climb the hill, another person joined me. It was dark now, so we took a flashlight with us. On reaching the top we looked everywhere and called out loudly, but we could not find him. Disappointed, we returned to the ashram. Upon reaching the ashram we saw the gentleman sitting with Maharajshri. He apologized for my going through so much trouble because of him. He had taken another route to visit the city. Both these incidents forced me to reflect deeply.

Every day Maharajshri would take a morning walk and I was assigned the task of accompanying him. During our stroll the following day, he mentioned the incident. "Don't be afraid. Whatever happened yesterday was for your own good. It is your duty to perform the tasks delegated to you with total commitment and steadfastness. You were sent with that gentleman so that you could accompany him back. However you left him alone and came back to the ashram. This was your mistake. As a result you had to climb the hill three times. Now you will never forget this mistake of yours, not for your entire life. If you are cautious henceforth, it will be beneficial for you."

I replied, "I realize my error. I will try not to repeat the same mistake in the future."

Maharajshri said, "The Guru-shishya [disciple] relationship is a very delicate but beneficial one. The Guru considers the disciple like his son and takes him on difficult paths, which the disciple cannot understand easily. So quite often, out of pride, a disciple disobeys his Guru. He ignores the wishes and the command of his Guru. Even if the Guru doesn't tell the disciple about his disrespectful behavior, the disciple is deprived of the possible benefits. For this reason, it is imperative that a disciple surrender completely to his Guru. You had to climb the hill three times to learn this lesson. Now you will never forget this lesson. Only a Guru can understand all the techniques he uses to convey a message to his disciple."

I was overwhelmed with Maharajshri's kindness. I said, "Maharajshri, I couldn't understand this fact. Until now, I had no experience of the Guru-shishya relationship. I did not even feel the necessity of this relationship. Now that I have come under your tutelage, I shall find the way."

2. My Initiation and the Science of Shaktipat

In those days most of the ashramites spoke Marathi. The Indian princely states had only recently dissolved. The official language of the princely state of Dewas had been Marathi. As a result, the dominance of Marathi was still intact there. Most of the visitors to the ashram also conversed in Marathi. I had just come directly from Punjab. I had been living in Himachal only for a short time. I was absolutely unacquainted with Marathi. How was I to understand it? I couldn't understand even one word. When Maharajshri returned from Nepal, I noticed that he spoke very good and fluent Marathi. People would talk amongst themselves and I would simply stare at them. The customs and practices, eating habits, clothing, language — everything was so different from Punjab. Of course, people would try to talk to me in Hindi, but I did not even know how to speak Hindi properly. On listening to my Hindi mixed with Punjabi, people would laugh. But what could be done about that? Slowly I began to understand the languages.

While living in Himachal Pradesh, I had grown accustomed to living without work. On coming to Dewas, I had a great deal of work. Every morning, I would accompany Maharajshri for a walk, then make tea for the ashram, then go to the bazaar for purchasing. In those days Maharajshri had a cataract in his eyes, so I had to read the newspaper to him and then get started on the activities of the ashram. I did not even know how to request initiation. I thought Maharajshri knew I had come for initiation and that was enough. "Whenever he feels it's time," I thought, "he will tell me."

Eventually that day dawned. The bramhachari from Garwhal was also awaiting initiation, and so was a gentleman from

Bombay. Maharajshri told me, "Tomorrow is the initiation for these people. You too, sit down with them." I said "Yes," but did not understand the meaning of "sitting down." When I asked someone I was told, "Tomorrow is your initiation. You also sit down in the cave. Go and get your stuff."

I said, "Stuff? What stuff?" I was completely unaware of such things and utterly ignorant.

He said, "A garland, flowers, fruits, sweets, a coconut, the material for puja and anything else you wish to bring, along with dakshina [a monetary donation]."

Now I realized that I did not even have a single paisa with me. While coming to Dewas, with the couple of rupees remaining from the forty rupees I was given, I had bought a small metal pot for water and a towel. Now where was I to get my offering? Was all this stuff essential for initiation? There was a gentleman who served Maharajshri, whom Maharajshri liked a lot and who also was fond of me. I, in turn, respected him greatly. I always had his support. On speaking to him, he gave me a rupee to go to the bazaar and buy whatever I wished. I went to the bazaar and bought a garland for four annas. With twelve annas left in my hand, I wondered what else to buy. Finally I decided that a garland was good enough and returned the twelve annas to the gentleman. The Garwhali baba gave me two bananas and an apple. My plate was decorated.

The next day, early in the morning, everyone came to the cave as scheduled. The man from Bombay had gathered so much stuff that half the cave was filled with it. The Garwhali bramhachari must have spent around a hundred rupees or so. I was sitting there with a plate containing two bananas and an apple. After the puja, Maharajshri started reciting some shlokas [Sanskrit verses]. Then he placed his hand on the head of each initiate. Even before Maharajshri had returned to his seat, my body leapt three or four feet up in the air with great force and fell down with a big thud. After that, very rapid kriyas [automatic movements] began. My veins tightened. I began to frown, tremble, sweat, cry and shout. After sitting for a while, Maharajshri left, but the intensity of my kriyas showed no signs of diminishing. Gradually all the other people got up and left, but at noon my kriyas still had the same intensity. At times I would start dancing and at other times I would roll on the ground. My eyes wouldn't open. The call for lunch struck my ears, but who wanted to get up? I was experiencing a unique bliss, even as I cried and screamed. The whole cave seemed to be spinning.

Around noon someone brought me outside the cave. I emerged as if I were in a state of intoxication. How could I eat my lunch? I just slumped down. I remembered an incident of the past. There was a babaji, a mendicant, in Nangal. In those days I was working there at the Sanatana Dharma Association Library. One day I met the babaji there. Afterwards he told someone, "That boy is good but his lock is closed, someone needs to open it." Had this closed lock been opened? Was Maharajshri the one who opened the lock?

Then I recalled an article by Swami Ramtirth, where he had written that all the sadhaks of the world are false. The only true sadhak is God alone. At the time, I couldn't understand the essence of that article, but now it seemed as if the mist before my eyes were thinning out. A human has pride, and with this pride he does his sadhana [spiritual practices involving conscious effort], but because it is done with pride, the effort is rendered useless. What is the need of pride in spiritual practices? God is the only one who can make his Shakti [power] turn inward and, through the medium of the mind and the body of the spiritual aspirant, perform spiritual practices for the benefit of the aspirant. God, nevertheless, does not feel proud, does not impose obligations, does not expect praise and does not demand a reward.

The memory of the banks of the Sutlej, in Himachal

Pradesh, came back. Solitude, peace and beauty were there, but I had no idea about these experiences. I began to feel that the joy I had experienced there was merely a perception. Will today's joy also end up being simply my imagination and my perception? I had been hearing that the awakening of the Shakti is very rare. Worshippers and ascetics perform long penance for this in forests, their eyelids droop as they study the exercises, the yogic postures and pranayaam [breath control], but still Shakti is not awakened. Yet all this happened to me in the wink of an eye with such ease. Should one call this fate or a result of Maharajshri's kindness? Possibly both. I was so fortunate.

As I thought about this my pride awakened. Now I could be called a sadhak! But at once my delusion of pride was broken and I became cautious. "What's this? Why this pride? And that, too, for something you haven't done." I began to sob. Possibly this was a kriya, too. This is how a kriya happens. Anywhere, anytime, when you are just sitting. My head bowed down at the feet of Maharajshri. Truly the scriptures and the saints haven't sung the praises of the Guru in vain. Now both the external and internal forms of the Guru were there in front of me. To understand the true nature of a Guru, the blessings of a Guru are essential. One should continue his efforts but acquisition is solely due to grace. I kept thinking about all these things or, rather, all these thoughts arose within me. Associated with these thoughts were knowledge, experience and emotion. Hurrah! Hurrah! O my Gurudev, by receiving your grace, I have been blessed with divine fulfillment!

But suddenly — what happened? Sparks of impurities began to explode inside me. Waves of passion started rising in the deep ocean of my mind. Only a moment ago I was sitting in an ecstatic state, then suddenly — what happened? One moment I would be detached from impurities and observe them, the next moment I would start flowing in the current of my impurities.

For a while I remained in this enigmatic state of attachment and detachment. My mind would fill with sorrow, then a ray of light would burst out. It seemed as if someone were throwing all the dirty things out of the house. But there was so much dirt! How long would he be occupied with this cleaning? I hoped he wouldn't tire out. And again my mind grew calm.

When we went for the next morning walk, Maharajshri initiated the following conversation: "Our lineage began with Swami Gangadhar Tirth Maharaj. A resident of Puri [a town in the state of Orissa], Swamiji was a spiritual aspirant who loved solitude. He thought, 'It's a frighteningly dark age. The wrath of indulgence, pride, selfishness, lust and anger is everywhere. Everyone is in an extremely unstable state of mind. Even if they wish to remember God, they are unable to do so. Hence they are caught in the whirlpool of this ocean of desires. They also do not have any support and, even if they do, it is only imaginary. However, if they somehow get a direct spiritual experience, a strong support will be available to them. Their spiritual practice will progress with its help. I am a sanyasi [renunciate]. I hope to find someone through whom the people can be given this experience.' Finally he found this person in the form of Swami Narayan Tirth Dev Maharaj. Swami Gangadhar Tirth Maharaj's resolve had great power because he did not desire anything for himself, neither wealth nor grandeur nor prestige. This is the nature of a true renunciate. As a result of the strength of Swamiji's resolve, spiritual aspirants initiated in Shaktipat are seen in all parts of India today."

Maharajshri continued. "The inner awakening of the Shakti not only provides support, but also gives strength for action, gives direct experience, places one in the frame of mind of an observer, and purifies the mind. Devotion is impossible without all this. By his divine grace, Swami Gangadhar Tirth Maharaj made arrangements for the well-being of mankind in spite of being detached from worldly activity. From this, one comes to know the great concern he had for the common masses."

Upon hearing this I asked, "Does a renunciate have to refrain from all kinds of action? To run an ashram, give initiation, give sermons and so forth — aren't all these activities for public welfare?"

Maharajshri replied, "There are different categories and different levels of renunciates. One person is slightly detached, another is more so, while a third is totally detached. The more detached a person is, the greater his renunciation.

"Many whom you consider renunciates are not renunciates at all. Desire to have disciples, attachment to the ashram, the desire to succeed, and pride in oratory or writing are typical of a worldly person, not a renunciate. Sanyas [renunciation] is an ashram [the fourth stage of life according to Hindu scriptures] and detachment is a state of mind. Renunciates who are full of pride are not renunciates at all.

"Someone who genuinely has a desire for public welfare, who does not have the feelings of attachment, ambition, love, hate, and so forth, or who has them but has overcome them with discipline, can surely be considered a renunciate. To him who is totally detached, all actions seem to be traps, however pure, sattvic [harmonious] or obliging he might be towards others. Hence he always prefers solitude. Swami Gangadhar Tirth Maharaj was such a great soul, an absolute renunciate. He did not involve himself in anyone's welfare or misfortune, nor did he visit anyone. He was not interested in anything other than spiritual practices. Due to his prarabdha [destiny], Swami Gangadhar Tirth Maharaj had to sustain his body, but while doing so he lived a life full of spirituality."

My next question was, "The Guru blesses the disciple by giving him his divine power. Does this mean the Guru loses some of his own power?"

Maharajshri replied, "The Guru does not give any power, he simply directs his kind attention toward the disciple. The power, Shakti, is already present in every being and there is no need for any external power. There is no other power existing outside. A living being needs the Guru-Shakti [the power of the Guru] only to awaken the dormant power which is extroverted, directed towards the world. The power and giving the support of that power are two different things. Out of sheer kindness the Guru extends support to the disciple. The Guru's power returns to him after awakening the dormant power within the disciple. This is Shaktipat. Many spiritual practices are prevalent these days that seek the support of the chitta [minds] of the saints; the biographies of saints are studied. People discuss incidents pertaining to the lives of saints, they sing divine songs composed by them. But all this is carried out with a sense of emotion, with conscious effort and with ego. This is not Shaktipat. Shaktipat, the descent of power, takes place only when it is conducted by a Guru. One does not seek the support of another mind, it is given. One gets the support of the psychic power of the Guru only when the Guru, out of his own resolve, extends his psychic power. This is Shaktipat."

My next query was, "But people will consider kriyas to be a bout of madness."

Maharajshri answered, "People do call it madness, but this is due to their ignorance. Kriyas appear to be madness, but if you think about it, there is a big difference between the two. People can see the body, but not the psyche. The infinitesimal changes that take place in the psyche do not meet their eye. The world is based on sight, whereas spirituality is a subject of the invisible. The world attempts to understand everything by direct experience or proof. If it cannot understand something, it is labeled madness, whereas, in reality, this itself is its own foolishness.

"There is one similarity in the kriyas during sadhan [effortless spiritual practice] and madness. The basis for both are samskaras [accumulated impressions]. These impressions do not become thinned out through madness, whereas in sadhan they come to an end. In madness the intellect is agitated, whereas in sadhan it remains normal. In madness there is a possibility of something unfavorable happening, whereas in sadhan there is no such possibility. The acts of madness cannot be stopped until the bout of madness comes to an end. On the other hand, the movements occurring during sadhan can be stopped at will."

Once again I commented, "When you were in Nepal, one day a sadhak was doing his sadhan in the cave. He was having kriyas — loud screams. At the time a policeman was walking behind the ashram. When he heard the screams he thought someone was being beaten. He climbed over the fence and came inside. He sternly asked who was being beaten and by whom. Many attempts were made to explain the facts to him but he was unable to understand. On hearing the commotion the aspirant came out of the cave. The policeman asked him, "What was the problem? Why were you screaming?" He said that he was doing his sadhan. When the policeman asked what sadhan meant, everyone started laughing. During sadhan such problems can arise. There are other people in the house; there are neighbors. People can interpret things in their own way. They will surely say, 'What kind of spiritual practice is this?' "

On hearing this Maharajshri laughed and said, "This is indeed a problem for spiritual aspirants who experience very intense kriyas. At times it is difficult to control them. Here the ashram is far from town. There is a cave for doing sadhan, so one can do sadhan here with a free mind. The kriyas will also happen freely. Where such a facility is not available, the kriyas automatically get controlled, either due to embarrassment or out of fear. So there is no reason to be afraid. Some aspirants have extremely violent kriyas and they can get out of control. If such a situation arises, it is the task of the Guru to reduce the intensity of the kriyas and bring them under control."

Maharajshri continued, "I remember when I received initiation, in Rishikesh in 1933. At that time I, too, did not know much about initiation. I had intense and strange kriyas, such, possibly, as no one else has had. I haven't met anyone with such an experience. Many people were convinced that I was mad. I rented a room in the city. Looking at the intensity of my kriyas, the landlord asked me to vacate the place. I felt there was no need for me to control the kriyas and even if I tried they wouldn't submit to my control. Now I feel that, if at that time my kriyas would have been under my control, then it would have been very beneficial for my sadhan. When kriyas become extremely intense it is like overflowing water spilling out of a vessel. The higher the intensity of the kriyas, the greater is the loss of power. The occurrence of intense kriyas is not a bad thing because whatever qualities are dominant in the mind will be expressed in kriyas, but it is also very important to have control. One should be able to stop kriyas at will. Hence my instructions to spiritual aspirants are to develop control along with the progress of their kriyas."

By now we had returned to the ashram and so our conversation ended here.

3. Sadhan and Sadhana

The subject was the same during our walk the next day: sadhan. Maharajshri was saying, "Sadhan is an intoxication that keeps us high without drinking. Sadhan is a killer that cuts sins without a sword. It is a poison that, without being consumed, causes the destruction of our ego. Sadhan lightens the burdens on our minds, fills our lives with joy, and grants immortality to the mortal."

I said, "Maharajji! Why is sadhana called sadhan?"

Maharajshri said, "No. Sadhana is called sadhana and sadhan is called sadhan. Sadhana cannot be sadhan. Sadhana is spiritual practice involving conscious effort; sadhan is different from that. Once these spiritual practices come naturally, sadhana becomes sadhan. [In Shaktipat, sadhan is what we call the automatic spiritual practices and body movements that happen after Shaktipat initiation.] The study of mind control is sadhana. In sadhana, the task of purifying the mind is secondary because the mind can never be purified by our efforts. In sadhana, an attempt is made to condition the mind in a certain way, even though the mind has impurities. This is analogous to the way we learn to ride a bicycle. After some days we get habituated to it. In the same way, the dominant characteristics of the mind are changed by suppressing negative impressions and by collecting new types of impressions, even though it is only for a brief interval of time. Sadhana is the practice of keeping the mind under control by being disciplined. It is classified under Anvopaaya [meditation involving effort]. When a living being continues to practice meditation or other spiritual exercises that are devoid of Shakti but full of pride, this is sadhana."

"If sadhana is Anvopaaya, then sadhan is Shaktopaaya [meditation performed by Shakti]. Hence sadhana is the spiritual aspirant's effort before the awakening of the Shakti and sadhan is the self-proven and self-perfecting spiritual practice after the awakening. In sadhana there is a sense of doership and in sadhan there is a sense of an observer. In sadhana there is some aim, some goal, whereas in sadhan the only aim is the kriya. Sadhana is the outcome of effort, while sadhan is the active nature of the conscious-self. In sadhan, the basis of activity is the accumulated impressions of past lives [sanchit samskaras], according to which kriya manifests. Hence, sadhan is called an automatic process.

In sadhana the spiritual aspirant performs some specific types of practices, by which he can carve out an identity for himself, like a Dhyana Yogi, who practices meditation, a Jnana Yogi, who practices study of scriptures, a Tratak Yogi, who practices tantra, a Bhakta Yogi, who practices devotion, and so forth. But in sadhan, there is only one spiritual aspirant who becomes at times a Hatha Yogi [one who practices yogic postures], sometimes a devotee, sometimes an accomplished singer, and so forth. As his impressions change, consequently the nature of his kriyas also changes. Sometimes the heart is filled with emotion and at times doubts start getting resolved within. In this way, two such categories are formed, the practicing aspirant [in sadhana], and the surrendered aspirant [in sadhan]. In sadhan one doesn't have to do anything except observe and surrender. There is no desire, no plan and no obstacles in sadhan. If sadhana is owing to one's own effort, sadhan is owing to the will of God. Hence, sadhana is done and sadhan takes place.

"It is simply your misconception that you believed sadhana and sadhan to be one and the same. Sadhana is like carrying your baggage while walking, whereas sadhan is a like riding in a railway train. In the train you set down your luggage and sit down. The train will take you to the desired place.

"Sadhana can increase your ego and your pride, whereas sadhan destroys your ego. I agree that in quite a few sadhaks who are at the level of sadhan an increase in pride has been noticed. This means that they are using sadhan in the form of sadhana. But the power that does sadhan is free from ego. If a spiritual aspirant feels proud about his sadhan, his sadhan deteriorates and falls to the level of sadhana."

4. What is Required for Sadhan?

Today I had decided what to ask even before we started the stroll. "Maharajji, what is required for this sadhan?"

Maharajshri said, "Nothing. That is the difference between sadhana and sadhan. That which needs the help of external tools is sadhana. Ours is sadhan, an internal sadhan. The kriyas happen within us; the power is awakened within us; the attention is kept inwards. The samskaras, too, are within, and they are eroded by internal kriyas. It is within that sentiments arise, the conscious-self [chaitanya] is within, too.

"The external world and our awareness of it are obstacles in self-knowledge. The chitta [mind-stuff], a product of the fundamental creative energy, works within. It acquires knowledge from the world but it is within that this knowledge is dissolved. All external things are a part of this world. The state of one's mind, introspection and surrender are the instruments of this sadhan, and they have no association with the world. Just as we remove our footwear before entering a temple, before entering the state of inner sadhan external things get left behind.

"As long as there are external spiritual devices, the focus of your attention is external and its impressions will continue to accumulate. In spirituality one has to purify one's self of all impressions and not accumulate them. When external objects are given up, not only does the accumulation of their impressions stop, but the erosion of past impressions also begins, through the medium of kriyas. When one has obtained the supremely powerful support of the grace of the divine power in the form of kriyas, why is there need for any external support?

"When one gets habituated to using external objects, it becomes difficult to leave them behind. The writings of saints have repeatedly mentioned that the alley of love is extremely narrow. Even crossing it alone is very difficult. Hence, while entering the path, external objects have to be discarded outside. But what can be done about habits? They stand in front of us in the form of obstacles. Rosaries, musical instruments, material needed for prayers, books, and for that matter even the body and mind, too. One has to rise above all these. Here the question is not of accumulating, but of emptying.

"These external objects are undoubtedly of value in practices involving conscious effort [sadhana]. To practice holding the mind steadfast, one needs a reference, a focus. But your question was in the context of our school of thought. I have answered your question accordingly."

Another question arose in my mind, "Maharajji, while giving Shaktipat initiation you did not do anything but place your hand on the head. Anyone can place his hand on the head, but kriyas are not initiated by that. Why is there such a big difference in the placing of a hand?"

Maharajshri said, "Anyone can extend his hand, but the subtle action behind it is missing. Merely holding the hand on the head is not important. It must be supported by a resolve. Behind that resolve should be the strength of the awakened power and behind that the blessings of the Guru. Initiation can take place even without placing the hand on the head. Initiation can be given simply by a glance, by a mantra, or even without these. People often throw glances, they speak, they also touch, but the effect is not the same. When there is darkness within us, how can we brighten the lives of others?

"Shaktipat, the descent of power, is a very subtle process. All its media are invisible, all its happenings secret. Everything takes place on the plane of the conscious-self [chaitanya]. Actions of the conscious-self also occur, without a doubt, on the basis of the chitta, which as expected, is gross. The state of the chitta and the kriyas also focus on subtle images. But why does one consider only these impressions, which occupy a place in the mind?

"Only the one who is affected by Shaktipat can experience it. At the time of initiation the power of introspection of many aspirants is not fully developed. As a result, even though they experience the inner effects, they are unable to understand them. The union of two conscious powers, their influence on each other, the introversion of the disciples power, the return of the Guru's power, all this happens in a secret invisible form on a very subtle plane. The gross world, which cannot even understand the nature of the conscious-self, how can it understand its activities and its knowledge."

"Okay, Maharajji," I said, "The mind is the main problem of a human, isn't it?"

Maharajshri said, "No, the mind is not the problem. Defects of the mind are the problem. When the mind is referred to as a problem, this always means the defects of the mind. When there are no defects, the mind is still there, but at that time it does not create problems. In reality, the mind is simply a purposeful or uncertain activity of the conscious-self, acting on the basis of the chitta. If there are any defects, it is this action that embodies the defects. If there are no defects, then this action is free from defects. The root cause of defects is desire and the root cause of desire is our accumulated impressions. As long as there are accumulated impressions there will be desires. As long as there are desires there will be defects, and until they are released the mind will remain a problem. A mind full of defects is bondage, whereas a mind free of defects is moksha [liberation]. Generally the mind is wrapped with defects, hence this has become accepted as the nature of the mind. Saints and devotees are determined to speak ill of it. Someone talks of destroying it, while another talks of suppressing it. Some try to please it, while others try to reason with it. In fact, a mind full of defects places a lot of importance on the world. It believes the world to be eternal and desires to live forever, but not a mind free of defects.

"When the mind is said to be very strong it means that the defects in the mind are very strong. They turn the mind in any direction they wish and can force the mind to do whatever work they want. But from a spiritual point of view this is a weakness of the mind. The result is it does what it shouldn't do. It thinks about issues that it shouldn't think about. This weakness forces a being to pursue worldly things. A living being has become so weak that he has no control over the actions of a defective mind. He dances like a puppet to the tune of the defective mind. His helplessness comes to him solely through his own actions. By surrendering to desires, attachment, anger and indulgence he stops considering right and wrong and accumulates the impressions of his undesirable actions. Those very impressions now take the form of desires and become the cause of further defects in the mind. This living being has accumulated such impressions within him that there is no opportunity for a good or auspicious desire to arise. The life of a living being has been reduced to one full of indulgence. Such a life, characterized by a defective, flirtatious and desirous mind, has obtained popularity in this world.

"But in fact, even good actions happen through the mind. Spiritual practices and devotional songs are done by the mind, and the love for God is also born in the mind. So how can the mind itself be the problem? It is the fault of those who have helplessly surrendered themselves to the defective mind. They shy away from the path of spirituality, then they blame the mind."

Old, deep-rooted tendencies [samskaras] also do not give up the chase easily. Before coming to Dewas, I lived with an altogether different ideology. I hardly understood Vedanta, but would claim to be a vedanti; without understanding the tenets of love, I would mix with the Sufis; without even having entered the field of yoga I considered myself a yogi. I would roam around in my own ego-filled mental world. My feet were trapped in the quicksand of my ego but my mind was flying in the sky. Even though the principles of Vedanta and Sufism are similar, what are the differences between these two schools? This question never occurred to me. Then I began to regard all the paths, the yogas, the principles and schools as different from one another and to compare. My viewpoint was totally comparative, and filled with pride. What more was needed? This is an example of the proverb, "One bitter gourd on top of a neem." [The fruits of both the plants have a very bitter taste.] My pride about my intelligence knew no bounds. Even without having a regular schedule of spiritual practices, I claimed to be a spiritual aspirant. In spite of being full of desires, I portrayed myself as totally detached. What was inside me was totally different from what I portrayed. I was proud of my good qualities and unaware of my handicaps.

At that time, my tendency to compare was becoming stronger. To see all spiritual practices as different, to judge good and bad, to be attached to my opinions and disrespect others — this was my nature. But when I came to Dewas at the lotus feet of the Lord, I could see that all my ways of thinking had begun to weaken. I could see a new road open up ahead of me, a path that integrates all the other paths, views and principles within itself. It did not dislike bhakta [devotees] nor did it hate jnanis [seekers of knowledge]. It was like the Sun, which gives light not only to the high mountains, but also to the deep valleys. It does not dislike anyone. In the same way, this path is so liberal that, from all viewpoints — conceptual, humane and practical — it respects all paths. It regards them as the same. However, my impressions of comparing various spiritual practices were so strong that they urged me, still, to accept the awakening of Shakti due to Shaktipat as a separate path. I felt as if this new path, even though it brightened all other spiritual practices and principles, was different from them. If it were different from them, wouldn't it be an addition to the number of spiritual practices?

Other similar thoughts were tossing in my mind. In fact, this wasn't such a serious matter, but the mind is sure to do some mischief. I reflected that old, deep-rooted impressions do not go away easily. I was in a strange confusion. Sometimes the mind would say that Shaktipat was a different sadhan. On other occasions it would say, "What difference does it make to you? Do your sadhan!" On one side were Maharajshri's strong arguments; on another side was direct experience; and thirdly, there were these old emotions, thoughts and impressions. Just as someone caught in a whirlpool keeps spinning at one place, I was unable to come out of this tangle. I had faith in Maharajshri; his talks would touch my heart; there was no choice but to believe in them. But memories of the past were blocking my way. I tried hard to convince my mind that the debate over whether this path were different or not was meaningless, but my mind wouldn't agree. Finally I decided to present the problem to Maharajshri. Maharajshri's way of explaining, I knew, was very scientific, logical and one which directly pierced the heart. His aim was perfect. He understood the problems and difficulties of the questioner very well.

The next day, while strolling, I presented the issue weighing on my mind to Maharajshri in the following manner, "Until now I have seen the jnanis mock the bhakta. The devotees consider the learned devoid of love and believe they acquire knowledge by mere reading. The yogis claim that yoga is the only solution, whereas the karma yogis consider performing their duties to be prayer to God. All of them argue amongst themselves, praising their own path and contradicting the others. Spirituality seems to be a large arena for debates. I, too, have considered my opinion and thought it to be of the highest order, befitting and logical. I cannot say that my thinking is fully developed, but its roots are quite mature. Now you have placed on top of all other sadhanas this new sadhan of awakening the power. Is this sadhan totally different and separate from other spiritual practices? I am unable to understand this matter. There is no reason to doubt your statement, but my past continues to hold me."

Maharajshri smiled and said, "This means that you have not yet understood the difference between sadhana and sadhan. I did not call any sadhana wrong, small or insignificant, nor have I compared one path with another. I have only talked about the level or quality of sadhana. Different spiritual aspirants practicing the same sadhana may do so at different levels. There can be a level where the sadhana [spiritual practice involving conscious effort] gives up its current form and becomes sadhan [effortless spiritual practice]. Then it becomes natural. This is not possible without the awakening of Shakti, because only then will the support of the sadhana rise above effort and manifest in accordance with the state of the chitta. This natural way of manifestation is called kriya. This is sadhan. Effort is replaced by naturalness; this is the only difference that arises. When the state of the chitta becomes the support, then in accordance to its nature, the kriyas of other sadhanas start manifesting themselves. As a result of this the debate of sadhanas and paths comes to an end.

"Most of the time the people who consider themselves to be spiritual aspirants aren't really aspirants. This is because they have no respect for other spiritual practices. Without becoming broad-minded and without acceptance, a spiritual aspirant can never advance towards destroying attachment. If there is a liking for one subject, then there will be for others, too, and there is sure to be dislike for still other subjects. In this way the aspirants mentioned above, due to their attachment to their own style of spiritual practice, get entangled in arguments, propose it as the only solution and, by living by it, continue to strengthen their attachment.

"The practice of awakening the Shakti is not a separate and distinct practice. The kriyas of devotion, knowledge and yoga are included in it, the same feelings and ideas, too; only the level of experience is different. The act of walking is the same, but one person may be going away from the house, another returning to the house, while a third person walks inside the house. The ego sitting within the person does not let go of him in any of these states. Superficially the person behaves as if he were ego-less, but this is just a facade. After the awakening of the Shakti, the process of melting the ego begins.

"Just as one person starts from Bombay, another from Madras and another from Calcutta; one person goes by bullock-cart, another by train and another by aircraft; one person proceeds by stopping along the way, and another keeps going straight down the road without halting, nevertheless all of them have to go to Delhi. In the same way, whichever path it is, wherever be the starting point, whether the rate of progress be very fast, average or slow, the goal is only one — the awakening of Shakti. On attaining this goal, the aspirant's state of sadhana transforms into sadhan. He doesn't receive any new sadhana, only its natural form becomes visible. Yes, the aspirant begins to have new experiences that give him a false feeling of newness in his sadhan. Ego, the doer, has changed into the seer. Because of this, too, sadhan seems to be new. But there is only one sadhan, a journey towards self-realization. All aspirants are pedestrians on this same path, moving towards this same goal, but the experiences of the journey are their very own. The task of intellectuals has been to propose various schools of thought on the basis of the differences in these experiences, and their followers have become attached to these ideologies and continue to argue among themselves. A spiritual aspirant doesn't have time for such arguments. He considers them an unnecessary intellectual exercise, in which nothing is achieved except a waste of time.

"The awakening of Shakti is also one stop along the way, not the final destination. It is the means not the end. It is the start not the finish. If there is no awakening, realize that sadhan has not yet begun. We are still roaming outside. The door of the house hasn't opened yet. Entry hasn't been made yet. If an aspirant believes sadhana to be the beginning of his journey, then this is his pride. Without entering the house, how can one sit inside the house? The awakening of Shakti gives naturalness to sadhana, which transforms it into sadhan. One begins to enjoy it, and as the accumulated impressions erode, new sadhanas take place. These are experiences or visions.

"Sadhana and sadhan are like the stairs needed to climb a mountain. While going up the stairs of sadhana, all of a sudden the awakening of Shakti comes before you. Sadhana becomes sadhan and the level changes. The mountain is the same, the stairs are the same and the traveler is the same, but the nature of the medium has changed. As the climber keeps going up, the view around him keeps changing. The places that seemed very high, now seem low. Earlier he could only see the scenery around him; now he sees over a long distance. This experience is the change. Has the path changed or the climber? Neither has. Only the level has changed."

I raised a new doubt. "Is sadhan impossible without the awakening of the Shakti?"

Maharajshri answered, "If there is no movement towards the house, how will you enter it? And once you enter the house, how will you reach the other side?

"I know that some people ask, 'What is this awakening of Shakti?' To know the answer you first need to understand one thing: When does the world exist for you? When your inner power starts flowing outward through your sense organs. They come in contact with the world and they obtain knowledge about the world. A living being becomes so engrossed in this knowledge of the world that he forgets his own self. That is why the knowledge of the world is said to be a cause for bondage. Now if someone seeks the dissolution of the knowledge of the world, then the Shakti, the inner power, will have to gather its spread and return back. The beginning of the return of the Shakti is called "awakening." It is possible that for some time an aspirant may not be able to experience it, but the awakening is definite."

"Agitation in the Shakti [latent power] is this world and its state devoid of agitation is the dissolution of this world. Similarly, on an individual level, the more agitated the mind is, the stronger is the reality and importance of this world. The starting point towards the agitation-free state of Shakti is awakening. Without this, how can one enter the realm of spirituality?"

My next question was, "Will there ever be a time when the Shakti will be absolutely free of agitation?"

Maharajshri said, "This question of yours is clearly an intellectual one. Your mental state is not yet ready for it. In spiritual practice, such a question is regarded as 'a right.' Nowadays neither does the person asking such a question reflect upon this right, nor does the respondent evalute the inquirer's right. The person asking such a question wants to know everything as quickly as possible without performing any spiritual practices and the respondent, for his part, wants to create an impression of his knowledge. As you have asked this question, I will try and answer it, but you do not have a right to it. All these are just your flights of imagination. I also know that you will not understand and everything I say will be beyond your comprehension.

"Only God knows the correct answer to this question, but from whatever I have understood from the scriptures and the writings of saints, I will say that the expanse of the universe is boundless. There are many, many solar systems like ours, in which the agitations of the conscious-self remain constantly active. Just as the stars keep twinkling at night, similarly the creation and dissolution of universes keeps happening continuously. At the rise of every agitation, many universes are created and at the end of every agitation many universes are dissolved. In a fraction of a second, many agitations are generated and many agitations are dissolved. It is difficult to say whether there will be a time when all agitations have subsided and no new agitation is being created. At that time, no universe will exist anywhere. Great men have experienced these things in the state of meditation and have been amazed at seeing the creation of innumerable universes. The creation and destruction of universes seems to be incessant like a river-flow. Anyone who has seen that incomparable play of God finds this visible world extremely insignificant and of no importance. The hollowness of his ego becomes clear to him.

"If all universes are considered as one single unit, then one cannot say whether the Shakti ever becomes free from agitation. No one has an instrument to see when and where an agitation takes place or ends. Even for a fraction of a second, if we agree that there is a specific instance when all the agitations in the conscious-self have stopped, who is going to see it? Because at that time all universes will cease to exist. That is the reason it is said that God alone knows his secrets. A human does not accept this logic because of his ego and tries to know the secret, imagining things and trying to guess, but who has unraveled the Lord's secrets?

"If you take one universe as a single unit, then surely an answer can be imagined. The scriptures and writings of saints are the only support for people who are not capable of a direct experience. Through their medium, one can imagine some answer or make a guess. Our universe at some time reaches a state of dissolution. One after the other, in reverse order, all the elements start dissolving and finally nature dissolves into its source. When the universe has ceased to exist, how will living beings survive? Their bodies are also a part of the universe. Then there is no one to be seen and no observer, thereby indicating that one agitation in the conscious-self has dissolved completely. But the property of agitation never goes away. Again an agitation occurs; again a universe comes into existence or seems to exist. Very few have direct experience of this; the majority of us proceed with the help of deduction.

"Then there is the living being, who represents a small universe within himself. This is called the individual level. The union of the gross and the conscious takes place within a person's body. He has ego, which refuses to admit that it is small. In the person, in the form of his inner self, there exists an inner universe, in which the memories of good and bad actions are accumulated. His body is created and destroyed. According to his memories, sometimes he is visible and sometimes not. In this way, in one life span of a universe, he is born and dies many times. If, at some point in time, good sense prevails over him and he takes up service and spiritual practices, then he can be free from birth and death and merge with the conscious-self. The union of the gross and the conscious is broken and the agitation of the conscious-self dissolves or contracts into a point. The goal of a living being is to remove the agitation in the conscious-self on an individual and personal level, not on a universal level. He cannot do anything at the universal level. He does not have the right to interfere in the activities of God."

I said, "Maharajji, this is an absolutely new way of thinking for me. Until now, I have only read the doctrines of Vedanta, and had begun to consider myself to be an intellectual. With your grace, secrets of the various spiritual practices are being revealed to me. It had never occurred to me how to incorporate non-dualism [advaita] into my spiritual practices. Acknowledging non-dualism and experiencing it are definitely two different things. Generally people only read sections dealing with the doctrines. The result of that is, they move around on the earth but fly in the skies."

Only a few days had passed since I had come here. But my thinking had started to change. Maharajshri's personality was right in front of me. In the past I had never felt the need of a Guru and now I began to consider a Guru indispensable. This is the grace of a Guru. I remembered those days in Nangal, when curiosity about a Guru arose in my mind for the first time, after hearing what the babaji had said. At that time I had been to the doorsteps of many Mahatmas [great souls], but all were merely vocal proponents, displaying pride every now and then, ever ready to get angry, without any modesty, nor kindness, nor a perception that noticed subtle things. Once a particular Mahatma appealed to my heart. His personality and his learning had a shade of spiritual practice. On thinking about it at night, the thought came to my mind repeatedly, "This Mahatma is good, but he is not your Guru." Today, I was in the proximity of a great man, at whose feet I had complete satisfaction.

I couldn't sleep at night. I was lost in memories of the past. In Nangal I considered myself a much greater devotee than other people believed me to be. If people called me to sing devotional songs, how eagerly I would wait for the opportunity to sing. I would feel very happy within on listening to their praises. My intoxication disappeared on seeing Guru Maharaj's personality. In my lifetime I had not seen such humility, simplicity, lack of ostentation and kindness in anyone. On top of that, he elucidated such intricacies of sadhan and experience, and was, again, so knowledgeable. There is no perfect being in this world except God. Even so, there was no one else in sight as close to perfection as I found Maharajshri to be.

Then I remembered that day in Nangal when I was sitting on the banks of the Sutlej in my hut and reading. I drifted off into slumber. In my dream, I saw a saint wearing a saffron robe. I was sitting near him when a person came with a glass of milk. The great soul drank half of it and then told me to drink the rest. I drank the milk. In the evening, a gentleman came along with *Devatma Shakti*, a book written by Maharajshri. The book had a picture of Maharajshri in it. The moment I looked at the picture, I realized that I had seen him in my dream.

I have heard that dreams are related to impressions accumulated in the past. These impressions arise from images in the chitta and create the world of dreams. I had accumulated some impressions associated with Maharajshri. Had he been my Guru in a previous birth, too? "Even after being blessed by the grace of such a great person," I had wondered, "why haven't my thoughts calmed down? Even now my mind troubles me a lot." I hadn't seen Maharajshri anywhere else except in my dream. Yet my mind was already attracted to him. It was at that point that I first began to correspond with him.

Now I was feeling remorse about my defects. My thoughts were racing on; my mind had become uneasy. The root cause of all defects is ego. It has to be crushed. For this it is necessary that the world hate you, ill-treat you, insult you. Your failure becomes known to the world — only then will your ego receive a jolt. This requires great tolerance. Whenever somebody's ego is hurt, how agitated he gets! It is said that when Kabir's fame spread, his ego was awakened, but he quickly composed himself and walked through the market place holding the hands of a prostitute. People were shocked and started abusing him. His misfortune spread everywhere. Kabir's ego was vanquished. Spirituality is not achieved by mere talk. One has to be ready to give up one's life with a smile on his face and even a sigh should not escape from the lips. One should wish everyone's well-being and love everyone, respect everyone. This is the path of lovers.

During the morning walk, I initiated the topic. "Spirituality is very difficult. One must bear many things and the ego is very troublesome. People wish to achieve it while sitting in an armchair, with a fat bank balance, with all kinds of facilities and luxuries. To the extent that spirituality is to be practiced by discussion, they will take interest in it. But they cannot bear even a small injury to their ego."

Maharajshri agreed. "This is the state of spirituality in this era. Everyone is full of anger and pride. They want tasty food to eat and desire all kinds of luxuries and services. First and foremost, they do not want to serve. Even if they accomplish something, they end up inflating their ego. "We are serving; we must be respected!" If someone else offers service, likes and dislikes are the result. They seek the help of intellectual arguments and resort to slyness. How can spirituality bear fruit under these circumstances? Spirituality is synonymous with burning one's self — burning desires and passions, burning defects and bad habits, burning attachments and aversions to the extent of even burning down the ego, becoming nothing. Only then will the light spread, only then will the fragrance spread. How can the mind become pure, without being scrubbed?

"But what can be done? The era is such. People are helpless against the influence of the mind. Not everyone is an opponent of spirituality and religion. There are many who understand everything and wish to act on this knowledge, but are unable to do so. Defects shackle them. The attraction of worldly things is very intense; slipperiness is all over the world. They walk carefully, yet they invariably slip. But there is no reason for spiritual aspirants to worry. It is only under such circumstances that good spiritual practice can happen. As the world pulls from all sides the aspirant remains engrossed in his spiritual practice. This is bliss. Such a spiritual practice is fruitful."

Then I said, "But the proponents of the path of devotion [bhakti marg] propound devotion by saying it is very easy. Even the saints have said that devotion is easy."

Maharajshri said, "They say this in order to generate faith in devotion. Ask Tukaram, Namdev, Jnaneshwar, Narsi Mehta,

Kabir or Meerabai, who took devotion seriously. They had to face so many difficulties. So many obstacles and difficulties they had to surmount! So many mouthfuls of insults they had to swallow! Yet a word of complaint was never uttered by these great personalities. Even though the world had strewn their path with so many thorns, they never said an insulting word about anyone. They respected and loved their enemies and their detractors. Can this task be called easy? Be it devotion or the path of knowledge [jnana yoga], detachment is necessary for all of them, and to acquire detachment is not an easy task.

"There is one more thing. Atheists did not cause them grief. They suffered at the hands of those who prayed, read religious books, knew scriptures, meditated, and those with braided hair and smeared foreheads. Who troubled Emperor Harishchandra? The great ascetic Maharshi Vishwamitra. [Vishwamitra means "a friend of the world."]. What kind of a world friendship is this? But the great personalities did not even utter a sigh. How much they must have had to bear within themselves! Whatever the branch of spirituality, whatever its principles and discipline, whatever the spiritual practice it prescribes, to pursue it is not easy. At every step difficulties, problems and pain come forth to block the way. This is because all have one thing in common: to purify the interior, to avoid the collection of filth within and to proceed in accordance with the Lord's wish. This flow is against the flow of the world. Nothing is to be collected; it is to be given up. We are not to be filled with likes and dislikes, but to spread love. To live in this world and proceed against it, can it be called easy?"

I asked with trepidation, "Maharajshri, I shouldn't be asking this, but the question is at the tip of my tongue. Did you have to face obstacles, too?"

Maharajshri said, "Yes. I, too, have faced many obstacles and difficulties. I have encountered many impediments. Worldly obstacles definitely exist, but the obstacles created by the deities are much more dreadful. The average aspirant is not evolved to such a level, thus the hindrances of the gods do not confront him. The beauty of the world holds no importance in comparison to the obstacles created by the gods, but the average aspirant is enthralled by the beauty of the world. If he attempts to understand all the obstacles in detail, an aspirant will learn a great deal. But the community of disciples does not want to consider the possibility that even their Guru Maharaj can be confronted by obstacles. This is not to their benefit. If they see the way in which we have overcome these obstacles, they might be inspired. Tolerance is extremely important for overcoming obstacles. There is a need for surrender to the Guru and a need for unceasing spiritual practice.

"There are obstacles in every walk of life, but a spiritual aspirant confronts more of them. Such are the rules on the path of spiritual practice. An aspirant does not enjoy many comforts, and on the other hand experiences poverty, suffering and calamities. An aspirant humbly rejects fame and receives insults. After the awakening of Shakti, the accumulated impressions begin to rise and come to the surface quickly, due to which pleasure and pain also come quickly. The pain has to be endured. The aspirant does not enjoy the pleasure.

"An aspirant also has to live his life in this world. His feelings, thoughts and point of view have nothing in common with the world. Every act of the aspirant is interpreted by the world from its own perspective. The whole world comes together and finds faults with him, but he does not see defects in anyone. Even if he notices them, he ignores them; he does not spread them. In this way an aspirant tolerates the insulting behavior of the world. He treats these ups and downs as a game and keeps smiling, even as he continues to be kicked by the world. To bear the pains inflicted by the world, its insulting behavior, its accusations, is a part of spiritual practice that removes all the trash from the mind. No one knows the accumulated impressions that rise and bear fruit, or from what birth they come. An aspirant, too, does not lose his composure because of obstacles and difficulties; he welcomes them. "Come, perform your act and go away." A worldly being avoids pain and seeks the support of charms and incantations. This is the difference between an aspirant and a worldly person.

"This was about worldly obstacles, now let us consider internal obstacles. External obstacles are, in reality, external manifestations of inner obstacles. Internally, on the basis of accumulated impressions, many desires begin to bloom, drawing a man towards pleasure. These urges are nothing but internal obstacles. They are products of indulgence, anger, jealousy, hatred, greed. Desires confuse the being; they make him dance; they take him for a ride. Spurred by desires, a person becomes blind, disillusioned and wicked. He forsakes the path of well-being and runs after worldly pleasures. Even if someone suggests that he consider his own welfare, desires prevent his heart from accepting it. These desires are the obstacle, in whose fire the whole world is burning. They arise in the mind in different forms, and sometimes allure and at times ensnare. The desires of common people are impure. Because of this the word "desire" is often interpreted as "impure desire." Desire is a fire that burns but cannot be seen. Desire is a tide from which no one can escape. Desire is an unfathomable ocean in which innumerable violent creatures do their mischief. Desire is a forest that seems to be extremely beautiful, but in which life is in peril. What more is there to say? Desire is a maze in which, if you get lost just once, you cannot come out. A spiritual aspirant always remains alert for this inner-obstacle-raising desire. His discretion gives him an early warning about its approach. He observes the desire and its activities from a distance, just as the audience remains separate from the play. The onslaught comes, shows its strength, and goes away. The aspirant keeps watching in the form of an observer. He who cannot do this is not a spiritual aspirant."

I asked, "It seems that in spirituality and the path of spiritual practice, there is nothing other than accumulated impressions [samskaras] and conduct."

Maharajshri said, "Actually purification of accumulated impressions and conduct are the most difficult problems of spirituality. Ignorance, egoism, attachment, aversion and fear of death are the five afflictions that add to the accumulation of impressions, and the impressions, in turn, strengthen them. But the moment an aspirant turns towards the path of spiritual practice, he confronts the accumulated impressions. Samskaras are the cause of lustful tendencies. They create prarabdha [fateful action] and give life a direction, a reference. They also influence our conduct. Spirituality is the process of extracting one's self from the quicksand of accumulated impressions.

"The goal of spirituality is self-knowledge, but when we talk about spiritual practice, samskaras take precedence. Impressions have accumulated and masked the self. The removal of impressions illuminates the soul. Accumulated impressions are the shackles of the world and their destruction results in liberation. Impressions take the form of the mind and make a person dance around. They become desires and generate wishes. They transform into worldly pleasures and disillusion the living being. Sometimes they make the being laugh and sometimes cry. If you remove the accumulated impressions and hold them aside, then there is no need to carry out spiritual practices. Thus if one's spiritual practice is based on accumulated impressions, these impressions will need spiritual practices for their destruction. For accumulation they will need karma [action]. In this way karma, impressions and spiritual practice affect each other. Karma, impressions, desires, tendencies and the mind — this cycle continues on. The goal of spiritual practice is to break it. Spiritual practice [sadhan] works continuously to break the cycle of karma and the same cycle of karma is ever ready to break the cycle of sadhan.

"Generally an aspirant wishes to avoid confrontation with his impressions. He would prefer to achieve steadfastness without touching them and let them live. Sometimes, temporarily, he may be successful in doing so. But after a while, when the impressions resurface, his mind becomes unstable again. Everything he has done is reduced to naught. Hence the path of spirituality is not to escape from our impressions but to destroy them. If you tell a worldly person that he is going to face a particular calamity, he will be frightened. He will search for astrologers and tantriks. But for a spiritual aspirant, the complete picture is clear. The ripened karma [prarabdha] must show its influence. What is the benefit in avoiding it and making it more powerful? He does not try to escape from his ripened karma. He does not resist it in any manner. On the contrary he bears it and ends it.

"A being stuck in the quicksand of accumulated impressions is like a mad elephant that keeps sinking deeper but does not wish to escape. He has sought happiness in this sorrow. Death is in front of him, but he doesn't see it. Spirituality makes him aware of his state, shows him the path of his happiness, and also helps him to free himself. Thus impressions are a subject of spirituality. Detachment, love for God, the practice of yoga, acquisition of knowledge, the company of pious men, and devotional songs and stories are for the destruction of samskaras. They are no longer needed once the accumulated impressions are destroyed.

There are two types of impressions: unripe and ripe, called "accumulated impressions" [sanchit samskaras] and "ripe impressions" [prarabdha], respectively. There is no way to destroy prarabdha other than to bear it with cheer and without agitation — to bear it without affecting the mind, without getting upset, without becoming happy or sad, without opposing it. This is sadhana, this is sadhan, and this is spirituality, too. Vedanta refers to this as titiksha [forbearance]. It applies not only to natural misfortunes, but also to psychological upheaval and to mental and physical joys and sorrows. Upon awakening, the Shakti, at the level of the mind, carries out the task of performing natural actions. At times it seems that, due to the impressions, the actions it inspires are undesirable. On such occasions it is essential for the aspirant to remain alert. If an aspirant loses the perspective of an observer, he surrenders to the desires that have awakened within. If the aspirant is affected, it can be disastrous.

"An aspirant must destroy his accumulated impressions through sadhan and his prarabdha through tolerance, and at the same time prevent the accumulation of new impressions. This is termed Karma Yoga. Only then is there a possibility of the purification of the chitta. As long as accumulated impressions and prarabdha exist inside, they continue to initiate karma [actions which generate further impressions]. As long they are present one must be careful. After they have been destroyed it doesn't matter whether you perform actions or not. Performing karmas by considering them as service to God, with a sense of duty, with tolerance, without getting agitated and without thinking of them as favorable or unfavorable, is called inaction or non-action [akarma]. This is the way of performing karma and staying detached from it."

5.   The Tea Predicament

While sleeping, the mind is strongly pulled towards the past. Sometimes it visualizes beautiful dreams about the future. Occasionally it worries. But most of the times it drifts off into the past. Today, while sleeping, my mind recalled a strange incident from the past. When I lived in Nangal, whenever I had time, I would visit Himachal Pradesh. The mountains of Himachal Pradesh are a mile away from Nangal. Once I was staying in a cave in the Bilaspur district of Himachal Pradesh. It was surrounded by forest. There were five or six houses at some distance. I would get two meals a day from one house and about one litre of milk from the other. I used to consume a lot of tea then. I decided that as long as I was living in this cave, I would not go anywhere to have tea. The bazaar was only four or five miles away. It wasn't a nuisance to go, have tea and come back, but I made a resolve not to go.

After five or six days had passed without tea, the memory of tea began to trouble me. My mind became restless, but I forcibly suppressed its desire. My mind would continuously remind me of tea, and I would suppress it. Generally it has become the nature of the mind to jump up and change the subject when asked to do a certain thing. It repeatedly brings forth things that it has been told not to. This arrogance of mind was harassing me. Out of the blue a cup of tea would appear in my mind. I would shrug it off. I would try to engage my mind with chanting. Sometimes I would read something, sometimes go for a walk. Tea did not leave me alone.

A fortnight passed by, and the craving for tea became very

intense. Spiritual practices, devotional songs were swept aside. Now my head started to feel heavy. The mind was continuing in its own rut. A picture of Bhairavji was carved on a wall in the cave. As Bhairavji did not have any place in my worship, I had not paid much attention to it. I was pacing in the cave and my mind was focused on the thought of tea. My resolve to not go anywhere to have tea began to weaken. I lowered my defense against the mind. I imagined going to the bazaar early in the morning and having tea. I was pacing and thinking at the same time.

My seat was on one side and Bhairavji was on the other. As I paced in one direction my seat would be in front of me and as I returned, I would be facing Bhairavji. That day, for the first time, I saw that on the chest of Bhairavji a niche had been made in the wall. I could see a whitish paper kept inside it. Initially I did not pay much attention to it. Then inadvertently my hand went into the niche. It was a small packet containing some jaggery, tea leaves and one anna. My happiness knew no bounds on seeing the tea leaves. My problem of tea had been resolved. I cannot describe the joy I experienced at that moment. I thought some devotee must have offered it. I had been living here for the last fifteen days, and no devotee had come. Perhaps someone had come prior to that. Whatever it was, for me this was a gift from Bhairavji.

The next day morning, I narrated this incident to Maharajshri and requested him to express his viewpoint. The essence of what Maharajshri said is as follows:

(1) "The first thing that is clear from this is how the mind plays mischief with a man. The mind repeatedly attacks him in different ways. Sometimes by posing as a friend, sometimes by cajoling him, sometimes by disillusioning him, sometimes by making him angry and sometimes by attracting him. All these are the tricks of the mind. The mind never gets discouraged. It will keep on

playing its tricks until a man refuses to accept defeat. The task of attaining victory over the mind is a very difficult one. The mind derives its strength from impressions. If the mind has to be defeated, impressions have to be destroyed, desires have to be wiped out, and defects have to be put an end to."

(ii) "Until impressions are destroyed, there is a need for strong determination to maintain restraint. The mind is bound to play mischief. Only strong determination can keep it under control. A slight relaxation and the mind will be out of control. You became weak and your entire restraint was wasted. If the lord hadn't helped you in the form of a gift, you would have collapsed."

(iii) "To maintain a strong resolve is very difficult for an aspirant. Upon becoming weak the mind is discouraged, thus along with strong determination, surrender is also a must. In that way, even if the resolve fails, the mind does not feel dejected. From this point of view, strong determination is needed to strengthen the feeling of surrender. What would have been the impact on your mind if you had gone to the bazaar to have tea?"

(iv) "If one has the opportunity and the convenience, one should periodically go into solitude and do sadhan for some days. In isolation the negative sentiments of the mind take a radical form and cause disturbances. An aspirant has an opportunity to understand his state of mind. Power is accumulated due to sadhan. Then, having returned to society, while performing his tasks he watches his mind. Sadhan is the never-ending act of watching the mind. An aspirant is never careless with his mind."

I asked, "Maharajji, it is difficult for worldly people to find an opportunity to go into solitude. What should they do?"

Maharajshri said, "They can find a little time daily, sit in a particular corner of the house and enjoy solitude. Solitude is said to be half-meditation [samadhi]. While going through their daily routine, they can watch the mind. They can try to surrender to God and do their work with a sense of service. Whenever possible, they can chant while working."

I observed, "It is possible that this happened as a result of some contamination or impurity from one of the houses from which I received my food and milk during my stay at the cave."

Maharajshri said, "Yes. That could have been the immediate cause, but not the major cause. The accumulated impressions are the major cause that keeps the mind continuously active. If you observe your mind, you will see that before and after this incident it experienced other upheavals. Thus there should be a reason that is predominant other than the immediate cause, and that can only be accumulated impressions."

Maharajshri's understanding and analysis were unique. It was accurate. Each and every word had strength. It was supported by continuous sadhan. As a result every word would directly enter the heart. His style of explaining was matchless. But he generally did not open his chest of knowledge until questioned. Once the window of knowledge was opened, knowledge would flow out in bursts.

Now I put forth a strange question, for which I was embarrassed later. But Maharajshri was neither offended by it, nor did he refuse to answer it. I said, "This era is not fit for great men like you. Why did you come to this world?"

Suddenly Maharajshri became serious. He said, "It is a separate question whether I am great or not, but one thing is sure: that no one can come into this world or leave it at will. When he is sent, he comes into the world. When he is recalled, he leaves. All this is in the hands of the one who sends and recalls. As long as God wishes, a being stays in this world and experiences joys and sorrows. No one can remain in this world even for an instant by his own wish.

It is a different story that, once they have been born into

this world, no one wants to leave. A living being undergoes suffering in this world, is insulted and gets angry, but he doesn't feel like giving up this world. He does not realize that, since the decision to come and go is not in his hands, he has no hand in deciding the duration of his stay. Yet living beings do not want to think about leaving this place. Even the animals, birds and insects wish to hold on to their lives. But has anyone been able to live in this world forever? Time comes along and takes us away in one sweep. Near and dear ones are left wailing behind.

"If we wish to invite someone into this world, we cannot do so. There are so many couples who yearn to see the face of a son, but coming and going is in the hands of God. How long one should be in this world is also God's decision. Joys and sorrows depend upon God. When he decides to send someone, that being cannot refuse. If he wants to take someone back, likewise the being cannot refuse. A living being is a mere puppet in his hands. If God says, 'Sit,' he sits down. If God asks him to speak, the being speaks. If he is asked to be quiet, he is quiet. A sinner, a good soul, man, woman, animals, birds — all are under his control. Let me ask: Have you come because of your wish and will you leave when you wish? People want to commit suicide, but all attempts are not successful. Only the person whom God calls can commit suicide. God creates some excuse or the other to call. He, being invisible, doesn't approach from the front. He pushes us — it could be through sickness, an accident or suicide. The truth is, it is God who calls you back."

6. Guru-Shishya Relationship

The only time I could converse with Maharajshri was during the morning walks. Usually we would be alone. Maharajshri was also in a healthy mood at that time. I did not have any respite from ashram activities throughout the day. There was no chance of sitting near Maharajshri. I queried, "Maharajji, I used to do sadhana and I also do it now, but the mind could never concentrate in the past, nor can it today. Kriyas happen; thoughts pass through. I cannot understand where my attention is diverted. Worldly thoughts keep coming. So what is the purpose of sadhan?"

Maharajshri said, "Why are you trying to put the cart in front of the bullock? You want to attain the state that occurs naturally after all the accumulated impressions are expunged before this has happened. Sadhana is not for attaining one-pointedness, but for removing all the accumulated impressions. One-pointedness is a natural state that never disappears but seems to have vanished behind layers of accumulated impressions. Once all the accumulated impressions are destroyed, it will appear in its original form. One-pointedness or concentration is against the principles of sadhan. Why would you aim at something that is not a goal of sadhan? Ask people how much single-pointedness their minds have achieved. There was a Mahatma from Ujjain. When he prayed to his Guru Maharaj for initiation into Sanyas [renunciation], he was told, "When your mind can concentrate for five minutes, come to me then and I shall grant you Sanyas." Even after twenty years, his mind had been unable to attain one-pointedness.

"One-pointedness is surely a natural characteristic of the mind, but as it is buried under unnatural characteristics, it is not experienced. There is no question of attaining one-pointedness of the mind. Since it is a natural characteristic of the mind, it is always there. The task is to is get rid of the unnaturalness, which requires sadhan. Unnaturalness increases by unnatural spiritual practices, and thus the mind keeps moving away from its natural tendencies. Yes, if the sadhan is natural, then the negative tendencies due to unnaturalness are removed and the natural one-pointedness of the mind can be seen and experienced.

"This state of one-pointedness is not a very advanced state of spirituality. According to *Yoga Darshan*, the restrained state of the mind, that is, the state of samadhi, is much higher than this. In samadhi all the modifications are inhibited. Consequently all the activity of the chitta stops and the chitta is totally inhibited. The observer [the soul or the spiritual principle] is established in its original form. Asamprajnat samadhi has been obtained. In asamprajnat samadhi the mind is without an object, whereas, in the state of one-pointedness an object is always present. The meaning of one-pointedness is that the attention of the mind is withdrawn from all other modifications and focused on a single object. This happens to an extent that one becomes unaware of one's ego and modifications dissolve. When there is knowledge of one object, the modification is objective and directed. But the chitta is working and all the modifications have not been inhibited. Whereas, in asamprajnat, the object totally vanishes. The knowledge of an emotion and the lack of it — both are lost.

"One-pointedness is not yoga, it is just the beginning in the direction of yoga. The journey may proceed forward or one could end up turning back towards the world. By the way, the deliberate study of yoga practice begins with an attempt to concentrate the tendencies of the chitta on a single object. It is initiated with an attempt to concentrate on some gross object. Initially a gross object is contemplated, then the object of concentration is reduced to its smallest, to such an extent that finally the pure substance, which is free from all modifications [asmita], becomes the object of one-pointedness. But yours is not such a goal-seeking sadhana. Yours is a sadhan of awakening of the Shakti, of surrender, and to let the awakened Shakti accomplish its work is your duty. Don't run after one-pointedness. Let the Shakti remove your accumulated impressions. You will attain one-pointedness and at the right time even the chitta will become inhibited. Thus courage has been given a very high position in sadhan. The action of the Shakti directly attacks the accumulated impressions. It purifies them. It cleans them. Whenever the accumulated impressions of one-pointedness come to the surface, one experiences one-pointedness in kriyas. When the chitta becomes saturated with sattva guna, the natural state of one-pointedness is manifest. Thus the awakened Shakti paves the way for the inhibition of the chitta.

"If the aspirant does not force his ego in the kriyas [activities] of the Shakti, the rate of progress will be extremely fast. But the ego is such that it repeatedly comes in between. It lets a certain kriya happen, a certain one not happen. It lets some other kriya be intense, and so on and so forth. It keeps on doing something or the other. Due to this the naturalness of the kriyas is destroyed and the speed is reduced. It is very difficult to get rid of the cycle of accumulated impressions."

My next question was, "When you were in Nepal, I had opportunities to converse with a number of aspirants. All of them talked frequently of great experiences. It seemed as if all were aspirants of a high order. But immediately discussions about attachments and aversions would ensue. Their talk reflected pride. Sometimes there would be arguments over simple things. At that time it felt as if they were common worldly men."

Maharajshri became more serious. He said, "Experiences

occur not just for their own sake. They create a state of consciousness, which is fully attained after the removal of accumulated impressions. What you have just described indicates that this state of the chitta has not been achieved. The ego, which is sitting inside the conscious-self of a human, prevents the creation of this state of chitta. Why feel proud about a sadhan which the aspirant doesn't do at all? But aspirants still feel proud. If the mind has pride, everything else follows behind. Whatever these aspirants say, they haven't yet qualified as aspirants. Pride raises the head; it doesn't sever it. Arguments over simple matters signify a lack of tolerance. Attachments and aversions denote a feeling that the world is real. If these traits exist in someone, what kind of aspirants are they? Being initiated and sitting in sadhan is not enough. Other things are required: seriousness, generosity, tolerance, humility, surrender, service, discipline and control over the senses, mind and speech. Then the accumulated impressions of an aspirant are eradicated in his sadhan. Tolerance gets rid of prarabdha [ripened samskaras] and service stops the accumulation of impressions.

"There is no shortage of people who weave stories in this world, but spirituality is not just a subject of discussion. If it were, the whole world would have been liberated by now. In spirituality one observes the state of his chitta, the destruction of passions and a lack of pride. Becoming eligible for God's grace is not so easy.

"It is not that I am unaware of these things, but as I look at the helplessness of these people due to their state of mind, I feel pity for them. I know that in their minds they are sad due to these shortcomings and wish to be freed of them, but are unable to do so. They are swinging on the swing of desire, stuck in the quicksand of accumulated impressions. Even as they attempt to get out, they go deeper into it. Now you ask whether they should be scolded or sympathized with. They sought the shelter of the

Guru on being pained by desires. While giving initiation, I was aware of their mental states and initiated them, considering them to be deserving of mercy. Now it will take time for them to escape the quicksand of desire. The accumulated impressions of so many births will surely not be removed in a day. Sometimes up and sometimes down, this will keep on happening. This happens with all aspirants. However one thing is sure: their internal journey has begun. After receiving the grace of the Guru-Shakti, the inner light has started to glow. But the fog of accumulated impressions rises again and again and covers the mind.

"Now I would like to tell you something in this context. Your attention towards defects in people cannot be considered proper. You saw the defects, not the awakened Shakti. You saw them falling, not their attempt to rise. You saw the fog spread on the chitta and not the emerging beam of light. Every person is busy fighting his accumulated impressions. In trying to defeat them, he often has to face defeat. In this struggle a being often forgets that he is waging a war, but the struggle continues. If your attention keeps focusing on the defects of others, you will never be able to rise above your own. Seeing defects in others indicates that these defects are still within us. By paying such attention, our inner defects are strengthened. So give up the attitude of hatred and surprise towards these people and fill your mind with a feeling of sympathy. Pray to God for their liberation and you too will be liberated. Attempt to help them, only then will you find a supporter. Wipe their tears and you will find someone to wipe your own. Spirituality is an extremely subtle path. One is not aware when impressions are accumulated, when they become strong or when they ripen [become prarabdha]. People spend their entire lives in carelessness and, in the end, piles of impressions are accumulated within. The impressions of the good as well as the bad qualities of an action accumulate continuously. To experience these subtle processes, to put an end to them, and to prevent the further accumulation of impressions is a part of sadhan.

"The auspicious and inauspicious, good and bad — both together pervade the entire world, outside in the external world and inside the body. It is up to you to decide what you want to see, what you want to associate with and what you want to accept. Thus saintly people always refrain from pointing out others mistakes, speaking and hearing ill about others, avoiding such attractions and aversions lest their minds become attached to evil. If you get involved in seeing evil in the world, then you will see only evil everywhere. If you want to look outward, see only the goodness. If you want to see evil, look inside your mind. Then you will come to know where you stand."

My mind was enchanted by Maharajshri's thoughts. These thoughts influenced me so much that the world seemed to be pleasant, beautiful, enjoyable and full of happiness. A fragrance had spread everywhere in it. The bodies of people seemed to be external coverings in which the life-force was shining. But this state did not last for a long time. This was the power of Maharajshri's words, which had taken control of my chitta. The moment this emotion broke, a negative feeling awakened. The mind started moving towards evil and again I began seeing the defects of others. Apprehensively, I placed my thoughts before Maharajshri. "Maharajshri, there are certain people who do not listen to you at all. They nod their heads in front of you but do exactly what they please once they go. What happens to these people?"

Maharajshri said, "You are still stuck there. You haven't yet grasped the essence of the Guru-Shishya relationship. The Guru wishes the well-being of his disciple at the time of initiation and he can never wish ill for him. If he ever sees something untoward happening to his disciple, his heart cries out. One thing is clear: that the heart of the disciple is impure. Otherwise why would he come to a Guru? He is filled with defects and desires inside. He listens to the instructions of the Guru with a polluted chitta. He has difficulty in understanding their meaning and essence. Upon awakening, the Shakti begins to work towards the purification of the chitta, but it takes time. Until then the disciple disobeys the Guru. The Guru, being a well-wisher of the disciple, continues to forgive his mistakes with a generous heart. Sometimes, for the disciple's welfare, he scolds him and sometimes he neglects him. How and when the Guru works should be left to the Guru.

"If the Guru has love for the disciple, the disciple, in turn, has faith and surrender for the Guru. There are different levels of faith and surrender. One cannot immediately expect a mature state of faith. A little faith exists from the beginning, but a lack of surrender is apparent. Surrender is the result of a sense of service and surrender adds a glow to service. Surrender grants maturity to the sense of service. It is surrender that makes the Guru-Shishya relationship profound. What more can be said, but that all sadhanas and sadhan end in surrender. Surrender develops sadhan and eventually encompasses it within itself.

"Pride is an enemy of surrender. Those who nod their heads in front of me and, upon going out, do as they please, do so under the influence of pride. Pride does not go away immediately; it requires long treatment. Love and surrender are needed. If the Guru becomes upset with the disciple and abandons him, who will treat him? In this world no one cares for anyone. Only the Guru thinks of his disciple's welfare. The Guru-Shishya relationship is based on this feeling of welfare. There is no attachment, no selfishness. Hence the Guru's attitude is very generous. Even if the disciple errs a thousand times, he will embrace him with love. The Guru's heart is tormented at the possibility of his disciple's misfortune.

"A disciple is like a small child. Sometimes he sulks, sometimes he is restless. As a wave rises from the ocean it reveals its identity. It takes up various forms and shows its playfulness. However, it attains peace only after merging in the ocean. The disciple too has his own pride, understanding, plans and restlessness but he does not have peace. He receives that only when he has surrendered at the feet of his Guru. That is why the saints and the scriptures have sung the glories of the Guru."

Today the Guru-Shishya relationship is in grave danger. There are many Gurus and many disciples, but the nature of the Guru-Shishya relationship has changed. The true nature of this relationship is seen very rarely. The level of both, the Guru and the disciple, is deteriorating. Hence the plight of spiritual worship is serious.

I was reminded of an incident from the Ramayana. During Lord Rama's period of exile he went to the ashram of Maharshi Atri and, in the presence of Sita, highly praised Maharshi's wife, Devi Anusuya. In response Devi Anusuya said, "I haven't done anything other than serve my husband with loyalty. I consider him to be my almighty. Due to this total service to him, I have obtained everything." The same thing can be said about a disciple. If a disciple places implicit faith in his Guru, always remains in his service, doesn't run after other Gurus and believes his Guru to be everything, then he needn't do anything else. But pride comes in the way. A disciple disobeys his Guru on a number of occasions. In the presence of the Guru, he lowers his eyes out of shame, but in the Guru's absence his mind runs wild.

I queried, "If the Guru's body has merged, then what does the disciple do?"

Maharajshri said, "Lord Rama's father sent him into exile for fourteen years and thereafter passed away. It never crossed Lord Rama's mind that, because his father wasn't alive anymore, he no longer needed to roam in the forests. Lord Rama fulfilled his promises to his father fully. Even if the Guru's body is not there, the spiritual practice given by him, his instructions and guidance, are with the disciple. And where does the Guru go? Earlier he was visible, now he is invisible. If the disciple is capable, he can see his Guru anytime. Even otherwise, the Guru is always there with an advanced disciple. If he obtains true knowledge of the Guru, then he is freed from the illusion of life and death."

Maharajshri continued speaking and I was dumbfounded. Trying to understand, as if a fountain of knowledge was flowing by, I kept drinking and quenching my thirst. But the thirst was not quenched. The more I drank the more it increased. Each and every word was impacting my heart. Every thought was showing a new direction, and every sentiment that arose in Maharajshri's heart was leading me towards a state beyond explanation. Now questions had stopped arising in my mind. What world? What attachments and aversions? Everything seemed to dissolve in front of me.

7. The Role of an Aspirant

Today my childhood memories were refreshed. The lanes of Lahore, its colors, began to dance in front of my eyes. No one knows the various images the mind holds. One day you open it and wonder at all that you have forgotten. You have no idea what the mind will draw out from within and hold before you. At this time there was no reason for, or likelihood of remembering Lahore, but my mind, as if forcibly, dragged me towards the past.

In those days I used to study in a school. When I sat down to eat, my bread would be hot so, in order to cool it down, I would remove the covering placed on top of it. My mother would say, "No, my son. It's not a good thing to remove the covering from anyone. You should not do it." Now as I thought about it, I realized that Mother conveyed a significant message through the medium of such a small thing. The whole world wanders around wearing clothes, but under those clothes everyone is naked — me, you, everyone. Similarly, everyone's body is clean but their minds are filled with dirt. Only the house that is concealed appears to be clean. Is there a house that has not been occupied by lust, anger and pride? We pull the sheets around us in an attempt to cover ourselves, but we do that by removing the sheets off someone else. We leave the other person to bear the heat and cold of the world. This is the way of all beings in the world, some more, some less. It is only a saint who gives away his sheet and covers others.

During our walk I mentioned this childhood memory to Maharajshri and he said, "This is the way of the world. Everyone you see is involved in pulling off the coverings of others. Seeing defects in others, speculating, imagining, hearing other's faults, believing them and reinforcing them, holding on to one's belief even after that person has proved that the allegation is false — the world does all this. It is said that those who live in glass houses should not throw stones at others. But here everyone is living in glass houses and throwing stones at others. Is there anyone who has not been touched by anger, desire and pride? Is there anyone not ensnared by lust, greed and attachment? Is there anyone who is not intoxicated by his intelligence, yet revels in others' defects without even noticing his own? He also spreads them rampantly. There was a great soul in Iran. A royal order was issued to stone him to death. People began to throw stones at him. Another great soul turned up while wandering and said that only he should throw a stone who has never committed a sin in his life. Every hand was stopped. Similarly everyone is blind, but everyone taunts and teases others for being so.

"No one has the time, nor the interest to think, to pause and penetrate to the root of the matter. They throw stones merely by looking at other people. They call those who are not throwing stones foolish. These people do not realize that although today it is they who are throwing, tomorrow they will be the target. Today you are busy exposing someone, tomorrow you will also be exposed. This is the rule of the world, what a person does to another today, the same will happen to him tomorrow.

"But the perspective of a spiritual aspirant is different. He considers this behavior of the world as the product of his prarabdha [destiny]. The world does not treat everyone in the same way. The treatment meted out to each being is according to his destiny. It is not necessary that his karma be the same today. If there is praise in his destiny, how can anyone criticize him? He does not see the world at fault in this. If he begins to see faults, he, too, will become a part of the world. This is the specialty of an aspirant. Where the world watches for defects and accumulates defects, an aspirant sees innocence and increases his own innocence. Hence an aspirant is not angered by the world's behavior, whereas a worldly person becomes sad. If a person exposes another individual the latter also starts exposing the former in response to his action. Be it true or false, factual or imaginary, somehow the other person has to be insulted. There is a competition in the world, as it were, for belittling others.

"An aspirant sees all this as the play of God. He considers it to be a blessing of God that he has made arrangements for the purification of the mind. In joy or sorrow he sees nothing but the grace of God. Possibly this is the job of Maya: to disillusion people, to make them commit atrocities and in this way purify the chitta of devotees. Maya deserves a salutation; it should be worshipped. If the whole world were pious, who would misbehave with the devotees and purify their minds? People speak ill of Maharshi Vishwamitra for causing grief to King Harishchandra, but only a devotee can understand the great favor that Maharshi bestowed on King Harishchandra by weakening his prarabdha.

"Therefore, if the world exposes you, let it do so. This, too, will remove the covers from your chitta. And don't uncover anyone, because that cover will come and layer your own chitta. Tolerate him who removes your covers, whoever it might be. Do not harbor any hatred towards him, because this will cast a layer of hatred on your own chitta. All this is a play of destiny. Bear it with joy and end it."

My next comment was, "Generally aspirants grow impatient. They wish to have a short cut for progressing in their spiritual practices, by which they can experience the Self as quickly as possible."

Maharajshri said, "Such aspirants either cannot perform spiritual practices or they don't want to. In fact there is no short cut in spiritual practice. If you receive the grace of God, that changes things, but consider all the tasks an aspirant has:"

(i) "To end the feeling of reality about this world. Whereas a worldly person imagines happiness in the world and chases it, an aspirant should see the world as a form of sorrow. Detachment is necessary for this. It is not an easy task to attain the state of detachment — a wholesome detachment full of discrimination and experience, and not a detachment that is a reaction or like a cemetery. In fact, attaining a state of detachment is the toughest part on the path of spirituality. The feeling of attachment is so strong that it does not allow one to withdraw from the world. It takes a long time to achieve this."

(ii) "Infinite love of God. Currently the love of a human is dispersed. Some is directed toward the world, some toward his body, some toward success, some toward power, and some happens to go to God. Love has to be turned away from all these and directed towards God. The world is visible, the senses are extroverted, God is currently invisible — a subject of feelings or imagination. To arouse infinite love of God is such a difficult task. So much effort and time is required."

(iii) "Purification of the chitta. Without the destruction of accumulated impressions and desires, neither is detachment strengthened, nor is the feeling about the reality of the world removed, nor is infinite love of God awakened. Spiritual progress remains a mere dream. Accumulated impressions have turned our tendencies outward through the medium of desires. How is one-pointedness of the mind possible with extroverted tendencies? It is possible only for realized souls to maintain a state of spirituality while tendencies are turned outward, while living in the world. The accumulated impressions are so deep-rooted that continuous effort and caution is required to destroy them. And man is still involved in accumulating new impressions. How will the mind be purified? It is not a small or an easy task. This is the most difficult task in the world. A man does not think twice before accumulating impressions, but when it is time to do spiritual practices he searches for shortcuts.

"These are the reasons why, as I said, people do not want to perform spiritual practices. They make excuses and prefer to waste their time. In fact, that which is the most difficult to achieve, the awakening of the Shakti, has been obtained so easily — isn't that a shortcut? In any case, sadhan has to be done with patience. Impatience in attaining results can disturb the continuity of sadhan.

"This is an age of impatience. The desire to accumulate maximum wealth without hard work, the desire to pass academic courses with good grades without effort, to drive a car at high speeds — these are all examples. The same mental tendency is at work while doing sadhan. Minimum sadhan is expected and the fruits should be obtained as early as possible. The ideal would be to meet a realized soul who places his hand on our head and samadhi is achieved. Thus the world doesn't have to be sacrificed and God is found. Who wants to go through the mess of detachment? It would be better to reach the final destination by a short route. Impatience, wasting time, carelessness and unnecessary tasks have become today's life style.

"In fact, this attitude is dangerous even in worldly matters, but in spiritual practice it causes the downfall of the aspirant in his sadhan. Patience is very important for sadhan, and impatience obstructs it. Another thing is that after the awakening of Shakti the aspirant doesn't perform any spiritual practice. He simply surrenders himself to the Shakti. If it is Shakti who performs spiritual practices, then it has the right to decide the goal of the practice as well as the duration. What right does the aspirant have to interfere? Is his surrender merely vocal?

"Yes, there is surely a shorter path by which you can be liberated, without destroying all your accumulated impressions. But if it is not impossible to walk on that path, it is almost impossible. All your duties, your desires, whatever house, family, wealth, grandeur, success or failure you have, offer it at the feet of the Lord. This surrender should not be merely vocal, it should be sincere. After that, whatever success or failure, gain or loss you have, everything belongs to the Lord. Your mind should not be affected. This is the shortest path, but the chitta must be suitable for such surrender. This state of absolute surrender is a very high state and to develop such a chitta much has to be done. This indicates that, although the path seems short, it is not really so. If such a feeling of surrender develops in the chitta, then the aspirant doesn't have to worry about the purification of the chitta, it is the worry of the one to whom the chitta belongs. He will or will not take care of your house and family. What do you care? Success or failure, everything is his. You are freed by placing all the burden on his shoulders.

"This path is short, but extremely difficult to reach. Pride does not let you surrender like this. It does not want to let go of worries and efforts. This happens due to lack of trust in God. Where there is no trust, surrender is not possible. Where there is no surrender, how is liberation possible? Thus I have said it is a short path, but only a rare person is able to walk on it. It is such a strange path that if you strive for it, even through lives after lives, that state of mind will not be reached. However, sometimes, without any effort, the mind is filled with emotion and this state arises. In any case, for a normal aspirant the right thing to do is to give up the wish of attaining quick liberation and direct the mind toward performing spiritual practices with patience. Spirituality is a long process. It is a task that is difficult to achieve. In spite of all the obstacles that come in the way of your spiritual practices, God's grace is always there. No obstacle is stronger than the power of God. There is only the need to seek the shelter of that power. This is surrender. The Shakti awakened within takes care of everything."

Due to my proximity to, and my conversations with Maharajshri, a new enthusiasm, a new zeal was arising in my mind. One after the other, the knots inside were being untied. Doubts were being resolved and guidance was obtained. Maharajshri would always remain in his own state of mind. Spiritual joy never distanced itself from his chitta. Neither did any defect arise in his mind. Even today that serene image is present before my eyes as it was. In spite of all this, the defects of my own mind were unwilling to accept defeat. Whenever they found an opportunity, they would show themselves, both in social interactions and in solitude. In solitude they would be more active. When I would do sadhan, or go to sleep or chant, or read, they would arise out of nowhere. Sometimes I would become so engrossed in them it was as if I had merged with them and taken on their form. I would resist, involving my mind in sadhan, but like the waves of the ocean the waves of defects would keep on rising, one after the other. My efforts did not work at all. Often my body would be working at the ashram but a storm of defects would pervade my mind. I did not know how to get rid of these internal demons. Finally I decided to place my problem before Maharajshri.

On listening, Maharajshri said, "You will become depressed and turn your face away from sadhan one day if you fight the defects within your mind in this way. First understand certain things very clearly in your mind:"

(i) "It is natural for defects to exist within a human or other living being. What else can be the result of the involvement in attachments for lives upon lives? When one does satsang [spends time in the company of good men] its effect or emotion encompasses the mind. Defects are suppressed but not destroyed from their roots. When the effects of satsang wear off even slightly, defects arise again and make one aware of their existence."

(ii) "For a long time these defects are not going to leave your mind. Many aspirants are involved in sadhan for years. They, too, have good kriyas, perform service and have good sentiments, yet their mental defects are fixed in the mind. Look at me! My whole life has been spent in sadhan yet, at times, defects arise and show themselves. After eons of residence, they are not going to leave their camp — the mind — so easily. Who gives up their power and kingdom with ease? You can make an effort — call God for help, do pranayaam [breath control], chant and read the scriptures — but the defects will not leave the mind now. If you suppress them, they will dominate you even more.

"If you try to fill your mind with sattva guna [good qualities], they will try to remove it. So such a path should be followed whereby, as long as defects are in the mind, they do not cause any trouble."

(iii) "Even in kriya-sadhana [spiritual practices involving kriyas] great caution must be exercised. The task of kriyas is to bring the accumulated impressions to the forefront, make them favorable, and give them an active form in the chitta. Sattva guna impressions will become sattva guna kriyas. Rajo guna [disturbing qualities] and tamo guna [inertia] impressions will result in kriyas of disturbing and inertial types, respectively. Impressions full of defects will cause kriyas with defects. The goal of the kriyas is to purify the mind, but many times when defective kriyas take place, the aspirant cannot bear them. He collapses and surrenders to the defect. The kriya is for purification of the chitta, but the aspirant accumulates many more impressions. Therefore kriya-sadhan requires great caution."

(iv) "By making defects the vehicle of your sadhan, you can proceed towards eliminating them. Here, instead of trying to directly end them, you will have to turn the direction of their flow towards sadhana. If you get angry, direct it towards your faults. If you want to beautify yourself, then beautify God or beautify your mind with good qualities. If attachment arises then love God. If the mind is filled with greed then the greed for achieving God's grace is the best. If you start using your defects like this, then instead of being obstacles they will become your assistants. Then you will start loving your defects, too."

(v) "There is one more solution that is prevalent in our school, which you possibly haven't understood or have forgotten. Do not fight the defects, just observe them. In the same way you observe other kriyas, similarly observe the defective kriyas. Let me remind you again that kriyas are for purification. If there is trash in the house, then trash will be thrown out during cleaning. Thus you should not be afraid of defective kriyas. Don't protect yourself from them, don't wish they never happened, and don't stop them. Keep your distance from the kriyas and, without any effort, simply observe them. The action of that defect will be pacified and the associated samskaras will be destroyed. The fruit of defective kriyas with inertial qualities [tamo guna] is the same as that of kriyas with good qualities [sattva guna] — that is, purification. Sat, raja, and tama represent three qualities. The power causing the kriya [action] is free from these three qualities. If we see it from the perspective of Shakti, then all kriyas are a play of the Shakti on the basis of the gunas [qualities]. From a spiritual perspective, just as tama is an impurity, sat, too, is an impurity. Therefore the solution is to remain separate from all types of kriyas and observe them. In contrast, the solutions mentioned prior to this one precede sadhan and involve an ego of action."

(vi) "You can arouse or develop a defect within you; you cannot destroy it. The job of a living being is to spread dirt inside and outside. It is not his job to purify, make sacred or cleanse. These are the works of the conscious-self and only in its pure light can the task of purification be initiated. That is the difference between a living being and the conscious-self. Even if a being attempts to purify, it is simply his false pride. The solution is to let the one responsible for the task perform it. The greater the interference, the longer it will take. Therefore, set your ego aside and simply observe. Let the conscious-self do the job.

"If the aspirant is simple, sensitive, devotional, and one who does not involve himself in unnecessary speculative arguments and debates, he can continue doing his sadhan with a sense of surrender. Aspirants who have an intellectual inclination are in the habit of thinking logically about everything. For them, clarification of doubts is essential, otherwise doubts will keep on ripening inside the mind and one day destroy sadhan. If you think in depth about these topics the subject will become clear to you. You must understand that waging a war against defects is a waste of energy and time. The more you suppress them, the higher they rebound. Tolerate the momentum of defects; do not surrender to them. If you wish to surrender, surrender to the inner awakened Shakti, which is a benefactor like a mother, a protector like a father, a giver of knowledge like a Guru, and a guide. This is sadhan."

I said, "Maharajji, when you were in Nepal, I had ample opportunity to listen to the conversations of aspirants. Some aspirants claimed that many people started having kriyas upon coming in contact with them. They believed this to be an achievement of their sadhan and claimed their state to be very advanced. What is your opinion?"

Maharajshri said, "This is a lack of control over kriyas of Shakti. Just as water spills off from a vessel while walking, Shakti, too, can be dissipated in the same way. The result is that the aspirant is unable to progress. The Shakti, instead of climbing up, keeps on scattering outside. For an aspirant, this state is of great concern and requires thought. An aspirant in this situation who considers his state to be advanced and is satisfied with his progress is mistaken. He is squandering the benefits of his sadhan. After some time there is a possibility of his own kriyas coming to an end. The more the Shakti progresses under control, the higher it rises.

"One reason for this dissipation may be that the aspirant has a desire to become a Guru. This tendency is fatal for an aspirant. Nothing has been achieved for the self, yet he has begun to show the way to the others. The purpose of becoming a Guru is not to be worshipped, nor to accumulate wealth. It is to assist the progress of others along with your own. For a Guru, the pride of being a Guru is the cause of his decline. It is natural for one to feel proud upon becoming a Guru if he has had a desire to be one, but as a result, dissipation starts."

I said, "But a road of welfare for other people is opened."

Maharajshri said, "It is not opened. When the aspirant's own Shakti flows without control, then how can he grant control to others. After only a few days, the flow of Shakti in other people could stop because it is not awakened. It is just a temporary influence of another person's kriyas, and thus only the so-called Guru believes himself to be an advanced aspirant.

"The subject of an aspirant is very intricate. A sensitive and innocent aspirant ascends the steps of progress on the strength of his feelings and devotion, but an intellectual aspirant must understand these intricacies. Here there is slipperiness at every step, a danger every second and a fear of getting lost at every turn. Such an aspirant has to forge ahead with extreme caution.

"After Shakti is awakened through initiation, the kriyas of Shakti progress under the control of the Guru's resolve. Otherwise uncontrollable kriyas start progressing. If there is a weakness in the Guru's resolve, the kriyas can be uncontrollable. This is a subject for the Guru to think about. If an aspirant pays attention to control in his sadhan, then he can manage his kriyas. An aspirant cannot control the Shakti because Shakti is independent, but he can surely control its kriyas because the basis for the kriyas is the accumulated impressions in his mind. However, one's control should not become an obstacle in the path of progress. During sadhan one should relax. If the kriya becomes so intense that it is out of control, then restraint is called for. If a disciple cannot do it himself, he should contact his Guru. There are many Gurus who give initiation but cannot control kriyas if they become uncontrollable. Giving initiation is like playing with fire. Eventually the kriyas will soften, and then only bliss will be experienced."

8. Sadhan and Social Conduct

Maharajshri considered social conduct to be sadhan. Social conduct makes a person turn away from sadhan, but it also inclines one towards sadhan. Social conduct produces attachment in the mind, but it also frees one from attachment. Social conduct is the door to sadhan and without entering it, sadhan is not possible. Whenever somebody blames conduct or social interaction, saying it should be rejected, he is talking about the rejection of conduct full of pride and attachment. Improper conduct will not go away on its own. Like a bullock at the grinding stone, a living being will keep circling around it. But pure conduct is discarded automatically after the mind is purified. Then if a person interacts with someone else, it is not painful or binding. In fact, to be freed from one's prarabdha [destiny] one must conduct oneself socially. For the destruction of rajo guna, too, social conduct is the solution. For a sense of service, too, there is a need of a social framework. In a Guru-Shishya relationship mutual conduct plays an important role. Without relationships the protection of this body is impossible. The essence is that social conduct cannot be neglected.

But a worldly person doesn't know how to conduct himself. He turns away from spirituality before he enters society. He believes that social conduct is everything. His conduct is not a means, it is a goal. It includes attachment, affection, likes, dislikes and pride. He takes the entire responsibility for doing his tasks and acquiring its fruit on his own shoulders. He even forgets that there is an all-pervading power that controls and drives this world. He plans and works tirelessly to succeed.

If the result is consistent with his wishes, he is overjoyed and credits his capability and hard work. If the result is contrary to his expectations, he becomes sad and blames God. His every action soils his mind. He believes that performing an action is karma yoga. He plans beyond his capabilities and dreams of things he does not deserve. The distinction between moral and immoral is lost to him.

On the contrary, the conduct of an aspirant is totally different. He treats social conduct as his sadhan. He only performs actions that are his duties, and discards actions beyond his duty like a straw. He considers the joys and sorrows confronting him as the law of providence and maintains his composure without letting the mind get affected. He performs every task with concentration but upon leaving it, mentally and physically distances from it. He never makes bad or unnecessary resolutions. He conducts himself with a sense of service. Whatever be the situation he does not get agitated. His conduct, too, is a prayer to God. He performs every task with sacredness. While performing his social interactions, his face glows with happiness.

Maharajshri understood the essence of action and knew at what level a human being was positioned. He was very well aware of where each being had to rise from, how he must rise and, while rising, what precautions he must take. He understood that a common man was incapable of immediately climbing to the peak of detachment. A common man was incapable of establishing harmony between spiritual practice and action. He would have to slowly ascend one level at a time. He would have to advance cautiously and with great care. While bandaging a wound a person recoils. Similarly an aspirant would probably try to save himself from performing his dutiful action, but the task of the Guru is to bring him on track. Thus the responsibility of a Guru is immense.

Maharajshri's style of explanation was unique. He would

take a very simple topic as the foundation and speak profoundly, making the subject crystal clear to the listener. The listener would not even imagine that such a small incident could have such a profound mystery hidden within. For instance, there were some fruit-bearing trees in the ashram — mango, chickoo, gromia, lime and so forth. Those who came to seek his blessings would attempt to pick them and take them away. The ashramites would object to this and occasionally there would be an altercation. Once such a situation arose. The ashramites objected, which resulted in a quarrel. It did not result in a fight but it was a heated argument. Maharajshri was in his chamber. On hearing the commotion he came out. The moment he arrived the argument ended.

Later, in discussion with the ashramites, he said, "You become excited even before you stop them from picking fruit, and thus you magnify the issue. Those people are surely at fault, but you are, too. You forget that you are not common worldly people. You are ashramites — different from common people. We haven't planted these trees for their fruit. The Lord gives us fruit without effort. We have planted those trees for beauty and elegance. If these people harvest anything, it is just the fruit. They do not spoil the beauty and elegance. To be attached to beauty and elegance is not beneficial. If tomorrow someone comes and cuts down the tree itself, you may fight with him, but you will not restore the tree. You cannot restore the lost elegance, so why fight? Why this agitation of the mind? If there is an altercation, do it in such a manner that neither does your chitta get agitated, nor is the other persons' chitta affected. Now have a look at your face, how the anger in your heart is being reflected on it. Life is not for being unhappy."

Then explaining further he said, "This instance reflects how you will approach the performance of actions in general. You all are ashramites — in a way renunciates. It is your duty to solve the mystery of karma facing the world. Unnecessary karma becomes evil karma. Either by performing a task the situation gets better, or else that action is unnecessary. If you answer that your duty is to carry out the karma and not focus on the result, then karma with attachment is not your duty. If there is attachment, the attention invariably turns towards the result. Getting into a quarrel as you have is unnecessary, which suggests attachment. Nothing but agitation will be obtained from this.

In such a manner a person wastes his time in unnecessary karmas. He keeps on accumulating impressions and keeps on revolving in this cycle of death. It is true that performing dutiful actions does not create a state of consciousness, but it creates the chitta necessary for it. Karma is the only coolant that can silence the fire of passion. Karma is such a Sun that can brighten a dark house. Karma destroys karma. Hence it is necessary that the pure, harmonious and spiritual nature of karma always be there in front of the aspirant."

I was sitting quietly, listening to everything. Then I asked, "The scriptures and the saints have called the world a delusion, therefore any karma performed in this world is also a delusion. They why is karma so important?"

Maharajshri said, "You are right. If this world is a delusion, then every incident taking place in it, every word uttered and every karma performed is a delusion, too. But to realize this delusion we must first deliberately bring the notion of the world to an end. Its falseness becomes apparent only after it is destroyed. In order for this notion to dissolve we must destroy it. It is like a dream that must destroy the cause of the dream before it can be interrupted. Even if karma is delusional it can be a cause for purification of the mind. Just as the state beyond emotions cannot be achieved unless the emotions of the heart come forth, the state beyond karma cannot be achieved without performing karma. Also, the dissolution of the impressions created out of ego cannot take place.

"A notion can be ended with a notion. You can also understand this idea in this manner: If this world is a delusion, then this ashram, these fruit bearing trees, the picking of the fruit by the guests, this altercation, this discussion — all this is a delusion. Then why are we agitated?

"Understand one thing. The principle of nonduality [advaita] is correct in its place, but all the rules of karma and spiritual practice are based on duality [dvaita], which indicates that while one does spiritual practice in duality, one has to achieve nonduality. A living being is in duality. If the discussion of nonduality is limited to a discussion only, then it is merely an intellectual indulgence. Only by performing karma and spiritual practice, and by thus purifying the mind, will the illusion of duality be dissolved. If, in the beginning, when the chitta is impure, one accepts the principle of delusion, then spiritual practice also becomes a delusion. This is inevitable for the state of nonduality.

"When you are hungry, you pounce upon food. Feeling hungry and eating food, both are delusional, but only eating satisfies hunger. In the same way the impressions that have accumulated in the chitta and the disturbing tendencies [rajo gunas] that have developed can be removed only by performing good karmas. We cannot overlook accumulated impressions, desires and the impurity of the mind. We cannot ignore them by calling them delusional. If we do so the delusion will continue to exist and we will remain in duality.

"Mere talking is not enough. If you want to get rid of karma then carry out karma and do so with a sense of service and duty. Inward contemplation [nivritti] arises out of social action [pravritti]. Hunger cannot be satisfied without eating food. Sleep is broken only upon waking up. The problem is most people do not understand the pure nature of karma. Some consider karma to be a cause of bondage. Others consider performing the act to be karma, while another performs a karma with attachment and driven by desires."

After initiation I stayed in the ashram for a while. Then one day the thought came to me that I had been living there for four or five months. It was improper to be a burden on the ashram for such a long time. The place in Himachal Pradesh where I had built a cottage and lived before coming to Dewas was on my mind. I like mountainous places a great deal. I enjoyed having brooks everywhere, crooked rivers and roads. Images of high and low greenery lingered in my mind. Frequently the memories of the divine mental bliss I experienced while living there would come back and touch my heart. Therefore the thought was in my mind that, after leaving this place, I would settle in a hill station, solitary, and spend my life immersed in sadhan, in renunciation and without distraction. One day, on finding a suitable opportunity, I proposed to Maharajshri in this manner: "I first came to Dewas with the intention of staying ten to fifteen days in order to be initiated. You were in Nepal at that time, so I had to stay here for two months, awaiting your return. You blessed me with initiation one month after your arrival. Now more than two months have passed since my initiation. Therefore I pray that you grant me permission to take leave."

Maharajshri asked where I would go, and I told him that I would stay at some suitable place and do sadhan. I hadn't decided upon a place, but most likely I would look in Himachal Pradesh. At this Maharajshri said, "Isn't this place suitable for your sadhan?"

I replied, "This place is the best. Guru Maharaj is seated here. There is much solitude. All kinds of facilities are here. There is a cave for sadhan. What place could be better than this? But out of embarrassment, concerned that others might think I have remained a burden on the ashram for a long time, I have considered leaving. In fact, I will always be available to serve at your feet. At one call of yours, I shall come running."

To that Maharajshri said, "People will say? Which people?

This ashram does not belong to the people. I reside here; I shall keep whomsoever I wish. There is no reason to be embarrassed."

I answered, "There is one more thing. There is solitude here, but not the kind of solitude where one is completely alone. Someone or the other always comes. When people come, they gossip. This can make the mind unsteady. My mind wishes that my attention remain undisturbed."

On this Maharajshri responded, "This is your mistake. The mind doesn't become restless due to external conditions alone. Inner impressions and desires also play a part. In reality, the actual cause of restlessness lies within. You want to break away from everything [nivritti] directly, but will not be able to do so. An uninterrupted state is attained only through the experience of social conduct. From what I see, you will not be able to hold yourself away from everything [in nivritti], therefore it is best that you follow a path comprising partly of pravritti and partly nivritti. Both these states are available here. While living among people in society, the study of nivritti is more beneficial.

"Hold the ideal of Swami Gangadhar Tirth Maharaj in front of you. If in the future you develop his kind of mental state, then you, too, can do as he did, if you wish, but you need to prepare a lot for that. The mental bliss you experienced in Himachal Pradesh would not have lasted long. Inner tendencies would have risen, become activated, and could have destroyed that bliss. Do not play with your mind now. Slowly purify your mind with service and spiritual practice. Prepare it, then you may live in pravritti or in nivritti."

I could not ignore Maharajshri's order and advice. I thought that staying at Maharajshri's feet for a year would give me the benefit of serving. Maybe my welfare was in this only. After a period of time I realized that it was due to my ego that I had made the decision to leave.

Once I had offered myself at the feet of the Guru, my mind

had no right to make an independent decision. If you think about surrender, it is a very far-reaching matter. Man wants to surrender and at the same time safeguard his ego. The same thing happens in sadhan. Who can resist from interfering mentally?

Whatever it was, it was my decision at that time to stay at the feet of the Lord and serve. I had no experience of living and conducting myself amongst people and society. It is a fearful era. People are well versed in stabbing while talking sweetly. Selfishness and pride reign in all the four directions. Under such circumstances one is scared to talk to others. How would I survive? As it was, Maharajshri's harmonious influence was spread over the ashram. Many bad qualities prevalent in the world were suppressed once they arrived here, but who can change the flow of the times? On the one hand, there was my desire for Maharajshri's company and service, on the other my fear of problems arising out of contact with people. The majority of the people at the ashram were inclined towards the Guru, but some were still self-absorbed.

As has been said earlier, at that time the size of the ashram was very small. Not many visitors came, but what a difference they made. Whenever two or more people get together, there is a possibility of some dispute. The world is the same everywhere. Be it an institution, organization, home, shop or office, there are actions full of attachment and aversion, push and pull, and selfishness everywhere. But Maharajshri, overwhelmed by a feeling for my welfare, had ordered me to stay here. It must be for my good.

Now that I had to live in the ashram, it was important to plan my direction. By now I had been living there for almost six months. This period was long enough for me to become acquainted with the activities of the ashram. People certainly did their sadhan, but the soil in the mind doesn't leave so easily. The impressions of many past lives are so solidly established inside that they make the mind unstable, make it follow them, and keep it wandering in the world. It was good that I had attempted to keep myself away from attachments and aversions here and, by the grace of the Guru, I had been quite successful. I would listen to everyone but remain quiet myself. Now the issue before me was that I had to spend one year here. The joy of proximity to the Guru was a great attraction for me and hence I rejected the joy of solitude. For solitude my whole life was still ahead of me.

Now the problem I was faced with was what kind of lifestyle I should maintain so as not to get entangled in any dispute. After deep contemplation and thought I reached the conclusion that, first and foremost, I should set some rules for myself regarding what to pay attention to, what to safeguard against, and what I needed to do. Once rules are laid down, they must be strictly adhered to. The following rules were finalized:

(i) To keep myself busy with more and more seva activity. An empty mind is a devil's workshop. It invariably comes up with useless things. In this way I would avoid hearing people criticize and talk ill about others. Even if someone wanted to talk to me, he would have to wait for some time because I would be busy with my work and would be able to listen only after I had finished. In this way, I kept myself free from an unnecessary environment.

(ii) To immediately go away from wherever there is a dispute, altercation or fight. Even if one doesn't utter a single word, doesn't interfere and take side or oppose anyone, he can still be called as a witness anytime. It is clear that whatever the witness says will be in someone's favor and against another. Whoever it is against is bound to become an opponent. The best thing is to slip away from such situations.

(iii) Since the beginning I had no interest in talking ill about others, gossiping or instigating people against one another. I remember an incident: A particular gentleman was talking a lot against me. At one point I had a talk with him about this and he said that I, too, could talk against him. At that time I said, "Then what would be the difference between you and me? It is better, when you speak against me, that I still not talk against you, but rather respect you and love you as before." The same rule I finalized again. "Do not listen to anyone's criticism, nor criticize anyone." This caused me a great deal of discomfort, but my mind remained calm. I recognize that it feels very good to criticize someone and to listen to others criticize. There is pleasure in it, but its results are very frightening. Due to this rule, I became less important in many areas.

(iv) To not to complain about anyone. I was in the personal service of Maharajshri. I had many opportunities to say things about people, if I wished. In some ways I was the *via media* between Maharajshri and people. I was also aware of the situations of the other aspirants. Some were jealous of me due to my proximity to Maharajshri, but I never complained about anyone. Complaining means making that person your enemy. In response, that person covers up the actual cause of complaint, and introduces other incidents, factual or imaginary, to defend himself. He starts raising unrelated arguments. A person who has made service his goal doesn't have time to give clarifications for such unnecessary things or get involved in them. Yet, in spite of taking so many precautions, sometimes, unnecessary arguments would invariably occur. Such is the world. It thinks according to its own mental state. The more you try to keep away from it, the more it surrounds you. But this rule gave me mental satisfaction.

(v) To avoid unnecessary arguments. When people make an argument an issue of personal defeat or victory, that argument becomes meaningless and unnecessary because the distinction between right and wrong ceases to exist. An argument is for understanding, for explaining your point of view and persuading. Upon losing, a participant may want to seek revenge. In this way unnecessary enmity can breed. To understand a topic, acceptable arguments are not unnecessary. But unnecessary arguments are a waste of time. It is a loss of service and a cause of an impure mind. At such times, get up and leave, immediately accept defeat or remain quiet.

(vi) To try to act in complete accordance with Guru Maharaj's wishes and orders. I would do everything to please the Guru. If this is not the case, then there is no point in serving. Talk humbly to Maharajshri and try to understand his intent. Follow Guru Maharaj's orders literally, in front of him and in his absence, too. Do not interrupt if Guru Maharaj is speaking to somebody, and do not try to establish my importance in front of other people. Remain close to him to be able to answer if he asks anything. When Maharajshri is seated amongst people and groups, either stand behind him or sit behind the people facing him. When he is walking, walk behind him and go wherever he wishes to go. Do any job exactly as he wants it to be done. Never argue beforehand and keep quiet when scolded.

My mind was certainly impure. There was clearly a need for much sadhan, for tolerance of many things, and for generosity in order to get rid of impurities. It is not an easy task to chop off your head with your own hands. The same is the case with sadhan. Chopping off the head of our ego is sadhan. He who wants to save his head cannot reap the fruits of sadhan. I knew this fact, but pride within was getting in my way. Even though I was following the rules, there was uneasiness inside. If pride did not find an occasion to come out, it would keep churning my heart inside. I would become sad. Many times, even though I wasn't at fault, and despite his being aware of the details of an incident,

Maharajshri would scold me and ask me to beg for forgiveness from some person. Upholding the command of the Guru, I would seek forgiveness, but internally I would writhe in agony. It was my ego that was being hurt and probably Maharajshri's intent was to inflict a blow on my mind. Also, it wasn't necessary for Maharajshri to explain his point of view to other people. Only a Guru knows about Gurus. Due to their impure chitta, people could have misinterpreted what he said.

I laid down rules, but it was extremely difficult to follow them. People do not judge a person based on his rules, feelings and conditions. They judge him through the blinders of their own feelings. They weigh him by their own thoughts. An aspirant who is in contact with the public and is involved in serving everyone encounters many difficulties. I repeatedly evaluated the competence of my mind, my tolerance and my capability. Eventually I decided to commit to my rules. If I do not walk, how will I get where I am going? I have to start some time or the other. If I make a mistake, I will be scolded. That, too, will be beneficial for me. Some of the qualities imposed by my rules already existed in me. I would have to make an effort for those that did not yet exist within. In the same way I made resolutions at the beginning of the last decade of the past century, but their mention here would be out of context. In the present selfish era, one encounters a lot of difficulties in following such rules. I, too, encountered them, but by the grace of the Guru I kept surmounting these difficulties.

The example of Grandsire Bhishma, in the Mahabharata, illustrates the inner turmoil of an aspirant. He had taken a vow and throughout his life had stuck to it. Dhritarashtra, the King, was blind with attachment. He thought only about his son, Duryodhana. Every decision of Dhritarashtra was clearly stamped by this attachment. Bhishma was bound by an oath to protect the king who occupied the throne, to follow every command of his and not to question anything. He would burn internally but endure his anguish. Neither could he say anything to anyone, nor could he utter even a word of complaint. He had to fight alongside Duryodhana's allies against his own wishes and also endure the insulting, disgraceful sight of Draupadi's disrobing. He tolerated everything with a distressed heart, but his resolve did not shake. The state of a tolerant, serious aspirant is somewhat similar to this. He endures insults, regarding them as the law of providence, without a word of complaint on his lips. He respects everyone, loves everyone. People condemn him; he keeps on listening. If someone misbehaves, he forgives. His goal is to subdue his mind, not to acquire the praises and applause of the world. But even in this inner fire he experiences joy. He regards the joys and sorrows experienced in the world as the fruit of his destiny. Joys and sorrows come and go. They leave behind a pure mind. Thus he hears criticism and does not react. If someone oppresses him, he forgives. He loves even those who consider him to be their enemy.

In those days I was responsible for an excessive amount of ashram activities. My schedule would start at three o'clock in the morning. In twenty-four hours, Maharajshri would have just one cup of coffee at half past three in the morning, and no more tea or coffee throughout the day. I would have to get up at three o'clock and finish my morning activities before making coffee at half past three. Then I would begin rendering services: clean Guru Maharaj's cottage, take Maharajshri for a walk, make arrangements for his bath, shop, do kitchen work, take care of the garden, look after visitors, and other things. Throughout the day I did not even have time to stop and converse. In addition to the personal service of Maharajshri, there was the responsibility of ashram activities. I was so busy that I would hardly get time for my sadhana. For that I would enter the cave at ten o'clock at night after Maharajshri had retired for the day.

All this service was nothing, neither in its effect, nor in my feelings. The head bows down with reverence upon reading about those who have continuously served their Gurus with an unbroken sentiment. I seemed like a dwarf in comparison to the untiring effort and sense of service with which Supreme Gurudev Swami Shankar Purushottam Tirth Maharaj, now one with the absolute, served his Gurudev Swami Narayan Tirth Dev Maharaj. No one can serve Guru Maharaj. Only he upon whom the Guru showers his grace and from whom he wishes to be served can serve the Guru. Therefore the credit of service goes not to the sevak [the one rendering service] but to the one being served. While rendering my service, at times I would get angry. Pride would arise at times. All this is against the dharma [duty] of a sevak, but the impurity of my mind would trouble me. A sense of service was the remedy for it, but occasionally service would become a harsh medicine instead of a good one. Then I would condemn my mind. At times I would end up crying over my mental state.

To understand the mysteries of the way of service [seva dharma] and to draw inspiration, in my spare time I would read stories of *Guru Sevaks* published by Kalyan Press, Gorakhpur. The feelings and the dedication with which those devotees served their Gurus are unparalleled. I was still raw and a novice, but I could still hold them before me as an ideal. This helped me in understanding the matter.

When Shri Guru Maharaj went somewhere for lunch, and if he took me with him, all my resistances would dissolve. I would not speak without being spoken to, nor comment on anything. I would eat whatever and however much was given, and attend to the protocols of rising and sitting. Even if the pulses or cooked vegetables did not have salt, I wouldn't ask for it. Guru Maharaj's love was infinite. It wouldn't be an exaggeration to say that he drenched me in a rain of love. But his reprimand had a color of its own. Whenever he resorted to reprimands, he would do so without any hesitation, leaving no stone unturned, but the next moment he would transform into his loving form.

I remember an incidence of Maharajshri's generosity. A certain ascetic came to the ashram. Some ashramites did not like his arrival. They believed that such wandering ascetics roamed only for food. They inquired of Maharajshri whether they could ask him to leave. Maharajshri said, "First give him food. It is inappropriate to ask a person who has come with a hope of food to leave without offering it. You are not aware of the difficulties of a wandering ascetic: where to eat, where to sleep. For them nothing is definite. Each day they are unsure whether they will get any food to eat or not. This is a form of sadhan." The thoughts of Maharajshri and other people were so far apart. On one side was the very personification of generosity and, on the other, a contracted heart. Spellbound, I was listening to Maharajshri's voice. The ashramites could not appreciate Maharajshri's words, but what could they do? It was an order. They served him food.

After resting for some time, Maharajshri was sitting in the courtyard. A person from the nearby village brought around twenty kilograms of wheat on his head as a gift. Suddenly Maharajshri shouted, "Call all those people who wanted to send the ascetic away without serving him food." After everyone had arrived Maharajshri said, "In return for the food you gave to that ascetic, receive this wheat."

Everyone looked at each other's face. No one had anything to say. Then Maharajshri said, "Do you think you have served him food? No one can serve anything to anyone, nor give anything. All eat according to their destiny, take according to their destiny. When a person walks, his destiny walks ahead of him. It is your misconception that you feed another. If it is not in your destiny, even if you possess everything in the house, you will still remain hungry. If it is in your destiny, even in a forest you will receive delicacies to fill your stomach. Anyone can be the medium." I have witnessed many similar incidents of Maharajshri, through which the generosity of his heart was demonstrated.

Maharajshri was always opposed to influencing the disciples of other Gurus and accepting them into his sphere of control. "Those who cannot commit to their own Guru, how will they commit to us? Even if they could, faith in one's own Guru is always beneficial. One should never interfere in the spiritual practice of someone else's disciple. If a disciple of some other Guru asked a question, the answer should be, 'Ask this to your Guru Maharaj. Do as he says.' Even if the sadhana is the same, there could be a difference in the system. The mixture of two systems can destroy the naturalness of the kriyas of an aspirant. Only the system of spiritual practice professed by one's own Guru Maharaj is beneficial to the aspirant."

In this way I would find myself at confusing crossroads. On one side were the attachments, aversions, lust, anger, greed, selfishness and other bad tendencies of the world. On another was the excessive burden of ashram services. On a third side were impurities within me. On a fourth side was Maharajshri's grace, his love-filled conduct and his simple, serene and spiritual personality. Sometimes my mind would incline towards one side and sometimes towards another. While serving the ashram, my anger and pride would assail me intermittently. Generally I would keep it inside, but my mind would lose control at times. In the world attachments, aversions, selfishness and other things have captured the minds of all people. While dealing with me, if someone invoked these bad qualities, my mind would be tormented within. But what can one do about this world? Neither has it improved, nor will it improve. The impurities of the mind keep on disturbing the chitta. As long as there is garbage in the mind, defilement is bound to be there. Guru Maharaj's personality was the only support. A single, sweet, love-filled smile of his would cool the depths of my heart. Every instructional word from him would put to rest old and festering doubts, and the system of sadhan given by him would wash away all the impurities of the chitta. Until now I had just been hearing the words "Guru" and "Guru-tattva" [the fundamental cosmic principle in the Guru]. Now their nature, their secrets and their difference began to clear for me.

I was enclosed in four walls, such that there was no door between the two walls of worldly attachments and aversions, and of the impurities of my mind. The wall of service had a small window that, nevertheless, had a persistent filter of pride and anger. Through it I could see the beautiful scenery outside and cool air entered inside. The fourth wall, that of Guru's grace, had a huge gate and, through that, one could pass without anyone stopping or questioning you. The Guru's grace is the only door to come out of this prison, that is, the painful illusory web of this world.

At Maharajshri's feet my faith increased. Now while carrying out the services of the ashram, going to the bazaar or in the kitchen, everywhere, every moment, I was experiencing the divine energy of Maharajshri. Everything happened on an experiential plane in my sadhana, and the same state also persisted in my conduct. While working, the mind would think of going to see Maharajshri. Fifteen minutes, half an hour later, I would make a trip to Maharajshri's room under some pretext or the other.

9. Seva Marg: The Path of Service

Now it was becoming clear to me how rigorous the path of service is. The world weighs the service of the sevak on the scale of selfishness. It tests his service against the touchstone of pride. It has nothing to do with the sentiments of the sevak. If the service of the sevak encounters someone's selfishness, that person does not abstain from insulting the sevak. I was serving Maharajshri, but the activities of the ashram, the responsibility for visitors — all these tasks were also a part of Maharajshri's service. People would forget the fact that I was Guruji's attendant and, because of the services I rendered in so many areas, considered me their own attendant. That's where problems would start. I was now experiencing what I had heard in holy company and read in books — that the path of service is the most rigorous of all. There was no shortage of pride and anger in me, too. At times I expressed it, otherwise I would burn internally. If a sevak does someone else's work a hundred times, but for some reason is unable to do it once, that person forgets the hundred instances and is bent on teaching the sevak a lesson.

People would come to see Maharajshri at their convenience after taking care of their work at home and at their business. There was no concern for Maharajshri's convenience, his health, or how much hard work he had to do during the day. That could be well understood only by a sevak who was in his close proximity. If someone was prevented from seeing him, it was the sevak's misfortune. Anything that seemed inappropriate to be done by Maharajshri and appropriate to be done by the sevak, if the sevak did not do, there would be a grievance against him. Generally people would be disappointed with the sevak who serves in the kitchen.

Now look at the sevak's plight: If he is a true sevak, then all the devotees of the Master are equally dear to him. No attachment to anyone, no aversion for anyone, no expectations of anyone. Serve everyone equally. He is like a bridge between the devotees and his master. He has to pay attention to the convenience of his master and at the same time serve the devotees. A sevak doesn't ask anyone for anything, he just serves. Even when others are sarcastic to him, even when he is praised, he bears everything and does not give up his service. But people are neither concerned about the master's comfort, nor the sevak's helplessness. The more a sevak serves, the more the world troubles him.

In those days I was so engrossed in serving Maharajshri that visitors thought I was a general servant of the ashram. I had an overgrown beard, naked feet and extremely dirty clothes, just like a servant who was kept for doing chores. Once a gentleman was visiting, accompanied by his wife and a servant. He would repeatedly send me to the bazaar for some errand or the other. Then he asked me to grind some soaked pulses. I refused because a lot of the daily work of the ashram was still pending. Then he complained to an ashramite, "This man of yours does not do our work. Even the soaked pulses had to be ground by my own servant because he refused." At that moment I passed by, so the ashramite said, laughing, "He is complaining about you."

Soon the gentleman erupted at me, shouting that I had said certain things to him, and that I avoided work. I replied, "I have a lot of work for the ashram. If you want to have something prepared in the kitchen, then you will have to make your own arrangements. You already have a servant." I left after saying this. Later the ashramite explained to him that I was not their servant, that I worked with a sense of service and they couldn't demand anything more of me. On hearing this the gentleman was surprised and came to me to ask for forgiveness.

In rendering my services I experienced many such difficulties. I had made a resolve to spend the period of one year in service. Often, when someone else took the credit for something I had done, I would feel very bad, but I would pacify myself by thinking that one doesn't serve for rewards. Getting an opportunity to serve was a reward in itself. Anyone who serves with the intention of winning a prize, fame or success is fooling himself and the one who is served. I would also feel bad when somebody would hold me responsible for a task that went wrong. But I had made it a rule not to complain or speak ill of anyone, and not to react if anyone criticized me. At first glance, it seemed that I had limited myself by making such rules. But all these things were a part of my spiritual practice. When I was scolded by Guru Maharaj, I would satisfy myself by saying that this, too, was for my benefit. Thus the path of eliminating my accumulated impressions kept opening, through tolerance. I would frequently remember Shankaracharya's words: *"Sahanam sarva dukhaanaam apratikaar purvakam."* ["Bear all sorrows. Do not resist."] Shankaracharya must have surely written this after deep contemplation and experience.

My mind was surely impure. Who knows from how many births filth had accumulated? Now new impressions were also accumulating. If this wasn't the case, why would my mind become insane, panicky and unstable. If the chitta was pure why did it need to wander? Only a diseased person goes to a physician. Only a being troubled with the issues of the world seeks refuge with a Guru. All saints and great men have had to deal with the tricks of the mind. All of them have cried about their minds, and all of them have named the Guru as a cure.

I have already written that I had a lot of ashram duties to perform, but all this service was physical. My stay definitely caused some financial burden to the ashram and I couldn't help this as I had nothing. I would see many other people who would provide financial support whenever required. Some would just stop by for glass of water and leave a gift as they left. On the other hand I was living there, a burden on the ashram, with nothing to offer. This thought began to weigh on my mind. This recurring concern also affected my physical service. My mind was unable to concentrate on my work. Finally, I came up with a solution. Why not take a small job somewhere? Whatever I earned, I would offer entirely to the ashram, just as all my time was already given to the ashram. My mind liked this solution. When I spoke to a couple of people they said that I could surely get some job or the other, but first I would need to make my request to Maharajshri and get his permission. I started looking out for the right occasion and at the same time started preparing myself for the conversation.

On getting an opportunity, I told Maharajshri, "A thought has been troubling me for some days. Everyone serves you financially. In contrast, I have become a burden on the ashram. I am thinking of taking some small job. Whatever I earn will become a service to the ashram. Physical service will continue in the remaining time."

Maharajshri remained silent and listened. Then he said, "How did this thought occur to you? The people who serve monetarily have a hundred rupees and they offer one rupee. But you have offered everything of yours to the ashram. How can their service be compared to yours?" Then he said, "I thought you were very mature, but now I feel I was mistaken." I felt ashamed on listening to Maharajshri's words. Now what could I say beyond this?

10. Attachments and Aversions

There was a priest who came to the ashram daily and meditated, but he was not on good terms with the managers of the ashram and one of the bramhacharis. After my arrival at the ashram he became quite close to me and whenever possible also helped me. He addressed me very sweetly. Maharajshri had gone out on a tour. The priest invited me to his house for a meal, which I accepted after some hesitation. The priest served me delicious food, strongly insisting that I eat well. The conduct of his entire family towards me was very loving and full of respect. However along with this, he continuously tried to corrupt my mind against the managers and the bramhachari of the ashram, which made the delicious food seem very bitter and poisonous. I started to see that family as a divine demon, sowing the seeds of demonic impressions in my mind. I repeatedly tried to change the topic, but after some time he would return to it. It seemed that he wished to give vent to all his frustrations in one day. It felt as if hot lead was being poured in my ears.

From a worldly perspective he might be a well-wisher, but from a spiritual standpoint there was no one more harmful than he was. Are such persons really well-wishers? No. While displaying a feeling of kindness and support they serve you sweet poison. They invoke feelings of attachment and aversion about someone or the other in your mind. An enemy is better than they are. At least his real nature is known, whereas these so-called well-wishers pollute your mind with poison, which their sweetness makes easy to accept.

At last I finished my meal with a burdened mind and took

my leave. All along the way to the ashram I kept thinking about the priest's conduct. Again and again I would feel pity for his mental state. Intermittently I would feel angry, too. Why did he attempt to spoil the mind of an aspirant? There was already a lot of impurity within me. I would feel pity because he was so helpless before the influence of his mental state. Thereafter I never gave the priest an opportunity to talk. Even if he said something, I would find some excuse to sneak away. But never did a feeling of hatred or aversion towards the priest arise in my mind.

There were several people who were determined to follow the wishes and words of Maharajshri, but others behaved very inconsistently. Sitting in the courtyard near Maharajshri's window, I would hear him giving instructions and the reply, "Yes, Maharajji," would also reach my ears. After coming out the same person would say, "He is a Mahatma. He is great. How does he know the conditions existing in the world? We are the ones who have to deal with worldly matters." I would be taken aback on hearing their contradictory talk. Is this the same person, who was saying, "Yes. Yes!" inside a moment ago? Why was there no courage to say the same thing in front of Maharajshri? If you have any difficulty, why not tell it to the Guru? But in front of Maharajshri they act like great devotees, aspirants. Upon coming out they become totally worldly. I couldn't appreciate this hypocritical talk.

Not that all people were like this. There was no shortage of those who took Maharajshri's words seriously. They would place their difficulties in front of Maharajshri. Accordingly they would receive satisfaction from him. Such people were my ideals. Maharajshri would say, "Here is the ideal to strive towards. Whatever you can apply in your own life, do at least that much. As you keep on doing so, your scope of trying will increase and eventually, some day, you will be able to walk naturally in accordance with the ideal. God will help." A majority of people could not do this.

They would nod their heads in approval, leave, and later contradict the instructions. Maharajshri would say that the influence of his talk lasts only for the time it takes people to step out of the gates of the ashram. One could see that the influence on these people had worn off even before they left the ashram.

Maharajshri would explain that attachment and aversions are the world. The world is important to him whose mind has attachments and aversions, and the world makes him happy or sad. Therefore moving away from attachments and aversions is spiritual practice. It can also be said that the goal of all spiritual practices is to end the feeling of attachment and aversion. Attachments and aversions are the cause of all mental defects. Anger, greed, attraction, and so forth are born out of attachments and aversions. I am not saying that I did not make mistakes. Due to attachments and aversions, often things would hurt me that should not have, but I would suppress them internally. Often I would get angry but not express it. In general, people in the world are ignorant. Their attention is never drawn towards these matters. They have no control over speech and action. They get excited very quickly. They cannot pay attention to things such as what to say, when to speak, where to speak, and so forth. Generally people develop a feeling or thought in one of four ways:

(i) **Imagination**. The mind is very efficient at imagining things. A person imagines something or the other all the time. He builds huge castles of imagination without any basis, then his mind keeps on wavering due to those castles, and speech becomes the medium of spreading them all over the world.

(ii) **Speculation**. Speculation is also built into the nature of a being. "So-and-so met such-and-such person and surely he must have said something about me." Then one considers many things on the basis of this speculation. "Could he have said something like this? If he has said something like this, I will certainly have to respond." Just on the basis of such speculation, one starts a campaign against another, and without determining how true or false it is, gossips about whatever comes to mind.

(iii) **Hearsay**. It is also human nature to believe anything that one hears, especially if it is something ill about someone. It is not a good practice to believe something simply because someone has said it, without verifying its authenticity. There is no shortage of people with bad qualities in this world. In fact, every person holds a storehouse of bad qualities within. No one pays attention to their own defects, but everyone is ready to take notice of the smallest infraction of others. Whatever you say to any person, be assured that it will reach many people.

(iv) **Factual**. Facts have their basis in truth. But people associate many imaginary and speculative things with facts and blow them out of proportion. As they travel from one mouth to another, their form expands. Facts are overwhelmed, and what remains is a pile of imaginary and speculative ideas.

I could see people entangled in all the above ways. I had to confront them, too. If there was a factual basis for a complaint, I did not have any problem in explaining or seeking forgiveness. But what could be done about imaginary, speculative and hearsay remarks? I would feel bad when such things were said, no matter who the speaker was. My detachment was not ripe, neither was I a Siddha yogi [a perfect being]. My mind would be in turmoil, but by remembering the teaching of Guru Maharaj that attachments and aversions are the cause of joy and sorrow, I would pacify my mind. I would repeatedly look inside myself. Upon meeting a person whose chitta was dominated by good qualities, it seemed as if a gentle breeze made my heart ecstatic. Upon encountering a worldly person, it seemed as if a hot wind had charred me from within. Guru Maharaj's state was exactly contrary to this. His mind would always be in the same state. How did Maharajshri attain this state? Would I be able to attain it?

Maharajshri used to say, "Even great intellectuals and ascetics can not rise above attachments and aversions." Then what is the chance of poor worldly people and raw aspirants. Here is an incident of one of those days when Guru Maharaj had gone on a tour:

I was almost alone in the ashram. There was no one to cook, nor any other ashramite. Due to Guru Maharaj's absence, there were hardly any visitors. I did not have much work to do. At such times only thoughts about gardening and planting vegetables came to my mind. I thought that when Maharajshri returned he would be happy to see vegetables planted. Pride and a desire to be praised had arisen in me. As the spinach, fenugreek, coriander, papaya, and so forth started growing, my pride, too, became stronger. Words of praise started ringing in my ears. I became attached to those vegetables. I would sit in the kitchen courtyard watching them and experience joy within.

In those days there were no walls around the ashram. As it was open on all sides, any one could come and go from anywhere. I was in the kitchen cooking. When I came out, some goats were making a meal of the papaya tree. I was enraged upon seeing this and, grabbing a stick, ran to beat the goats. What chance had I of catching the goats? I chased them over a long distance. I was panting, so I came back. My body was burning with rage and, disarming myself, I lay down. My pride and desire to be praised had been crushed. I did not even feel like having lunch that day. I fell asleep while lying down. I saw Maharajshri in my dream. He said, " Had you not developed an attachment for that farming and those plants? Was there not a desire in you to earn praise? If you had done all this with a sense of duty and service to the Guru, and if you had understood the secret of dutiful action, then you wouldn't have had to bear this dejection and sorrow." I awoke immediately. Maharajshri's words were still echoing in my ears. The mystery of desireless work [Karma Yoga] was still not clear to me. I thought of asking Maharajshri about this on his return, but one thing was clear: Instead of a sense of service, the desire to earn praise was dominant in my mind. This hope was the cause of my dejection.

11. Sevak Dharma: The Essence of Service

When Maharajshri went to visit his disciples and devotees or traveled to different places, a bramhachari or other people would always accompany him and leave me behind at the ashram. Once when Maharajshri departed for a tour, leaving me behind, I felt very bad. I thought that my position was limited to serving and keeping watch over the ashram. "Whenever Maharajshri visits his disciples, he never takes me with him!" My mind was very depressed and dejected. It was evening and some people came as they always used to. One gentleman was fairly resolved and also very kind to me. He ended up asking me why I didn't go with Guruji. His question gave me an opportunity to open my heart and reveal it to him. I said, "When do I have such good fortune? I only take care of the ashram. There are many people available to go out with Maharajji. How will I get a chance?"

Seeing me dejected he said, "Don't be afraid. One day you, too, will go with Maharajshri and tour the whole country. Why are you upset?" Then explaining to me further he said, "The path of service is very subtle. A sevak doesn't have any personal ambitions. Wherever his master puts him to work, he remains dedicated there, considering it to be his good fortune. He does not desire honor or luxury, nor does he have any ambition for himself. This depression of yours does not suit the duty of a sevak [Sevak Dharma]. You should think seriously and generously about the duty of a sevak. It is your good fortune that Guru Maharaj has considered you worthy of his service and assigned you work. It is not important what that work is. What is important is that he has trusted you and assigned you a service. Therefore, continue to do your work without any pride, full of a sense of service, with total commitment. Therein lies your welfare. In the future, when Guru Maharaj finds you suitable for some other work, he shall give it to you."

After listening to him my mind became peaceful. I said, "You have cleared the misconception from my mind. I had succumbed to pride even while performing service. I was harboring many hopes in my heart, and when these hopes were not fulfilled, I was unhappy. Now there is no dejection in me."

I was freed from my dejection, but I cried a lot over my mental state. I was so ignorant that I could not even understand such a small thing. In fact, all these things had been known to me from the beginning. I would explain this to others, but I became confused due to the impurities in my mind. When I met a guide I began to see the way. I thought very deeply and very seriously about dutiful action [Seva Dharma] and by the grace of Guru Maharaj the aspects of Seva Dharma that arose and shone within me are given here:

(i) **Pride is an opponent of the sense of service.** Even if a person filled with pride renders service, there is a fear of his falling away from it. Often a proud man starts feeling that the importance of his master is a result of his support. If he withdraws his service, he believes, then his master will lose importance. He does not realize that he has been favored by receiving an opportunity to serve.

(ii) **A sevak never wishes for any form of respect.** A desire for honor is contrary to the sense of service. A sevak does not think that because he is rendering service he should gain in status and be consulted for everything; that if people come together, he should be offered a special seat. He always wishes for his master's honor and is personally satisfied in being his attendant.

(iii) **A sevak never brings the thought to his mind that he is a** sevak. He is grateful to his master or to the one he is serving for their infinite grace in giving him the opportunity to serve. Thus he demonstrates that he is not responsible for his service; on the contrary his master deserves the credit. It is the Guru who chooses who will serve — someone whom he finds suitable, or whomever it pleases him to select.

(iv) **It is not necessary that a master give clear orders to his sevak to do something**. If at a particular time he expresses a certain desire, the sevak does not treat it as any less than a direct order. He always remains engaged in the master's welfare in accordance with the master's comfort. The sevak does not have anything of his own. Whatever he has, everything belongs to his master, to such an extent that his body, mind, time and inner tendencies all belong to his master.

(v) **Anger makes a person insane**. In anger a person loses the distinction between right and wrong. He is not aware of what to say, to whom and when. An angry person at times is unable to respect his master and says things that shouldn't be said. Therefore an angry person is totally unfit to serve. Greed, attachment and lust also fall under this category. There is only one feeling in the mind of a sevak, the feeling of service to the Guru. He only wants the happiness of his Guru and nothing else.

(vi) **The personality of the Guru represents welfare**. He always wishes for the welfare of his disciple. Often the disciple cannot understand his Guru's actions, but only a Guru can know when and in what manner to bring about the welfare of the disciple. Therefore the welfare of the disciple lies in his accepting the Guru's word without finding any fault in it.

(vii) **A Guru has many disciples**. Everyone wants to personally attend the Guru because it is considered to be the highest form of service. This is a misconception. It is not possible that all disciples be engaged in personal service. Another consideration is, if all disciples gather around the Guru, who will do the other work? Cook, clean, water the garden, shop, welcome visitors and many other tasks — all are a part of service to the Guru. A Guru's mind is very generous. The whole ashram is encompassed in it. All his disciples are like his children. The service of a disciple who remains silent, at a distance from the Guru, involved in other activities of the ashram, cannot be considered inferior.

(viii) **Along with service to the Guru, it is important to remember that one must maintain love and goodwill toward other sevaks.** Often there is dissention between sevaks, which can never be in their favor or beneficial to their service. Ultimately it is the work of the Guru that is compromised. The energy that should have been spent in some task is spent in conflict and the pleasure of the Guru is not obtained.

(ix) **It is important for a sevak to have a generous heart.** People from outside come to seek the blessings of the Guru. They, too, wish to serve him. It is the duty of the sevak to give them an opportunity to do so. Giving others a chance to serve is also a service. This does not reduce the importance of the sevak; it invariably increases it.

(x) **Maharajshri used to glorify the cultivation of a life devoted to service.** He used to say that if some time was spent in serving and the rest was spent in conduct involving attachments and aversions, it would be difficult for the aspirant to achieve the desired goal. It is true that it is better to do some service rather than none, but for spiritual elevation every moment of life and every action carried out by us should be like service.

(xi) **This tendency is commonly seen among serving aspirants:** to follow all the Guru's orders while in his presence, but, in his absence, to slacken. Their belief is that Guru Maharaj is not there.

They do not believe in the omnipresence of the Guru-Shakti [the power of the Guru], hence they cannot identify with it. The commands of the Guru should be followed in the same way, whether in his presence or when he is far away, by believing in the power and omnipresence of the Guru-Shakti.

(xii) **It is not beneficial for a sevak to become agitated.** A sevak is the epitome of tolerance. He must restrain his mind a lot and yet keep serving. An aspirant who gets excited at small things cannot serve for a long time. Many such aspirants are seen who, upon getting excited or having an altercation with someone, give up their services and move aside or go away. According to their viewpoint, their pride is more important than their service. Only a tolerant person can continue to serve.

(xiii) **It is the duty of a sevak to obey his Guru's orders.** To explain your viewpoint to the Guru in an attempt to change his opinion is contrary to the duty of a sevak. Who knows what is in the mind of Guru Maharaj? Who knows what he wants to achieve through a particular task? If a sevak tries to impose his opinion, then there is a possibility that the goal that Guru Maharaj wishes to achieve will be left aside. There is a possibility that the well-being of the disciple was involved in his performance of the task. The disciple is unable to understand this.

(xiv) **If the Guru is served with tolerance, good feelings and love**, then it helps in ending the destiny [prarabdha] of the disciple. If the service is in a pure form, then it does not accumulate any impressions because the sevak doesn't have any desires, wishes or attachments. In this way service causes the destruction of one's accumulated impressions.

(xv) **Service is definitely important.** Here we have been talking about physical, mental and intellectual service, but along with this it is important to mention another type of service. That service is the progress of the spiritual practice [sadhana] imparted by the Guru. As much as possible, one should do sadhan and regard it as a service to the Guru. If the Guru-service aspect is taken away from sadhan, then pride will arise. Pride is the cause of bondage. Only a sense of service is capable of suppressing pride. Humility arises out of a sense of service. In service the person being served always remains in focus. Even if the person to whom service is rendered is absent, a proximity is maintained with him.

The above thoughts on service are applicable to the aspirant community, but my contemplation at that time was for my own self. Now that I had surrendered myself, there was no other choice but to struggle. Due to this deep contemplation, not only was the disappointment in my mind pacified, but it also gave me inner strength. A new zeal and a new inspiration to serve arose in me. When a man is falling, even the support of a reed is more than enough. I had recovered, as it were, after receiving support.

12.   Controlling the Mind

During those days the thought came to me that, along with sadhan and service, prayer, reading and chanting were also important. Sadhan is not possible all the time. While serving, too, the mind at times becomes unstable. Sometimes the mind wishes to just leave everything behind, to go to some isolated place and do incessant sadhan. It has become the nature of the mind to uproot a man from the place where he is and drive him away. The mind derives pleasure from this. Thus a continuous control and watch over the mind is needed. If the control of the mind becomes loosened even a little bit, it will run away and make a person run along with it. Through sadhan, service, chanting, prayer and reading, the mind can be kept in control all the time.

   Thus I thought of reading the Gita daily. In the first place, I was already studying the Rudraashtadhyayi [the eight chapters on Rudra, i.e. Lord Shiva] in order to perform worship of Lord Shiva, but the Gita is a very special book on Indian spirituality. Secondly, I had also recently come out of a retirement full of solitude and had just started on the path of social action. Under such circumstances there was no better book than the Gita for my guidance. But my difficulty was that I was responsible for so many activities at the ashram that I did not have time to sit in one place and read. I am writing this for people who whine about the lack of time. Lack of time is a mere excuse. If there is a strong resolve in one's mind, then one surely finds the time. Generally humans waste a great deal of time during which a lot could be achieved. But even if there really is no time, one can still find time.

I used to go to the bazaar for shopping. I needed to go two or three times a day. I kept a pocketbook version of the Gita with me. I would read the first chapter while going to the bazaar. Once I completed it, I would start again. After reaching the bazaar, when I had to shop, I would keep the pocketbook in my bag. Once the shopping was finished, I would begin to recite the first chapter. In a few days I memorized the first chapter. Now I was reciting the first chapter daily, so I started reciting the second chapter while going to the bazaar. I would recite the Gita while working in the kitchen, while working in the garden, while cleaning Guru Maharaj's cottage, or while carrying out any other task, wherever it was possible to recite. Once the second chapter was memorized, I started the third chapter. Once a chapter was memorized, I would recite it without fail at least once a day. The one I wanted to memorize, I would keep repeating it again and again. In this way, in spite of being very busy, I memorized the entire Gita. Then the job became very simple. Whenever I had the slightest opportunity, I recited the Gita. This incident has been written here for the guidance of other aspirants.

13. Maharajshri: A Unique Personality

I received a lot of inspiration and guidance from Shri Guru Maharaj. Often I would generate doubts in my mind in order to test Maharajshri, which was merely my stupidity, but each time my faith and respect for Guru Maharaj increased. Maharajshri's personality was singular and extraordinary. Once there was no one to cook in the ashram. The brahmin who did this job had left. A serious search was going on, but an appropriate person had not yet been found. An old woman proposed to offer her services to carry out this task. She said that she would come twice a day and prepare meals, but she herself would go home and eat. Maharajshri asked her why she needed to go home to eat. "Have your meals here."

The woman replied, "I cannot eat from a Mahatma. I can only serve."

Maharajshri replied, "The one who cooks must also eat. This is my principle. I do not consume the food cooked by a person who himself doesn't eat." Maharajshri refused to accept her services.

Maharajshri would be very happy upon feeding others. His fundamental principle was, "Share and eat." His heart was generous and big. It was not in his nature to eat alone and not invite others. Once a devotee visiting from outside was staying at the ashram. Before going out he asked Maharajshri, "Will you eat bananas? If so, I will get some."

I was standing nearby. Maharajshri asked me how many people were in the ashram. I told him there were approximately twenty-five people. Then he asked, "Did you count the laborers who are building the house?" I said that there were around ten of them.

Maharajshri told the visitor, "If you really want to bring bananas, then bring seventy of them. Everyone will eat about two each. I will also take one." I was very impressed after hearing this from Maharajshri. Until that point, I, too, would sometimes close the door and eat. If someone was present, I would wait for him to leave so that, once he left, I could eat. However, after seeing Maharajshri's generosity, I was ashamed of myself. This shame provided me guidance for the future.

Another quality of Maharajshri which impressed me a great deal was his total lack of greed. I have seen advanced aspirants, great souls and lords of devotional organizations who speak grandly, but, when tempted by greed, lust, anger and pride, seem worthless. Maharajshri's personality had less talk and an abundance of spiritual qualities. This was because Maharajshri never pursued wealth. Even when, on occasion, someone made a donation, he would consider the capacity of the person giving the gift and, also, whether or not he really had a need for so much money. There was no bank account in his name, nor was there any property in his name. He did not have a safe. He used to say that his treasure was kept with Lord Shankar, who gives what he feels is reasonable at appropriate times. Thus the income of the ashram was not much.

The main source of income was Guru Purnima. In those days things were inexpensive. One could survive on a very meager income. Some donations would come throughout the year, but most expenses would be met through the income obtained during Guru Purnima. By the time Guru Purnima arrived, the funds from the previous one would be exhausted and new funds would come in. One day the gentleman who maintained Maharajshri's accounts came to me and said, "Guru Purnima is still far away and I have only four hundred rupees. How will the expenses of the ashram be met?"

I was still new to the ashram and had no experience in such matters. My faith in God was not firm either. Pride was also in abundance. I started getting worried. Finally we decided to ask Maharajshri to go on tour. On one hand, the expenses of the ashram would diminish in his absence. Secondly, donations would come in from outside. We went before Maharajshri and explained the complete situation to him, suggesting that he should embark on a tour. Maharajshri thought seriously for a while and then said, "Okay. I shall do as you say. Where should we go?" It was decided that a trip to Gujarat would be appropriate. Following the decision, letters were written and the replies of correspondents were received. They all expressed their happiness about Maharajshri's visit to Gujarat.

One day when I went to Maharajshri's room, I found him in a pensive mood. He said, "Listen, I have never gone anywhere with the intention of acquiring wealth and you people want to send me out in that hope. I will not go. Whatever happens will happen according to Lord Shankar's wishes and in that only lies our welfare."

When I pleaded that the letters had been sent and that replies had been received, he suddenly said, "No. I will not go anywhere. Write letters to everyone saying that the program has been canceled. You have wheat. We shall bide our time by eating dry roti with salt. How can the monk who roams around desperately trying to acquire wealth be a monk? A monk should cultivate a habit of carelessness and be happy under all circumstances. One should develop a habit of living according to what God gives."

I reflected upon Maharajshri's greatness. The letters cancelling the program were written.

The subject of contentment is very important in spiritual practice. As long as there is no contentment, there is no spiritual practice, no removal of accumulated impressions and no purification of the mind. Contentment is the mother of tolerance. Contentment is the treasure of spiritual practice. A contented person is never upset. I witnessed contentment in Maharajshri's personality, which is rarely seen in the world. Maharajshri knew that he simply had to go on a tour, collect money and return. But then it wouldn't be an act of faith in God. It would be an act of faith in money. There would be no contentment, there would be greed; no removal of samskaras, but accumulation. That is the difference between an aspirant and a worldly person.

A similar incident took place on Guru Purnima. A certain gentleman presented forty thousand rupees in service of Maharajshri. When Maharajshri saw the large amount, he asked about it. The gentleman said, "It is offered in your service."

Maharajshri said, "No, No. I do not require so much money. What would I do with so much?" The gentleman insisted.

Maharajshri said, "This wealth does not belong to you alone. Your wife, your son, your grandsons and granddaughters are all partners in this. First, go home, divide your wealth, give them their share, come back with your share, and then we will talk." The gentleman went away. Maharajshri eventually accepted only one hundred rupees from him.

One more incident. In the upper portion of the ashram near the cave was a building, which is not there now. In those days the building was under construction, but due to lack of funds it remained incomplete. Five thousand rupees were needed to complete it. When Badwani Maharaj came he saw the unfinished house. He asked Maharajshri why the house was incomplete. Maharajshri said, "As long as we had money, work progressed. Now we don't have money, so it has stopped."

Upon hearing this Badwani Maharaj offered a check in his service. (Now I don't remember what the amount was, but it was much more than five thousand.) Maharajshri saw the check and at once said, "What will I do with so much money? Only five thousand is required to complete the house." Then he returned the check. Eventually Badwani Maharaj gave a check of five thousand rupees.

Maharajshri was never greedy for wealth. He used to say, "Lord Shankar is the master of this ashram. He alone runs it. He alone looks after it. The ashram will function as long he wishes. When he doesn't wish, it will close down. Why should we take unnecessary worries upon ourselves. All we have to consider is whether we are doing our duties or not."

Maharajshri told me the same thing in 1965 when he declared me his successor. "The ashram is not yours. It belongs to Lord Shankar. Your duty is to serve and remain on the path of duty. If you have to worry, worry about service and spiritual practice."

14. On Anger and Aversion

In general I never interfered in any way with any decision of Maharajshri. I only followed orders. But as far as matters related to initiation were concerned, I surely never interfered. The fact is I wasn't a very important person in the ashram. There were many people who were initiated long before me. From the perspective of initiation, I was very junior and my role went no further than service of the ashram.

There was a panditji who was learned and performed prayers and recitations. He was also considered well-versed in astrology. He would come to the ashram periodically. Whenever he came to the ashram, for reasons unknown to me, I did not like him, although we had never spoken to each other, nor was there ever any dissension between us. There had been no dealings between us, nor any sort of altercation. I do not know from which birth these mutual samskaras arose, but I did not like him. I often tried to explain away the situation to my mind, but the negative thoughts did not leave me. Maharajshri respected the man a lot. Once when he came he prayed to Maharajshri for initiation. Maharajshri agreed and gave him a date and time for his initiation. I did not like the acceptance of his initiation. I thought, "Why is Maharajshri giving initiation to him?"

When the date set for his initiation arrived, Panditji did not come. That evening we were informed that the night before he had suffered from diarrhea, because of which he could not come in the morning. I was very happy that at least one problem had been avoided. He did not come to the ashram for the next four to six months. The next time he came he requested initiation and again Maharajshri gave him a suitable time. Maharajshri said, "Panditji, you have already received an approval. There is nothing to think about." Again when the time came, Panditji did not turn up. We learned that his employer had sent him away on some project.

I was taking walks with Maharajshri in the morning. Most of the time I would be alone with him. While strolling Maharajshri would discuss various spiritual topics. On seeing an appropriate occasion I asked, "That Panditji who comes — I have no dispute with him. I don't converse with him. I don't know why I don't like him. Every time you gave him approval for initiation, I did not like it."

Maharajshri laughed loudly and said, "Now I know it is your resolve that is blocking Panditji's way. That is the reason why he has met some obstacle or the other and hasn't come." Then explaining in detail he said, "Accumulated impressions keep on affecting the chitta. Sometimes we feel very happy for no reason. Sometimes we become very sad for no reason. We like a person naturally whereas other people find the same person evil. I, too, dislike certain people without any reason. All this happens due to past impressions. The impressions influence the mind internally. No one knows from which births the impressions arise, gain strength and influence the mind. It is the duty of an aspirant to observe these inner ripples and resist getting carried away in their flow. However much your mind urges you, you should neither like, nor dislike Panditji's initiation.

I started thinking, "Why had a resolve against Panditji surfaced in my mind?" I started thinking that I had wronged him. I started praying to God for Panditji to come back and be initiated so that I might atone for my sin, but Panditji never came back. I felt regret in my mind.

I would be very careful in dealings related to the ashram. One thing was that my mind was weak, full of desires and defects. A house of anger and pride, even though I rarely got angry in a way that was evident, I would keep burning internally. Generally the people who came to the ashram were very nice. They wished to be freed from desires and bad qualities, hence they had come to the feet of Guru Maharaj. But the world is not the same everywhere. How can any part of a house, office, organization or nation remain untouched by defects? All places are afflicted with defects, even though the people are good. How can attachments and aversions emerge so quickly? How can one save one's self from gossiping and backbiting? In a way I was new to worldly dealings. Where was the solitude of the green valleys of the Himalayas? I would try to keep myself in solitude even in a crowded environment, but sometimes the mind would still be affected. The anger would boil internally. Just as a volcano erupts after many years, similarly, suppressed anger manifests in a fearful form.

I remember one such incident. Once I had a dispute with an ashramite who was worthy of Maharajshri's special grace and trust and served him wholeheartedly. He also loved me a lot. My pride awakened all of a sudden, my body trembled with rage and I could not control myself. I had no right to comment about that ashramite, but I exceeded my limits. It seemed as if my body was on fire. You already know that in anger the intellect is constrained and there is no awareness of right and wrong. In such a state an angry person ends up losing control. Neither did I remember my responsibility and my service, nor my respect for Maharajshri. In the darkness of my anger the divine form of Guru Maharaj disappeared from before my eyes. Only one thought came to my mind" "Leave the ashram!" Repeatedly thoughts about Himachal Pradesh, the place where I had been before coming to Dewas, came to mind. "Solitude is so much more blissful! No arguments with anyone, no fights. Just sing devotional songs and seek alms. I came here and was ensnared in complications. It would have been advisable to leave immediately after my initiation!"

In this state of anger I went to Maharajshri and told him that I could not stay. I was leaving. Maharajshri tried to reason with me, but does an angry person listen to anyone. He has already lost his senses in his agitation. I even refused to listen to Maharajshri's explanation and remained firm in my decision to leave. The train was scheduled to leave at 9 A.M. the next day. I announced that I would leave the next morning. I went to my room and lay down. Neither did I eat food, nor did I go to Maharajshri again. Neither did I talk to that ashramite again.

That night I tried to sleep but couldn't. By that time my anger had subsided and the churning of thoughts had already started. The whole incident was playing before my eyes like a movie. It had become my habit, while contemplating, to observe my own mistakes first. Due to this sequence the occasion to look at others mistakes never arose. I will not say anything about that ashramite being at fault or not; I was seeing nothing but my own mistakes.

Guru Maharajji adored that ashramite, and I should tolerate everything in the interest of Maharajshri's happiness. Where does a disciple have the right to hate, dislike and get angry at someone whom Guru Maharaj adores? Besides the ashramite also loved me a lot. He cared for me a great deal. Even if he said something I found unpleasant, he did so considering it as his right. But I disrespected his authority. The saddest thing is that I did not even respect Maharajshri's words. Who could be such a sinner and egotist before such a Guru Maharaj, at whose words a disciple should sacrifice everything he has. I kept holding on to my ego. Because of these thoughts my mind filled with repentance. I felt like going to Maharajshri right away, holding his feet and begging for pardon. I also felt like apologizing to the ashramite, but it was late in the night. I thought it advisable not to disturb their sleep.

However morning seemed too far away. Perhaps the

ashramite, too, could not sleep throughout the night and was awake, thinking. I do not know the nature of his thoughts, but when we woke up in the morning he was not to be seen anywhere. He had left. Later a person coming from town informed us that he had seen him heading towards the bus station. Due to the departure of this ashramite, I delayed my own.

My mind became very uneasy. Again and again I would remember the ashramite — that neither had he forgiven me, nor did he give me an opportunity to ask for his forgiveness. Now I was hesitant even to look at Maharajshri. I was the sole cause of the ashramite's departure. If I hadn't had a conflict with him, he wouldn't have left. What had happened to my rules? Where did my tolerance go? Where was that plan to love everyone. What had happened to my decision to serve for one year in silence? I cried a lot over my condition. What had happened to me? Where had my discretion gone? Is this the life of an aspirant? I condemned myself again and again. Now I was scared even to go before Maharajshri. When it was time for lunch, I went to invite him, but Maharajshri did not say anything. His silence spoke volumes.

This incident shook me up. My pride and anger became like orphaned calves. My pride did not die but it was definitely suppressed. After four months the ashramite returned. When he arrived, I apologized to him. I do not know if he forgave me or not. Still my mind did not calm down. The mind was burning in a self-ignited fire. I started following my rules even more strictly. It was becoming clear to me how helpless a being is in front of destiny. When desire exerts its force, great warriors fall to the ground. I was also discovering how difficult it is to fight against one's own mind. In the face of this inner battle even the greatest battle in the external world is meaningless. When someone falls, we laugh. The next day we ourselves fall flat and others laugh at us. God alone knows his games. What we see are games of the mind.

I resolved to try again, but this time it felt as if I were starting from scratch. I became like a stone lying in the street, even though it was contrary to my nature. I would get kicked as people came and went. People did not even realize they were kicking me. A stone doesn't resist. It rolls in the direction it has been kicked. Neither does it complain, nor does it scold. It just lies silently. It is the nature of the world that the more you serve, the more you love and the more you tolerate, the more it troubles you. When I made myself a stone on the road, the world played with me more openly. Sometimes, when the blow was severe, my reaction showed in my face or a sigh escaped my lips. I would explain to my mind again and again that all this is destiny. How can anyone understand this inner turmoil? No one has the time to understand it. What was the point, then, in being upset or complaining about the world? A very large and strong support was available to me: Shri Guru Maharaj. If someone can hold on to such a support, it can take him to the ultimate goal.

By the grace of Guru Maharaj, I had realized that social conduct has a close relationship to spirituality. Conduct can cause a downfall and conduct can be the means to purify the chitta. Conduct leads you to hell and conduct, too, shows the way to heaven. For purification of conduct, the path of social action or the path of dutiful action is necessary. Conduct paints the mind with the colors of the world and it also washes these colors away. Just as solitude is necessary for spiritual practice, so purification of conduct is possible only through social involvement. Perhaps this was the reason why Maharajshri stopped me from leaving the ashram and going into solitude.

Due to a lack of discretion I was unable to understand the essence of this. Like other people I wished to progress spiritually as quickly as possible. I wanted to find a shortcut. Thus I wanted to take a big leap and build a hut on the banks of the Sutlej in Himachal Pradesh. I wished to escape into nivritti [inner contemplation] and occupy myself with sadhan. This was my mistake. Nivritti does not arise in this manner. So long as the natural state of nivritti is not attained, what is nivritti? I would compare nivritti and pravritti [social action].

The understanding that if one wants nivritti he first must embrace pravritti came from Guru Maharaj. Guru Maharaj was very well aware of the fact that the destruction of my prarabdha was possible only on the path of pravritti. Thus he took care of me and stopped me from going into isolation to do sadhan. It is Maharajshri's infinite grace that he showed me the ephemeral nature of the world through experience. No one is for anyone in this world. All relations are based on selfishness. The world is covered with lust, anger, greed and attachment. The world continuously changes its appearance and its qualities. He inspired me to live in the ashram and carry out my service and spiritual practice in order to give me first hand experience of all these things.

15. A Writer's Pride

Maharajshri would often explain that the actual support for progress in sadhana is the state of the chitta. If purity of the chitta is not attained, it does not matter how well the sadhan is going. Whatever be the kriyas, the aspirant is far from his goal. One day I was lying on my bed thinking about this. The state of my chitta was before me. I felt that its purification was very far off. I would recite the Gita daily, but the characteristics of a devotee as described in the Gita were absent in me. It was fine that I had accomplished many things, but much more was yet to be done. I could sense that. Thinking in this way, I remembered a tale. The tale is as follows:

There is a cult of ascetics in Punjab called "Suthra" who wear iron bracelets on their hands and, by playing them against a wooden stick and singing, seek alms. This tale is about their founder. At a certain place people were having spiritual discussions and singing devotional songs. The Suthra went and sat with them. When one bhajan [spiritual song] was over, the Suthra sat with his face turned to one side. After the second bhajan ended, he turned his back to the singer. After the third bhajan, he got up and started walking away. People found his behavior very offensive. Some young men ran after him, caught him and began to beat him. An old, experienced gentleman came by. He said, "Why are you beating him like this?"

The young men told him what the Suthra had done. The old man asked the Suthra, "Dear Sir, why did you do this?"

He replied, "When the first bhajan ended, I felt as if someone had hit my face with a stone. I turned my face away. The second bhajan ended and one more stone came. I turned my back in that direction. When the third bhajan ended, it seemed as if someone had struck me hard on the back. I couldn't bear it and walked away. All of you who face stones and slaps daily and yet remain seated, you are great."

I felt my state was somewhat similar. I was reciting the Gita daily and I was also in Maharajshri's company daily. My services and sadhan were also continuing. But it seemed that everything was just passing over. The heart, it seemed, remained untouched and the knot of the mind was not untied. As a result the state of the chitta showed no signs of changing. The state of other people might also have been similar to mine, but how did that concern me? It was definite that the state of my chitta was not changing. How could it?

"The saints and the scriptures scream and scream and become silent, but man takes absolutely no heed of it. He hears it through one ear and lets it out from the other. Possibly God has given us two ears for this specific purpose. The reach of a sermon, at the most, is only as far as the intellect. The heart remains untouched. How will it be affected? There is a layer of illusion over the intellect. How will it listen and act correctly?" This was my state. I was reciting the Gita with my mouth. It had nothing to do with understanding. Then there was the question of incorporating it into my life. "People say that I am a great devotee. I have memorized the complete Gita. I recite it daily, but I alone know my state. I recite, but only verbally, like a parrot. It has nothing to do with understanding." The saying, "A hollow bean makes a lot of noise," was perfectly meaningful here. Thinking this way, my state distressed me. Sitting alone, I started to cry. I fell asleep amidst these thoughts.

Maharajshri was very kind. He would take care of me under such circumstances. At night he came to me in a dream. He said, "Recitation is certainly done with the mouth, but it should also be done with all one's heart. Understand the meaning with the intellect and the feeling with the heart. Your mind is somewhere else. Your lips keep on moving. The scripture that you recite does not reach the mind. If it doesn't reach the mind, how will it become a part of your life?"

When I went for the morning stroll with Maharajshri, I told him about the previous night's dream. He said, "It is an auspicious sign when you see your Guru, a great soul, any form of God, a temple, and so forth in a dream. It means that at the time of the dream sattva guna [harmonious qualities] was dominant in the chitta. If instructions are received in a dream, one must try to carry them out. This dream can be called an initiation. Shaktipat can take place in a dream. The instruction you have received in your dream is clear in itself. Try to control the mind. One cannot control the mind by simply moving the lips."

Attachment is the cause of social activity and thus is a cause of bondage. Attachment gives rise to enthusiasm towards the world and also blocks the path of inner progress. I still remember an incident related to this. A retaining wall was being built in the ashram. I was helping build it myself with whatever time was available. This task had taken many days, but it still was not complete. A bramhachari and I decided that we must complete it one day. While we were engrossed in this work, the time for evening satsang [spiritual discussions] arrived. Maharajshri was in the satsang hall. We decided to skip the day's gathering. In those days discourses on *Yoga Darshan* were held. Maharajshri looked at the audience; the two of us were missing. He asked our whereabouts. He was told that we were building the wall. Maharajshri got up, came to us and said, "You have developed an attachment to the task of building the wall. Attachment is an obstacle. There is a feeling of sweetness in attachment. Attachment restricts the intellect. This is the time for satsang. You should have been present in the hall. Leave this work and come to the satsang." We left the work.

In his discourse, Maharajshri shed light on the topic. "People get involved in the world on a mental and physical plane, and as a result they are unable to perform a task at the time when it is to be done. They keep on doing the work to which they have become attached, due to which other important tasks suffer. Then problems arise and the mind becomes agitated. All this is due to attachment. Attachment prevents a man from making the right decision at the right time. This makes the mind weak. You all know that weakness of the mind is the greatest problem of a human. Habituate your mind in such a way that it takes interest in what is to be done and, when it is your duty to put aside the work, that it withdraws itself from it. This is the summary of the sermon of the Gita. Without such a habit of the mind, it is impossible to perform the spiritual practice of yoga [yoga-sadhana]."

Throughout the night that followed, thoughts kept on coming. At one moment I would laugh at my foolishness and later sadness would overshadow my mind. When I went for a stroll in the morning with Maharajshri, I was rather out of sorts. Maharajshri asked, "What are you thinking?"

I replied, "I am thinking about yesterday evening's stupidity."

To this Maharajshri responded, "This is the means of attaining nivritti [freedom from worldly affairs]. When one's duty is to leave an activity, no matter how great the attachment, one should give it up physically and mentally. Retire from it totally. In this manner the mind will learn to give up attachment and grow accustomed to performing dutiful actions. Once the chitta is purified, even dutiful action will withdraw and nivritti will arise. People simply discuss nivritti. They do not do anything to attain it. As long as one is living in pravritti, one is bound to remain there. There is no benefit in wearing a cloak of false nivritti."

I said, "This is very difficult for a common person. He has many obligations in the world that keep him engaged in inappropriate and unnecessary activities."

Maharajshri said, "Stop worrying about the world. Due to the weakness of its mind, the world imagines different types of obligations. Your path is different from theirs. You are free to do many things. If you fail to recognize your independence, then it's a different story. Now just consider yesterday's incident. If the wall is not completed in one day, what calamity will befall us? Even if it takes fifteen days, what do we lose? The services you carry out are for your spiritual advancement. If they do not result in spiritual advancement, then there is some flaw in the way they are being rendered or in the feeling with which they are performed."

One day the thought came to my mind that, although Guru Maharaj had written so many books that were full of spiritual secrets, there was no proper arrangement for their sale. They were not reaching the common people who were thereby deprived of a possible benefit. During our stroll one day, I discussed this issue. "Wouldn't it be nice to organize the sale of your books in an orderly fashion? You have written such good books with such effort, but they do not reach the common man."

Maharajshri remained silent for a while and then said, "I had a desire to wear a coat. I went to the bazaar, selected the cloth, had it sewn and wore the coat. My desire was satisfied so I hung the coat on a hook. Now it makes no difference to me if the coat remains on the hook or someone takes it away. My interest has either way been satisfied. I did not write the books with a desire to become famous as an author, nor to make a business out of them. I wrote them to understand the subject myself, to provide some guidance to myself and for my own satisfaction. After writing them, when they get published, I distribute them among the aspirants. That's the end of it. My interest in it is over. I have hung the coat on the hook. Whatever happens after that is fine with me."

I requested again, "Maharajshri, your interest is satisfied. But what harm is there if your books benefit the public?"

He answered, "He who is worried about his own welfare will find his way by some means or the other. What is the use of knocking on the door of a person who is not concerned? An effort towards public welfare is, in reality, for our own benefit."

What more could I say? I became silent. After returning to the ashram I pondered his words. Maharajshri's perspective was quite practical and accompanied by sound logic. Study and writing can be made a part of sadhan. If they are not approached as sadhan, they become a source of pride and attachment. I had such an experience when my first book, *Sadhan Path*, was published.

In 1960 I suffered from sciatica. At the time I had many experiences, which is another topic. Much of the time I would lie in bed, moaning. For almost a month, even when there was some relief, I could not walk or move about. What could I do lying in bed? For my own guidance, I would write small notes regarding sadhan. At the time I was in Ahmedabad, where a gentleman had taken me for treatment. My knowledge of Hindi was only average, so I wrote the notes in Urdu. Maharajshri knew Urdu. Upon reading my notes he said, "Okay. Translate them into Hindi."

After I translated them into Hindi, Maharajshri wrote a preface and said, "Send them to Rishikesh for printing." I was speechless upon hearing this.

"Maharajshri, how am I a writer? I have written all this for myself."

He answered, "This is the way writers are made. This is the beginning. Send it to Rishikesh."

I sent off my Hindi translation and the booklet arrived after it was printed. Maharajshri said, "Don't consider writing to be your main sadhan. It is just a supporting limb. I, too, have written things and thus I understand a little about the state of the chitta while writing. Many people will make fun of your writing and will advise you not to do this work. But as a supporting limb it is good for sadhan. It leads to the churning of thoughts. It is the way in which doubts are clarified. The sentiment in the heart grows. But do not get influenced by pride. The ego that says, 'I am an author,' deprives one of the benefits of writing."

Nevertheless, this was my first book. My mind was filled with pleasure. The pride within me was awakened. My stride became defiant. I began to think, "No other aspirant has ever written a book before. Only I have done so." Again and again I would look at the book. I would see my name on it and my pride would double. Whenever I saw someone reading the book, I would hope for praise. Whenever somebody praised the book, my mind would be overwhelmed internally. On the outside, however, I would act very humble and say, "All this is the grace of Guru Maharaj. Otherwise, how am I a writer?" My friends exacerbated my shortcomings by piling heaps of praise on me. My pride kept on growing.

This pride of mine could not remain hidden from Guru Maharaj. A Guru cannot tolerate the pride of his disciple. He knows that if the disciple's pride remains intact, his downfall is sure to follow. He did not tell me anything directly, but in the evening discourse he expressed his feelings in the following manner:

"If a singer does not express the anguish in his heart, filled with emotion before God, then he sings for the entertainment of the audience. His attention is directed towards how the singing affects them. His pride in singing increases. If the priest of a temple does not worship God with a sense of service, then his attention is directed towards what particular devotees have offered. Greed increases in him. A reader, an intellectual, moves away from the real goal of searching for God and instead begins to impart knowledge to others. Assimilating darkness within, he tries to show the light to others. His pride increases. Similarly, if a writer becomes neglectful of his defects and begins to write for fame or wealth and in this way begins to regard himself as a great writer; if, instead of considering writing to be the supporting limb, he considers it to be the main trunk, it is natural for pride to arise in him. Whatever the amount of writing done by such an aspirant, he does not attain anything."

It did not take long for me to realize that his observations were directed towards me. I was very ashamed. His statement was correct. To attain heavenly joys, to acquire wealth and pride — these are not our goals. These are hurdles on the path. Who am I to write? We do not know what power holds the hand and makes one write, or who gives rise to thoughts in the intellect and feelings in the heart. Why have pride?

16. Tolerance: The Means to Mental Peace

I am very grateful to sciatica for destroying a number of my attachments. It crushed to bits my pride about a number of things. Some whose friendship I was extremely proud of did not come to my help. I saw those whom I thought were dear to me turn away. In 1960 I had very severe sciatica. Standing, sitting, walking — everything became arduous. I couldn't find a position in which to hold my leg in order to stop the pain. I would scream throughout the night. Many times Maharajshri would come during the night and try to pacify me. I almost stopped eating and drinking. Even going to the bathroom was a problem. There was a person who would lift me and take me to the bathroom, but he wasn't always around. I wondered, "Who will sweep my room? Who will change my bed and give me a bath?" On Sundays a gentleman from Mahu would come. That day my room would be swept, the bed would be changed, my clothes would be laundered, I would get a bath, and so forth. When I went out people were probably thinking, "Who would serve such a sick person? He should go back to his house." But once I had left my house, what was the point of returning? In the first place visitors would hardly enter my room. Those who did so would observe how painful it was and go away. The people whom I had treated lovingly, whom I had respected, for whom I had made tea — not one of them even peeked inside to have a look. I was no longer of importance to the ashram. According to many, it seems, I had never been more than an attendant.

I have no grievances or complaints about anyone. In fact, I am grateful to everyone for helping me see the true nature of the world. I saw how nearsighted and forgetful the world is. I would lie in my room groaning and people, hearing it from outside, would go away. Many people from those days are no longer in this world. I have good relations with those who are. I have never complained to anyone. I just convinced my mind that this is the way the world is. What was my status in the ashram anyway? I was neither a sanyasi, nor a bramhachari. People thought I was a servant. Then with whom was I to be upset? What authority do I have over others? This is, in fact, an opportunity for the mental state of a sevak to be judged. He doesn't serve in order that he be served in return. He serves because it is his duty, without any expectation or intention. The more anguish he suffers the more his mind rises. At last someone's dutiful sight fell upon my pitiable state. He took me from Dewas to Indore, and there he looked after me. I underwent treatment and, on recovering slightly, returned to Dewas.

Sciatica clarified the insignificance of the world to me. It opened my eyes. Sciatica made me experience what is not understood even after reading the scriptures and listening to spiritual discourses. No one is for anyone in this world. All relations are based on selfishness. Do not trust anyone. All these things became clear to me. Now for me the world was only a place for performing my duties, performing service, for the suppression of Rajo guna [disturbing qualities] — only a medium for removing impressions.

I actually would have preferred not to talk about this matter, but I couldn't remain silent. I talked to Maharajshri. He understood my state of mind. He said, "This world is like the waves of an ocean. It keeps changing its form. One wave is tall while another is small. One wave goes over your head but you remain dry, whereas another drenches you. One wave returns after washing your feet, while another turns back at a distance. Similar to the waves of the ocean, changes continually take place in the mind and waves of lust, anger, greed, indifference, pride, selfishness, and so forth keep on rising. When these feelings arise in an intense form, the waves rise very high. The crest and the trough of the wave can be measured by comparing feelings. You see a wave rise in the distance just as another engulfs you. In this way you sometimes feel honored, sometimes insulted, sometimes happy and sometimes sad. Sometimes it impacts you more and sometimes less. The impact of these waves is related to one's destiny. The indifference and neglect that you had to face must surely have been in your destiny. Therefore it is meaningless to blame others. In themselves they are nothing but statues of false pride in whose inner mind, too, waves are rising and urging. Every action related to you is carried out by your own destiny, through that person."

I said, "Maharajshri, when someone behaves in an insulting manner for no reason, then one naturally gets angry."

Maharajshri said, "There is a reason but it is not visible to you. The reason is your destiny. That person has simply become the medium of your destiny, bringing it to the surface and, by behaving in accordance with it, doing the groundwork for clearing your destiny. You should be grateful to him. If you bear it with patience then that portion of your destiny will be cleared. If out of anger you end up behaving improperly, then it will develop into a more intense form. Accept this negligent behavior of people with a pleasant state of the chitta, considering it to be the result of your own actions."

I asked, "Can sciatica also be related to my destiny?"

Maharajshri answered, "It might be and it might not be. It could be the destiny of this birth due to improper eating and drinking, or it could be due to accumulated impressions of past lives. Be it sciatica or any other disease, honor or disgrace, happiness or sorrow, you must bear it with delight. In this way you will be protected from the instability of the chitta, and impressions will not be accumulated for the future."

I said, "Maharajshri, it is very easy to say this but very difficult to achieve. Isn't there another way to clear one's destiny?"

At this Maharajshri got slightly irritated and said, "You talk like this in spite of being a sadhak. There is no other way than to endure it. It is indeed difficult, but not impossible. What great man has risen without enduring his destiny."

Then I said, "Isn't there any role of the awakened Shakti in all this?"

He replied, "There is. The awakened Shakti increases your rate of bearing fruits, but it is still you who must endure. As you do so, your tolerance will increase. Tolerance is a state of sattva guna [harmonious qualities] that destroys tama and raja. Tolerance is the road to destroying your destiny. Tolerance is the solution to mental peace."

17. On Cheating God

Surrounded by devotees, Maharajshri was looking very pleased today. Some light social and political talk was going on when the talk turned toward spirituality. Craftiness with God does not succeed because he is a witness to all the feelings and actions within the being. Then how can one tell him a lie? How can somebody cheat him? How is trickery possible? On this subject Maharajshri narrated an incident prior to his ashram days, which is very interesting and educational:

"It is an incident from the days when my kids were very young. My elder son must have been around eight years old. In New Delhi there is a famous Hanuman temple. We would go there frequently. Once, on a Tuesday, I went there with my family. We brought laddoos [round shaped Indian sweets] as an offering to Hanumanji. When the priest used to make an offering there, he would return a small portion in the form of prasad [a portion of the offering that is returned to the devotee after being offered to God] and retain a major portion for himself. The priest, too, was a worldly being. He, too, was not untouched by greed and attachment. I had planned to set aside half of the laddoos beforehand and make an offering of the other half. In this way we would have enough laddoos for ourselves. When a person stoops down to craftiness, he doesn't even spare God. How low he stoops!

We had darshan inside the temple, offered the laddoos, collected the prasad and returned very pleased. Now we were not at all short of laddoos because we already had half of them with us. After reaching the street we hired a tonga [horse cart]. The tonga must have gone only a short distance when the horse was startled, the tonga was overturned and all the laddoos were scattered and rolling on the street. On the face of it, it is a very common incident, but there is a lot to be understood and explained by it."

Someone asked a question. "One should not deal craftily with God, but is it okay in the world?"

Maharajshri said, "It shouldn't be done even in the world. After all God resides in all beings. He knows and sees everything. He laughs at your craftiness. The God within you makes a note of your craftiness. This is the righteous form of God."

I sat there listening to this whole discussion. Forgotten events from the past were passing before my eyes like a movie. I remembered the times when I had tried to cheat God. Even in the ashram, I had not refrained from it. Often I had made fun of the offerings to God. It had pleased me then, but now I repented. When the priest would come to collect the naivedya [food for the gods], I would set the boxes of good sweets aside for myself and offer the remaining ones for naivedya. I started feeling dejected about such acts. Are these the qualities of a devotee? When God watches me setting delicacies aside out of greed for rich food, what must he be thinking? At such times one only reflects upon the taste in the mouth, not the words of Guru Maharaj. I started feeling uneasy internally. I saw my stature as the smallest of everyone. It is possible that other people, too, were doing the same thing, but what had that to do with me? My progress or downfall was not because of what other people did or did not do. Only one's own actions bear fruit. I was so narrow-minded. I did not even refrain from cheating God.

The problem would not be solved simply by repenting. I would have to go to Maharajshri and acknowledge my mistake and that, too, in front of everyone. This was the only way to ensure that I did not repeat my mistake.

In the evening people were sitting with Maharajshri. I said, "Maharajshri, the mistake that was discussed this morning — I have committed it quite often. When the priest comes from the temple for offerings, I keep the good food aside and give from what is remaining."

Maharajshri said, "This is the influence of the Kali Yuga [the present, dark age]. In fact there is good as well as bad in all the yugas, but the proportion of bad becomes very high in the Kali Yuga. Even good people frequently do inappropriate things. Attachment and aversion, anger and pride reach their zenith. The generosity of the mind weakens. Spirituality is restricted only to discussions. I, too, had an interest in spirituality, and performed prayers and recitations, but when it was a question of laddoos, I cheated Hanumanji. Whether one is a Mahatma or a devotee, everyone has to flow with the times. Those who continue to do spiritual practices, their heads rise above the water level. But everyone has to flow.

"Don't worry about anything. Pay attention to your service and sadhan. The mind will keep on doing mischief in between, but God takes care of everything. He protects. Even a great ascetic like Vishwamitra could not protect himself from the influence of Maya, even though his was the Satya Yuga [also called Krita Yuga, when dharma was at its peak]. Maya is very powerful in all the yugas. You are fortunate to have direct experience of the actions of the inner power. Imagine the condition of those people who proceed merely on the basis of emotion and imagination. Keep trying to make your mind as generous as possible. Pray to God for that. He is very kind. He will surely listen to you one day. My blessings are also with you. Do not let service, duty, sadhan, tolerance, humility and unpretentiousness slip away from your hands.

"Do not be afraid of people. They will talk. Their job is talking. He who climbs the slope will fall, and fall again and again. Those who stand below watching only talk. Keep moving towards your goal honestly."

18. Significance of Guru Purnima

Today is the holy day of Guru Purnima, the first Guru Purnima of my life. On this day people go to the ashram to worship their Guru and seek his blessings. Today this is what Guru Purnima has become. Who cares if, at any time, it had any other form or purpose? Now it has been reduced to a social festival. People meet and interact with one another, consume sweets and delicacies, sing and play musical instruments, and debate. There are complaints and gossip also, and worldly discussions too.

So this was my first Guru Purnima. It was an occasion of great curiosity for me. Food was being cooked on one side. People were coming and going. Others were sitting and chatting, or talking to each other in loud voices with bloodshot eyes. I had much work to do, but there was peace in my mind. Maharajshri's sermon took place in the evening.

Maharajshri said, "The fruit of worship on Guru Purnima should be like initiation." I did not have any such experience. At the time of initiation, I had felt the awakening. Kriyas had occurred — crying, laughing and screaming — but this time, nothing happened. Had my worship been meaningless? Did I not receive any blessings? I began to brood. Possibly other people had experiences. Was I the only one who was empty handed?

The only time I would be able to talk with Maharajshri was during the morning stroll and it was an appropriate time. When I expressed my concern, Maharajshri laughed at once. He said, "Either you did not hear the complete talk or you did not understand it. If the preceding and succeeding content, the context, is removed, then the meaning is distorted."

He continued, "The first thing I said was that the fruit of worship on Guru Purnima should be like initiation. I did not say that it is always like that. So many people came to worship. Do they do sadhan daily? Do they endeavor to purify their conduct? Is everyone's feeling pure? If not, how would they get that kind of result? Even in initiation, does everyone experience the same advancement? It is dependent on the state of the chitta, the accumulated impressions and the state of the gunas [qualities]. One person's advancement takes not even a moment, whereas someone else has to wait for a long time. This is also the case with the worship on Guru Purnima. Aspirants should come to worship with total faith, feeling and surrender. Only then will they receive results similar to initiation.

"If you did not experience anything today, one possible reason is that your mind was not in a state to be influenced. You have a lot of work and your attention has been on work. You somehow managed to break away from your obligations. You came running and performed the puja [ritual of worship]. But even while worshipping your attention was not on the puja. It was on work. The donor gives, but if the recipient does not receive, how will he obtain anything? In the same way, if the donor does not give or is incapable of giving, then nothing can be obtained. What I said about worship on Guru Purnima was in the context of Shaktipat. Do not worry about anything. You are with me only."

I had heard Maharajshri's sermon the previous day during my busiest moments. I was unable to hear it completely. There was no possibility of my getting the context right and understanding the essence of the sermon. However, I was satisfied with Maharajshri's explanation.

19. Lust, Anger and Greed: The Doors to Hell

Maharajshri was extremely good at explaining the abstruse aspects of spirituality through the medium of minor events. Once, I forgot to take proper care of the milk. At night I did not store it behind its protective mesh curtain. In the morning the kitchen door was open. I came in and saw that the cat was drinking the milk. I was furious. I threw a stick at the cat. On hearing the sound of the stick, Maharajshri came out of his chamber. I had picked up the stick again and was standing with it in my hand. The cat had run away. It did not take Maharajshri much time to understand what had happened. He said, "The cat drank the milk because the milk hadn't been stored properly. If the milk had been behind the mesh, then how could the cat have drunk it? If a cat finds milk, it will definitely drink it."

That same night I forgot to bring Maharajshri's chair inside from the courtyard. The chair had a cushion. At night a dog had come and slept on the soft cushion. When I opened the door in the morning, I saw the dog sleeping on the chair and was filled with anger. I had already forgotten that just the day before Maharajshri had scolded me for hitting the cat. Again I picked up the stick and hit the dog with it. The dog ran away yelping. I also forgot that Maharajshri was standing right behind me. Maharajshri said in a reproachful tone, "The mistakes are yours and you go around beating dumb animals. If the chair had been kept inside, how could the dog have come and slept on it?" I stood there like a criminal.

After some time Maharajshri called me into his chamber. He observed, "Man curses the world and things in the world but does not take care of his mind. Whenever the mind is not taken care of, like the milk and the chair, then sense objects, like dogs and cats, will surely launch an attack. When the mind is weak and careless, that is when the storm of sense objects carries it away. They distort its form by assaulting it continuously. Man doesn't understand and blames the storm, just as you failed to learn from yesterday's incident and pounced upon the dog today. The milk and the cushion were ruined anyway. And most importantly, you became angry. That is a great loss.

"Do not forget the quote from the Gita, that lust, anger and greed are doors to hell. I am not worried about the milk or the cushion, but about you getting angry. An angry person can neither do his sadhana, nor can he be victorious in the race of life."

I stood silently and listened to everything. Then I said, "Maharajji, whenever such an incident occurs I get angry."

Maharajshri said, "Why did such an incident occur? Wasn't it due to your own negligence? When the mind is negligent, the attack of sense objects takes place. The mind must be continuously alert until such time as the natural state of the chitta has risen. Keep a constant vigil on the mind and only then will you emerge victorious in the great battle of sadhan. You still have much to do in life. It is a very long journey. You will be able to walk only if you do so with care."

I said, "But I don't get angry often, only sometimes."

Maharajshri said, "The anger that comes only sometimes is more dangerous. You get angry. That is enough to be concerned about. Do not forget that history is filled with turmoil caused by anger. Ascetics and knowledgeable people, too, on succumbing to anger, have lost control of themselves."

I listened to everything silently, but many question marks gathered around my personality.

20. There Is Only One Dharma

During his walks, Maharajshri would say many good things. At that time his mood would be excellent. In the first place the time was early morning. Second, he would have just got up after doing sadhan. And thirdly, no one else would be present to interrupt us. I, too, would introduce topics, usually in order to avoid a discussion about politics, construction or some other social issue.

One day I asked, "Maharajji, what is dharma? In some places in the Gita, karma is called dharma, in some places yajna [religious sacrifice] is called dharma, and in some places duty. Generally aren't Hinduism, Islam and others religions considered dharma?"

He said, "There is only one dharma: to realize God. That is, to clear the misconception that God is not realized, which means to establish oneself in dharma through dharma. Everything else is a display of words. Understand the essential meaning of karma as dharma. Karma full of attachment is not dharma. Detached karma is called dharma because it purifies the mind and is instrumental in clearing misconceptions. Where yajna is called dharma, remember that japa [chanting] is the most superior amongst all yajnas. Doing japa to attain something is not yajna. Yajna with the sole intention of realizing God and not for obtaining anything else is dharma because it destroys misconceptions. Performing one's duties is called dharma because achieving results is treated as secondary in this. Performing one's duty without desiring any fruits is dharma because it removes desires and destroys misconceptions. This issue is present in all types of spiritual practices. The goal of attaining God is identical in all paths. Wherever realization of God is not the goal, it is not dharma. Dharma is a devotee worshipping, a karma yogi performing his duties without any attachments, the knowledge arising in an intellectual from within, and a yogi performing meditation to realize God. A householder living in accordance with the scriptures to achieve detachment, the sacrifice of sense objects by an elder, and acquisition of knowledge by a celibate [bramhachari] is dharma. All these are helpful in leading towards God.

"Hinduism, Islam and other religions are not only dharma, but also doctrines which suggest the means of moving towards dharma. Some are action-oriented, some japa-oriented, some sentiment-oriented, some worship-oriented, some prayer-oriented, and some service-oriented. The distinction of Hinduism is that it is not based on the means but on the state of the chitta. The state of the chitta is not the same for all beings. Everyone's accumulated impressions, sentiments, faith and tendency are different, and thus one doctrine or spiritual practice is not appropriate for all. The doctrine of Hinduism acknowledges all ways and grants one the right to practice what is suitable for him."

I asked, "If all doctrines lead to the same God, then why this mutual animosity and argument?"

His answer was, "Attachment has become the nature of man. However unnatural it is, nevertheless, a human is helpless in the face of it. He gets attached to his school of spiritual practice and its doctrine and starts considering his way of thinking superior. He wants to forcibly impose it on others. If one is broad-minded and understands the true essence of dharma, then the fight comes to an end. The work of dharma is to destroy misconceptions while purifying the mind, and to establish a person in dharma by giving a direct experience of the immortal, pure, intelligent, *satchitanand* [harmonious, conscious and blissful] qualities of the Supreme Being. Only through dharma can one get established in dharma."

I asked, "What place does Shaktipat have in dharma?"

"Shaktipat is a pragmatic school of spiritual practice, devoid of ego. Correctly speaking, it is not even an independent school of thought. It is the science of advancement of all schools. Just as devotion is the dharma of a devotee and contemplation the dharma of a jnani, surrender is the dharma in Shaktipat. It is a way of advancing internally in a natural way and becoming established in one's own self. In all other spiritual practices, effort and the ego of doership on the part of the aspirant are involved. But Shaktipat is self-proven, accompanied by the sense of an observer. In fact, this dharma is easier than egoistic dharmas."

I mentioned that some people believe that Shaktipat is tantrik, and thus they are afraid of it. Maharajshri replied, "In the first place, such people have a wrong notion about tantra. They consider only tantra involving sacrifice of animals as tantra. However the actual nature of tantra is spiritual. At one time the practice of tantra involving sacrifice of animals became dominant. It was widespread and, as a result, many great souls criticized the tantriks [those who practise tantra]. By reading and rereading their writings, many people have nurtured negative opinions about tantra. Shaktipat is, indeed, a tantrik art, but it is not just tantrik. It is also vedic [in accordance with the *Vedas*], pauranik [in accordance with the *Puranas*], yogic and devotional in content. It can be explained in the context of all philosophies. An aspirant can explore the theories of Shaktipat according to his interests.

"Tantra does not contradict any vedic or pauranik texts. It explains their principles in a different manner. The tantras are called the supplements of all other texts. Whatever the nature of the tantrik practice, external or internal, it requires detachment, control over the mind and control over the senses. Tantrik sadhana also removes the extroverted character of tendencies and turns them inward. The important thing is inner awakening rather than philosophies, paths, doctrines or feelings."

21. The Role of Kriyas

Some people were sitting before Maharajshri. They were gathered in the open space adjacent to the temple. The discussion was about sadhan. Maharajshri said, "There is no reason to be afraid of kriyas. Only the fortunate have this experience. If someone is frightened by his kriyas, they stop. During kriyas, if fear arises from within, that, too, is a kriya, caused by the accumulated impressions of fear coming to the surface. Just like other kriyas, the kriya of fear should be experienced with the sense of an observer."

One gentleman asked, "What is the meaning of the kriyas of crying and laughing? Some people believe that crying is a punishment inflicted by the Guru. They call the kriya of laughing madness. When I have the kriya of crying, I control it out of shame."

A smile graced Maharajshri's face. He questioned, "Shame in sadhan? Then you cannot do sadhan. Just as kriyas stop when you are frightened, they also stop when you feel ashamed. Crying reflects the feeling in your heart. It could be a feeling of love for God, a feeling of separation from God, the pain of not being free from sense objects, or repentance upon remembering some sinful act. The essence is that when past impressions rise, by whatever means, the heart of the aspirant may scream with anguish and tears may flow from his eyes. He might, in fact, cry loudly from the suffering of his mind. It may be that he does not understand the reason for his cries, but they still come. Only a person unfamiliar with this style of spiritual practice would blame the punishment of the Guru.

"Similarly, laughter reflects the happiness of the heart. When one experiences joy and is filled with love for God, impressions of laughter come to the surface. One remembers a humorous incident and the heart is overwhelmed . Even though the reason is unknown, the laughter doesn't stop. This is a manifestation of the joy in the heart. Laughter can take place individually, and also in the form of a collective kriya while sitting for sadhan in a group. Once collective laughter begins, people hold on to their stomachs and laugh. No one knows the reason. This is the kriya of humor.

"Remember one thing: that all kriyas are for removing accumulated impressions. The act that accumulates an impression also removes it. At the time of accumulation the act is equipped with the ego of doership, whereas at the time of removal it is devoid of ego, a kriya of the Shakti accompanied by a sense of observation. Generally karma takes place in the world and the kriya within. At the time of accumulation the ego unites with the karma, whereas during cleansing a separate identity of the ego is retained. Dust accumulates when the house is dirty and spreads even while cleaning. After accumulation the house is dirty, but after cleaning, dust is nowhere to be seen. That is the blessing of Shakti. All spiritual practices are for achieving this goal. That is the reason why ascetics and renunciates wander in the jungle. By the grace of the Guru, you have received this blessing while remaining at home."

22. I Cannot Initiate You

Maharajshri was sitting outside in the courtyard on a chair. The time was around four o'clock in the afternoon. A young man came and prostrated himself before him. Maharajshri asked, "Who are you?"

He replied, "I am a resident of Dewas. I have a job, and have come to serve you and request initiation."

Maharajshri asked, "Who lives with you in your house?"

He received this answer: "My mother, a brother and a sister. My father has passed away."

Then Maharajshri asked, "Have you received the permission of your mother for initiation?"

The youth said, "What is the need for my mother's permission?"

Maharajshri said, "You may not need it, but I do. Anything can happen tomorrow, so it is advisable to be cautious from the beginning."

The youth remained silent for some time and then said, "My mother doesn't even speak to me. From whom should I get permission?"

This surprised Maharajshri. "Doesn't speak to you? Why?"

Then the young man began to talk rudely about his mother. "My mother is very harsh. She doesn't know anything and talks incessantly. She always sides with my brother. How much more can I tolerate?"

From this Maharajshri understood the entire situation. He told the young man as follows: "I cannot initiate you. It is best that you leave, and do not ever come back to me. If you do come,

come with your mother. Only on her recommendation will I consider initiation." The young man departed.

After he left, Maharajshri said, "A person who speaks ill of his mother today will speak ill of his Guru tomorrow. The mother is the first Guru. A true Guru cannot turn his disciple away from his parents, neither will any understanding mother or father try to distance him from a Guru. A mother, who nurtures her child with her own blood for nine months, feeds him her milk and raises him, is always worthy of worship, whatever her nature. A child can never be free from his obligation to her. How can one forget the obligation towards one's father, who with his hard earned income bears hardships himself and makes provisions for the upbringing of his child, who helps his child stand on his own feet and always wishes well for him? The Guru, who always desires the well-being of his disciple, shows him the path of absolute truth, forgives hundreds of his mistakes, and loves him like his own child. If a disciple betrays such a Guru, he is a sinner. He who doesn't have faith in his mother and father will extend the same thread of disbelief towards his Guru.

"In the spiritual culture of India, it is said, *'Matru devo bhava, pitru devo bhava, acharya devo bhava.'* ['The mother is God, the father is God and the teacher is God.'] It is such a great ideal, but in this present age, who believes in it? But I am a believer in the old traditions. How can I give initiation to that youth?

"The practice of spirituality begins at home. At home, too, the child encounters his mother first. From there he gets affection and also scolding. But this affection and scolding are filled with motherly love. In them are beautiful dreams about the child's future. The next confrontation is with the father, whose blood runs in the veins of the child. Being of the same blood, there is bound to be a feeling of closeness. Just as a Guru wishes for the well-being of his disciple and God desires his welfare, in the same way parents desire the welfare and good fortune of their child. Thus one is instructed to see God in parents. I understand the state of mind of that youth. He has an aversion for his brother. All the children are the same for a mother, but the young man perceives partiality. This bias is not in the mother's conduct, it is in his chitta. A chitta full of such aversions and an interest in initiation?"

23. Tolerance

On finding a suitable occasion, I made a request to Maharajshri. "Yesterday during the evening discourse, when you were talking about titiksha [tolerance] by quoting examples from Shri Shankaracharya's book, *Vivek Chudamani*, the tendencies of my memory urged my mind in such a fashion that I became engrossed in previous experiences. As a result I could not listen and understand properly that part of your sermon that dealt specifically with titiksha [tolerance]. Bhagwan Shankaracharya said, '*Sahanam sarva dukhanaam apratikar purvakam.*' Could you please oblige me by explaining the meaning of this?"

Maharajshri said, "Tolerance is the life of spiritual practice. Control of the sense organs and control of the mind are related to tolerance. Cleaning out accumulated impressions [samskaras] and the tendencies of past lives [vasanas] also have a very close relationship with tolerance. Physical tolerance is important, but mental tolerance is more important and much more difficult. One must bear psychological turmoil, anger, insult, failure, and so forth without reacting. Even great ascetics get frightened and move away from tolerance.

"Physical tolerance involves the control of sense organs, but it cannot be totally separated from control of the mind. For physical tolerance a strong mental resolve is required, the absence of which can lead to the undermining of the will. When happiness and sorrow, enjoyment and consumption take control, the objects of the world attack the sense organs. When natural calamities cause sorrow, bearing them without getting upset, without surrendering to the attractions of sense objects and without reacting to them is physical tolerance.

"Mental tolerance requires an even more determined resolve. If the aspirant is ever honored, he must resist pride. If he is insulted then he must not let his mind go astray. He should not get attached to friends. He should not have aversion towards those who consider themselves his enemies, and if he runs into such people, he should give them respect and love. One has to endure a great deal for all this. The mind must be suppressed often. An enemy shows indifference and you still love him. Someone insults you and you endure it without offering a reply or clarification. This is not an easy task.

"A tolerant person undergoes suffering for the benefit of others and this purifies his own mind. A tolerant person fully understands that honor, insults, success, failure, joy, sorrows — all are the fruits of his own karma. The world can neither give success, not failure. The world is only a support on which our destiny is displayed. An individual feels pride, but for everything he does he is merely the medium. Every incident that takes place through him is a kriya of the active Shakti, which a person, under the control of pride, transforms into karma. He believes that others are the cause of honor and insult. The only solution is to endure it, live it and thus end it."

I asked a question. "If the active Shakti clears accumulated impressions through the medium of kriyas, then what is the need for tolerance?"

Maharajshri responded, "The active energy transforms accumulated impressions [samskaras] into kriya. Destiny [prarabdha] can be ended only by living it. If prarabdha is not borne with tolerance then it continues to accumulate impressions. Then the prarabdha never comes to an end.

"Titiksha [tolerance] is such a unique word. It has very wide implications in the field of spiritual practice. It lifts one from individuality and establishes one in the atma-tattva — the ultimate reality. Externally it is the cause of purification of conduct and internally it is the provider of a sense of observation in kriya sadhan. But nurturing it is an extremely difficult task. People are able to carry out difficult spiritual practices, but not tolerance. Sadhan cannot progress without tolerance.

"There are many kinds of tolerance, but it can be divided into two main levels: deliberate and natural. On the deliberate level the aspirant has to keep the mind disciplined. Repeatedly the mind refuses to tolerate. It gets restless, gets agitated, but the aspirant keeps the mind suppressed. In natural tolerance, forbearance becomes the aspirant's nature. He endures adverse situations with simplicity. A third level is higher than these two that, in fact, it is not really tolerance. When you reach that level, tolerance is ended. At that time the natural qualities of the soul are manifest.

"Tolerance can be achieved in two ways: through one's own power and through God's power. Yogis and jnanis have confidence in their own power, whereas a devotee is under God's shelter. Tolerance is achieved, on the one hand, through effort and, on the other, through surrender. The only difference between the two is the sentiment."

I asked, "Why do tolerant devotees have to undergo so much suffering? People with a worldly perspective enjoy themselves, but the one who has embraced tolerance must suppress his rage."

Maharajshri said, "He does not suppress his rage. It is the worldly person pursued by various types of fears who must suppress his fury. A devotee does not react, nor is he worried about anything. He always remains blissful. Others might think that he is sad, but his mind is always joyous. One should learn from devotees how to remain happy during times of sorrow."

I said, "Maharajji, this is very difficult. The world inflicts sufferings upon sufferings, launches one attack after another. To bear everything with a calm mind, not let a sigh escape the lips, love everyone and keep the mind pleased — a common man cannot do this."

Maharajshri said, "When did I say that this is an easy task? This is an extremely difficult task. To behave like this in the world is most difficult. Only a brave warrior can do this. He falls down a number of times, but stands up again. He balances himself and proceeds ahead."

24. Your True Self Has Awakened Now

Today when Maharajshri started his morning walk two gentlemen from outside joined him. Today was my day to remain silent and listen. On most occasions, in fact, I would talk less and listen more. Maharajshri used to say that the less one talks, the more one acquires. He who talks a lot has very little capacity to receive.

One gentleman placed his issue before Maharajshri in the following manner: "I am unable to do my prayers and recitations. I used to serve God daily in the morning. I would bathe him, adorn him, worship him, and later sit in front of him and recite the Gita. But now when I sit down to do this I just sit. I go into a kind of meditation. I experience joy in simply sitting there. I wonder what has happened to me? Is God upset with me that he does not accept my services? When I sit down to recite the Gita, the book just remains open in front of me. I even forget the shlokas [stanzas] of the Gita that are on the tip of my tongue. The situation with chanting is similar: I forget the mantra. Even if I try to remember it, I cannot do so. It seems as if all the activities of the mind have stopped — no thoughts, no feelings, no resolve. It is as if I have died while still alive."

Maharajshri listened very seriously and then said, "It is very strange that you are worried about this state. Ascetics perform penance, intellectuals seek knowledge and devotees cry and sing in front of God to achieve this state. Only a rare person attains this state beyond feelings. This state is not the state of total restraint of the chitta, but is quite close to it. In this state, the mind becomes free from resolutions and uncertainties, no sentiments arise in the heart, tendencies are silenced, the samskaras are pushed to one side and the chitta, in this state of beyond feelings, sees only chaitanya [conscious-self]. In the *Narada Bhakti Sutras* this very state is called atmaram [resting in the self]. This is the samprajnat state [conscious concentration] in Yoga. After this comes the asamprajnat state [seedless and without support].

"You bathe and decorate God only through your senses. When all the sense organs become introverted and cease all interactions, how can they serve God? When the sense organs have given up all efforts and become inactive, then how can they chant? When speech has become silent, how can you recite? Your efforts are possible only so long as the sense organs and the mind are active. In the state you describe the chaitanya [conscious-self], which, on giving life to the sense organs, is called chetan [consciousness], withdraws its activity, which is dependent on the sense organs. But its vibrations are still there in the innermost recesses of the chitta. Thus the chitta is not fully restrained but its external activity comes to an end. This is samprajnat."

Then the gentleman said, "But Maharajji, if our external activity has come to a halt, if there is no ego, what is the use of this life?"

Maharajshri said, "You think in this way because you are attached to your life and ego. But if you think about it, your real life and your true self has awakened now. Now the time to enjoy life is near. The dark night is about to end. The closed door that you have been knocking on so long is about to open."

"Until now you have been attached to a world that is meaningless and has no stability. Now you are advancing one level after another and moving toward a bliss that is lasting and eternal, in which there is no sign of sorrow. What you consider life is just momentary. No one knows when the lamp will be extinguished. It is only a mirage. There is movement, walking and everything else, but no power of one's own. This life is surely going to slip from your hands. Why not move towards that life which is eternal and filled with bliss?"

The gentleman again spoke. "Whatever the case, Maharajji, my mind only wishes to serve God and chant. What do I have to gain from the direct knowledge of chaitanya [conscious-self]? I derive joy from singing devotional songs."

Maharajshri said, "If you eat food your hunger will be satisfied. When you sing devotional songs various states are its fruits. Whether you like it or not, you will inevitably attain them."

While talking about these matters we reached the ashram and the conversation stopped. For me this discussion was very interesting and inspiring. It forced me to think and understand many things.

25. Surrender to Kriya-Shakti

I don't know why, but my mind was sad today. I was in no mood to talk to anyone or to listen to anyone. All I wanted to do was pull the blanket over my head and remain in bed. However, I was helpless; there was a lot of ashram work. Somehow I completed my chores. When I was finished, I went to Maharajshri to pay my respects. My face was drawn. Maharajshri asked, "What is it? You are looking very sad today."

I replied, "Even I don't know the reason, but my mind is very sad."

Maharajshri asked, "Did anyone say anything to you or are you missing your home?"

I replied, "Neither is the case."

During the morning walk Maharajshri again mentioned the incident. "Sometimes we do not see the reason but our mind is very pleased. Sometimes we become sad without cause. The reason for this is not in the outside world, it is inside the chitta. In fact, the world that diverts the mind is only within the chitta, which may be regarded as a reservoir of accumulated impressions. These accumulated impressions make up the state of the chitta. It is fine to say that an incident in the world influences the mind, but the root cause of the incident is our accumulated impressions. These impressions inside the chitta, while changing their own state, change the state of the chitta at the same time. When impressions of joy are awakened and exalted, they give rise to tendencies and bring them to the surface. As a result the mind is filled with happiness for no apparent reason. Contrary to this, when impressions of sadness arise one feels sad but is unaware of the reason.

"Your condition may be somewhat similar to this. People in general pass through this state, but it occurs more often among aspirants of Shaktipat as the Kriya-Shakti brings accumulated impressions to the surface. Sometimes one gets angry at minor things. Sometimes foul and vulgar thoughts arise. Sometimes a feeling of forgiveness comes, and at times pride increases greatly. An aspirant has to bear all this with a calm chitta. It is not the case that these kriyas of Shaktipat happen only during sadhan. The Kriya-Shakti is always active. Kriyas during sadhan are clearly manifest, whereas at other times they are not. Even during social interactions, when the attention of the aspirant is not on his sadhan, the kriyas continue internally. Under such circumstances, it is not surprising when sadness arises in a kriya, affects the mind and is expressed in the face."

I said, "Even when kriyas happen in this fashion, are samskaras still destroyed?"

Maharajshri said, "Destruction of samskaras is not due to kriyas. The job of a kriya is to bring the samskaras to the surface and exalt them. It depends on how you react to this exalted samskar. If you are provoked, there is no destruction of samskaras. They gain more strength. If you bear it with tolerance without getting provoked or angry, then the samskar will show its strength and become feeble."

Then I asked, "When a samskar arises, if our reaction is in our own hands, then what is the meaning of surrender?"

Maharajshri answered, "You have asked a very good question. It is a matter of understanding. When the samskar is exalted, the Kriya-Shakti does not motivate our reaction, the samskaras do. Acting according to the motivation of the samskaras can never be called surrender to the Kriya-Shakti. Some people say, incorrectly, that they have acted according to the orders of the Kriya-Shakti. They do not acknowledge that the Kriya-Shakti exalted the samskaras but that they acted under the influence of those samskaras. This is a very important matter and must be understood. A normal aspirant forgets this and under the name of Kriya-Shakti ends up surrendering to his samskaras. Thinking about surrender in a chronological manner will clarify the matter."

(i) **"After awakening, the goal of Kriya-Shakti and the sense of surrender towards it should always be maintained.** Kriya-Shakti is divine power, all-knowing and beneficial. Every kriya of Kriya-Shakti is in the interest of the being. Thus it is in the interest of a living being that more and more of his kriyas are manifest. The more resolutions a being makes, the more the kriya of the Kriya-Shakti becomes subject to the control of those resolutions. The meaning of kriya is independent movement based on samskaras. One must surrender to the independent power of Kriya-Shakti by leaving all kinds of resolutions and efforts aside. A being is bound by hopes and desires and is incapable of considering benefit and loss. So why not surrender to that Shakti, which is always beneficial? Even if one surrenders to someone in the world, one should experience the Shakti in that."

(ii) **"If there is welfare in the kriyas of the Shakti, then why not let them happen with uninterrupted immediacy?** Mental resolve is an obstacle in a kriya. When a kriya comes under the influence of resolve, it is reduced to a karma and an impression is accumulated. Thus the mind should not be allowed to hinder the kriya. In other words, one should not interfere in kriyas. As the Shakti is all-knowing, it is aware of everything and knows when and which kriya you require. All decisions about kriyas should be left to the Shakti and one must surrender to it."

(iii) **"Kriya-Shakti brings both types of samskaras — sanchit [accumulated] and prarabdha [ripened] — to the surface.** The force of the sanchit samskaras is within the chitta. If an aspirant is influenced by that force, his behavior in the world is affected and he accumulates new samskaras. If he endures the force and does not allow his chitta to be influenced, then the samskar to which the force belongs, becomes feeble. Now remains the issue of prarabdha. When the Shakti brings it to the surface, joy and sorrow are expressed externally as well as internally. Though this joy and sorrow are definitely expressed by Shakti, prarabdha is their cause. There is no other solution but to endure the fruit that has ripened. An aspirant's surrender is towards the Kriya-Shakti and not towards prarabdha. His reaction, on the other hand, is not towards the Shakti. It is towards prarabdha. An aspirant can have only one reaction towards his prarabdha, and that is to endure its effects with a calm chitta. The surrender towards the Shakti does not interfere in this. Even if one listens to the Kriya-Shakti, just as sadhan without the mind being affected is one's duty, in the same way enduring the fruits of prarabdha without the mind being affected is also one's duty. It is sadhan. It is surrender towards the Shakti. It is the quality of Kriya-Shakti that in spite of coming in contact with your samskaras, it remains unaffected by them. You, too, have to absorb this quality of the Kriya-Shakti. Only then can your sense of individuality come to an end. The means to incorporate this quality in you is internal and external surrender towards Shakti."

26. The Dilemma of Good and Bad

Once some people made a request to Maharajshri. "This place is your residence, not an ashram. Why do we need to feed and provide shelter to those who use the name of God for food, to wanderers and vagabonds dressed as monks?"

Maharajshri said, "I don't agree with you. The place where a monk lives, where there are bramhacharis [celibates] and ashramites, where people from outside come and go and do sadhan, where there is a kitchen and meals are cooked, where daily prayers are conducted in a temple — if this is not an ashram, then what is? Your perspective is narrow and that is why you think like this. If a monk arrives, then he eats in this ashram and so you are troubled. But this is a monk's ashram, not the house of a householder. Actually, according to old traditions, there are explicit rules and duties for householders, too, regarding wandering monks. Times have changed, but it is advisable that you do not impose the influence of time on me."

Everyone was disappointed upon hearing this, but they still did not lose heart. They said, "If we have to serve meals to monks who come and go, then we must at least see who is deserving. There should be some investigation."

At this Maharajshri said, "You are talking of identifying a good or a bad monk. Now, first and foremost, who among you has such judgment? When one's own mind is a house of desires, how will he identify a monk free from desires? Secondly, the day you start testing for good monks, the true monk will stop coming. Why does he need to take your test, and that, too, for just two chapatis [Indian bread]?

"It is best that we treat all monks as deserving. Why would you involve yourself in the dilemma of good and bad? Why would you even have the feeling that someone should determine whether the monk you are feeding is deserving? Isn't the sentiment that, "However he is, as far as we are concerned he is good," a better one? Whatever the nature of the monk, your mind will remain healthy with this sentiment. In these times, however, we have come to accept the idea that, although it doesn't matter to the world how we ourselves are, the world should be good. We are committed to improving the world. But the world does not improve and neither do we.

"Forget the idea of issuing a certificate of good or bad to the monks who pass by here. The greatest evil in you is that you see good and evil in the world. Why grow thin worrying about the concerns of the ashram? The ashram is not going to run by your worrying; this is Shankar's [Lord Shiva's] ashram. It functions the way he runs it. We cannot differentiate between good and bad. He who comes to eat, let him come. Who knows who among them is good? It is not a costly proposition even if we have to feed a hundred thugs to feed one good monk.

"The basis of your relationship with the ashram is sadhan. Strengthen that relationship. If your sadhan gains strength, then it doesn't matter how many people eat and leave. God makes arrangements to fill the stomachs of both the honest and the dishonest. He does not keep the dishonest hungry. Then again, do all the aspirants who come to the ashram each day have pure minds? If one starts considering purity and impurity, then hardly anyone will be able to come here."

27. Why the Ashram Is In Dewas

One day a devotee asked Maharajshri a very strange question. "You have toured all over India. You must have seen very beautiful places — Kashmir, the Himalayas, the seashore. Why did you choose Dewas for your ashram. Maharajshri laughed aloud and then said, "Your question is proper in its own way. I chose Dewas for four reasons:

The first and foremost reason is prarabdha. Don't sanyasis [ascetics] have prarabdha? Dewas was written in my fate and thus situations arose that led me here. Supporting ideas kept on coming to me. To consume the food and water of Dewas, to walk on the land of Dewas — this was predestined for me. Thus the ashram is in Dewas. After all, who can avoid fate?

The second reason is the command of Guru. When I asked Gurudev Yoganandji Maharaj where should I go, he told me to go south and settle somewhere near Indore. Remember that Guruji's residence was in Rishikesh, which is to the north of Dewas. First I chose Mahu; then I settled in Dewas. In those days Bankebehari lal Saxena was Secretary to the ruler of Dewas. I was in Ujjain suffering from malaria. From there he brought me to Dewas. In this way I arrived in Dewas in 1948. In those days a Mahatma named Swami Narayananand Saraswati was based at Narayan Kuti. He asked me to share a cottage with him, but at the time the cottage was too small. After sometime Narayan Swami passed away. The cottage was empty. People tried to bring me here and I came. Circumstances helped in this way.

The third reason is the air and water. The air and water here are neither excessively cold, nor excessively hot. Kashmir and the

Himalayas are definitely very beautiful, but it is too cold there. The seashore is also beautiful, but it is hot. In Dewas it is neither too cold, nor too hot. And Dewas is a small and silent place.

The fourth reason is geographic. By geographic I do not just mean the terrain. Dewas is exactly in the center of India. If you consider India to be a Sri Yantra [an auspicious tantrik symbol, consisting of circles and triangles, representing the universe], then its midpoint is Dewas. There is a temple of Chamunda Bhagwati on the hill, and right at the foot of the hill is Narayan Kuti. That is another reason why Narayan Kuti appealed to my mind. By sitting here and doing sadhan, one makes direct contact with the Goddess Shakti [divine power]. You all know that the midpoint of a Sri Yantra is sacred. If you consider the human body to be a form of Sri Yantra, the midpoint is the Kundalini. Even today many realized souls live in an invisible form in and around this midpoint, Dewas. They wander here and there and bless and help serious aspirants. That is another reason why I chose Dewas.

Question: "Have you seen or felt the presence of any such great soul? Did you get any help in spirituality from them?"

Answer: "It is inappropriate to express one's experiences related to sadhan. Neither should one ask such a question. But one thing is definite: If I am speaking of it, then there is some basis to it."

Question: "But do people feel the presence of such great souls?"

Answer: "I have used the phrase 'serious aspirant.' Common worldly people are incapable of having such an experience. Those who are advanced aspirants will surely experience it."

Comment: "In that case, Dewas is really very good for aspirants. First, the temple of Mother Chamunda; second, Narayan Kuti; and on top of that, the company of a saintly person like you. It is icing on the cake."

Response: "In the sadhan of Shaktipat there is no need for any support or help. However saintly people and the atmosphere can definitely add intensity. The word 'Dewas' can be interpreted in two ways: First, 'the abode of Gods,' deva plus vas. [In Sanskrit, 'deva' means God and 'vas' is the root meaning 'to reside.'] Gods are present everywhere. But in Dewas they are benevolent towards aspirants. Kashi, Vrindavan, Haridwar, and other names also have the same etymological meaning. The other meaning of 'Dewas' is, 'That in which a prayer is offered to the Gods to permit us to reside in their worlds,' so that we can proceed further towards our spiritual goals."

28. The Nature of a Saint

From the following incident one sees the wide gap existing between worldliness and social interaction, and the thinking of saints:

Construction activity was going on in the ashram. When there was a lot of work, laborers were hired as needed. In a few days most of the work was completed, but the laborers remained. There was very little work, not enough to keep all laborers busy. As a result they passed the time wandering here and there. Still the ashram had to pay their wages. Some ashramites were uncomfortable about this. They said to Maharajshri, "The construction work is almost complete. There is very little left to do. Why not reduce the work force? There is so much unnecessary expenditure."

Maharajshri stood up at once and said, "Your way of thinking and mine is different. All these workers started the job together and they will finish at the same time. If some of them are let go now, how will they feel? They also have families and children, and everything is so expensive. Now their expenses are taken care of. There is no guarantee when they will get another job or even whether they will get one or not. Let them stay until the job is finished. It doesn't make a difference to us, but it makes a big difference to them."

Then Maharajshri started talking about a certain Mahatma from the days before he entered monastic life. "In Haryana, where this body [Maharajshri's] was born, there was a Mahatma, Hanumandasji. Hanumandasji was a devotee and recited the Ramayana regularly. He received many donations. He was greatly respected by the people. In the village there was a shortage of water and what little there was, it was salty. Thus Hanumandasji started a project of digging a huge lake. Whatever donations he received he would distribute the same day to workers, paying them in advance. The workers ended up collecting advances for a year or two. But who maintained the accounts? He said that digging the lake was simply a pretext. It gave some people a livelihood. I had a great deal of faith in Hanumandasji. I would go to see him often. The samskaras of my faith in him were inscribed in such a fashion that they are still there."

Now the discussion about Hanumandasji had started, and other stories related to him were told. When Hanumandasji's Guru Maharaj passed away, the question of his successor cropped up. It was everyone's opinion that Hanumandasji was a deserving and strong choice for this. Everyone was determined to appoint him to that position. Hanumandasji was totally detached. He was not willing to get involved in the complexities of the ashram, but people tried to persuade him. Eventually Hanumandasji thought of a trick to save himself from this situation. The next day the village sweeper-woman passed by carrying chapatis in a basket on her head. He went running, picked up a chapati from the basket and started eating it. Simultaneously he began screaming that he had eaten the chapati of a sweeper-woman and now was no longer a brahmin. In those days untouchability was a big issue. Hanumandasji's problem was solved.

There was only one well in the village and that, too, of salty water. It was difficult to get sweet drinking water. One had to get it from a distance. Once a wealthy man came to Hanumandasji and offered him twenty rupees. In those days twenty rupees was a lot of money. He asked Hanumandasji to use the money in the construction of the lake for drinking water. Hanumandasji asked someone to bring a bucket filled with water from the well. When he received the water he asked the wealthy man to drink some of it. The moment he drank the water, the wealthy man said, "How did this water become sweet?" Hanumandasji asked him to take back his money. Later on he said that the income of that person was not earned through honest means, thus he had rejected his service.

After that Maharajshri said, "Tell me: How can I release those workers with such samskaras?" Everyone was silent. What could they say? Nothing came to the mind. Eventually everyone touched Maharajshri's feet and departed.

29. Maya

Today there are many buildings in the ashram, but in 1960 it had a very different look: a temple that was too small, a kitchen extremely small in comparison to the one today, and Maharajshri's place of residence. The rest of the space was open. The ashram was situated at the base of a hill, built almost halfway into it. The town of Dewas was at a much lower level. In those days even the retaining walls were not like today and the ground was hardly even. Flowers of xenia and marigold bloomed everywhere. The ashram was open on all sides and, as a result, the flowering plants had spread out over a long stretch of the hill. There was a deep canal on one side and towards the lower side of the ashram there was an abundance of flowers. Due to this the ashram looked very pleasant, as if it were a big garden. When I arrived there on the first day, I was simply awestruck. Nearby, and even for some distance from the ashram, there were no buildings. Only the newly-built, shining railway station was visible in the distance. The rainy season had just ended. There was greenery everywhere. More than anything else, there was the influence of Maharajshri's personality.

One day I told Maharajshri, "The ashram is so beautiful, surrounded by flowers on all sides, with solitude, silence, slithering of snakes, the mischief of squirrels. The mind wants to drown itself in this beauty."

Maharajshri laughed and said, "This beauty and ugliness is the misconception of Maya [illusion]. Maya manifests itself by taking various forms. Sometimes it attracts by beauty and sometimes it frightens through ugliness. If there are skyscraping mountain ranges, then there also are very deep valleys. There are saddening troubles of the past and golden dreams of the future. There is the kind, cool shade of motherly love and heat from the insensitivity of the heart. All these are the conspiracies of Maya. If it ties you in a bond of love with a friend, it also ties an enemy with a rope of hatred and anger. Friendship and enmity both are bonds. In the same way, beauty and ugliness both influence the chitta, destabilize it, and inscribe memories on the mind. Every person desires happiness in the world. Everyone wants a beautiful form, sweet voice and a delicate touch, but all these are as dangerous as ugliness. Actually, these are much more lethal.

"Now take your example. You visualized beauty in the ashram and you thought of drowning in it. You forgot that all this is Maya. Maya has many different types of weapons. She knows how to entice, entangle, ensnare, mislead and provoke. If at times one of the weapons does not work, she uses another. If, after her explanations, you do not give in, she will become a lover and influence your mind. Greed, attachment, anger, fear, love, trick or fraud — whichever can succeed on a living being, she takes up that weapon. Sometimes she calls you to the world by taking a beautiful form, at other times she pushes you into the world by showing her ugliness.

"Thinkers, yogis and devotees refuse to succumb to the incitements of Maya. They retain their mental poise. If at times the mind gets excited, they apply the restraint of discretion or love and bring it under control. They know that Maya is standing in the background of the beautiful and the ugly, thus they refer to Maya as an actress, a female thug and other things. She is very efficient at changing her form according to the situation. She can make something beautiful look ugly, and make something ugly look beautiful. She can make someone drink poison by making it look like nectar. By suggesting ideas about duty and ideals she can make someone go to the gallows. She can make big look small and small look big, an evil person look virtuous and a virtuous person look evil. She is so powerful that she has also hidden God within herself."

On hearing Maharajshri's words, I stood gaping as if I had been swindled. For quite some time I could not figure out what to say. It was as if the mind had frozen. Then somehow I composed myself and asked, "Maya is of such a form? I have never imagined it. Our ancient rishis and sages carried out their spiritual practice resting in the lap of nature. They preferred the murmuring of brooks and fruit-bearing trees. They thought it was more fruitful to stay far from cities and pass their life in the splendor of nature. Such samskaras have made a home inside me. That is the reason I said such a thing."

Maharajshri said, "The rishis were well-acquainted with the tactics and doings of Maya. In a city there are more means for slipping. Thus they thought it more appropriate to carry out their spiritual practices in forests far from the cities. As long as this body is here, safety and satisfaction of hunger is a necessity. Water is definitely required. Thus they preferred to be near fruit-bearing trees and rivers and springs. Even in a forest there is fear of wild animals. However they considered desire to be more frightening than this fear. This in no way means that they were attached to the beauty of the forest. They knew that the root problem was attachment, whether they were in a city or in a forest."

I said, "A normal, worldly householder who is an aspirant and has many responsibilities cannot even think of leaving the town, staying in a forest and performing his sadhana. What should he do?"

Maharajshri said, "I am aware of the difficulties of a householder. I have personally endured them. They can at least give up attachment. Living in a forest is not important. The state of the chitta is. Great saints, too, have lived as householders. If there is no attachment, beauty and ugliness, attraction and repulsion, happiness and sorrow all become the same."

Question: "As you mention in your sermons and as I know from the study of your books, the sacrifice of attachment is very difficult. Yogis, ascetics and devotees, too, experience difficulty in giving up attachment. So is it correct that the perception of beauty and ugliness can never come to an end?"

Answer: "So long as the natural state, the state in which attachment comes to an end, is not achieved, one must practice restraint. The perception of beauty will continue to distract your mind. In every assault one samskar [impression] or another will be removed. If one loses tolerance, then the samskaras will become stronger. This is a long spiritual practice that requires great patience. Along with the erosion of samskaras, attachment will also weaken and over a period of time the perception of beauty will come to an end. Even if one falls from the path of spirituality, one should compose oneself and get back to sadhan and not give up."

30. Service and Sadhana

A gentleman came from Delhi. He seemed to be very devoted. He said to Maharajshri, "I have two sons. With your blessings, both of them have good jobs. They are happy in all ways. They and I, too, want to serve you in some way. Thus if you grant permission, I can tell my sons. They will send something on a monthly basis in your service."

Maharajshri said, "We have no system of monthly service. Other people have expressed such a desire but I did not grant permission. If I grant permission to you, what will other people say?

"Another reason for not granting permission is that I do not want to become dependent on anyone. An aspirant should only be dependent on God. The thought invariably comes to the mind, 'Something is coming from that person monthly. Why worry?' Due to this monthly schedule an aspirant begins to wait for the postman. 'The money order should have arrived today. I don't know why it did not come. I had to buy a particular thing. I had to pay for it.' And so on and so forth.

"It is your duty to serve, but not through monthly payments. If you come here on Guru Purnima or once in a while, you may give when you wish. You may even send it via money order. I am a sanyasi. My work keeps on progressing. However you don't have to serve by depriving yourself, by cutting your household expenditures or by borrowing. Serve according to your capability and only so much as you can bear. Actually true service is your sadhana. Through that the task of your Guru becomes easier because it ties a disciple to his Guru. If he does not do his sadhan then he is like a heavy stone tied to the Guru's feet."

31. The Supreme Personality of Maharajshri

Often the thought would come to my mind that Maharajshri was a devotee, a yogi or a jnani. His personality was such that it encompassed each of these forms. When scripture was being discussed, he would explain it in one uninterrupted stretch. Be it the Tantra or the Puranas, Vedas or the Gita, he had equal mastery over all of them. His commentary on *Saundarya Lahiri* is incomparable, whereas *Upanishad Vani* contains the essence of the Upanishads. He never gave lengthy explanations, but he gave them in such an appropriate manner that the listener could draw many things from them. Those subjects that couldn't be understood even after listening to many discourses and much study he would clarify in a moment. This was the form of a jnani.

A Shastriji [religious scholar] came to Maharajshri. He was proud of his knowledge and erudition. He did not even feel it necessary to follow the common custom of salutation. He came directly and sat down. Maharajshri understood his sentiment. He began to ask questions.

Maharajshri said, "Shastriji, A question may be asked from many different perspectives."

(i) "If you are questioning to exhibit your knowledge, then I accept that you are a great scholar."

(ii) "If you are here to test someone, then in that case, I declare myself unworthy of your test."

(iii) "If you are here to defeat someone in debate, then I accept my defeat and your victory."

(iv) "If you are here to pass the time, then in that case I would say that you are wasting my time as well as yours."

(v) "If you are here to satisfy your curiosity, then in that case please ask a question and I will definitely try to answer it."

Such humility and lack of pride can only be a quality of a devotee. Shastriji was ashamed. The disturbance of his mind became visible in his face. He said, "I am asking a question out of curiosity. I accept that until I came to you I was filled with pride at my learning, but in the force of your humility, all my pride is dispelled." Then a spiritual discussion began. Shastriji asked questions to his heart's content and Maharajshri resolved all of them lovingly. This was the jnani form of Maharajshri.

One day a saint came and a discussion on tantra began. Upon hearing Maharajshri's experiential and learned analysis of mysterious subjects, it seemed that tantra was his specialty. In addition he has written a commentary on *Pratyabhijnaahridayam* and the *Shiva Sutras*. The basis of *Saundarya Lahiri*, too, is tantra, and his commentary on this scripture is his definitive composition. I was unable to determine what kind of Mahatma I should consider him. Just as many different tributaries converge, join a river and assume a grand form, in the same way different disciplines of knowledge were illuminated in Maharajshri and his personality kept glowing more and more. His knowledge and experience of the yoga path was singular. His heart was full of divine sentiments. Astronomy, practical knowledge, politics — there was no subject left untouched, to such an extent that he even had a good command of the art of cooking, of construction activity, of architecture, of gardening and of social science.

Not only that, but even in the field of sadhan his reach was without parallel. As one considered his experiences of sadhan, other aspirants seemed like dwarfs. His specialty was the absence of pride. This is fitting because if there is pride, how can one progress in sadhan? Pride is for worldly people and not spiritual aspirants. His nature was like that of a small child. Even if he became upset, the next moment he would be happy. I was continuously surprised that such a simple person could be such a great soul. If he made a mistake, he would feel no hesitation in acknowledging it. His ways of living and dress were very simple. No trickery, no deceit.

He was very regular in his morning walks. Be it summer or winter there was no interruption in that. In the rainy season he would carry an umbrella. His state of sadhan would remain throughout the day. He would say, "That pleasant state of the chitta, which comes occasionally while sitting in a chair, comes with great difficulty even in sadhan." I experienced very frequently that he was far from attachment. It would not be an exaggeration to say that he always remained in a state of divine bliss.

A life devoid of ostentation was his nature. Once it was winter. One sweater wasn't enough. He wore a long-sleeved sweater and a half-sleeved sweater on top of it. I felt it was very strange, but he said, "It is only to protect me from the cold. If people laugh, let them."

It would also be appropriate to say that his entire life, every incident and thought in his life, was a form of kriya. You know that karma is filled with pride and kriya is natural. There is pride in ostentation, not in naturalness. Trying to show something that is not there is ostentation.

He was an ocean of kindness. Once a monk came to the ashram. Maharajshri welcomed him in an appropriate fashion. The monk said that he had to go to Bombay but he did not have money. He would be obliged if some arrangement could be made. Maharajshri said that some arrangement would be made. In the midst of their conversation, the monk lied about something, which upset Maharajshri. He asked the monk to leave. After the monk departed, Maharajshri remained serious for a while. Then he called someone and told him that the monk had gone to the railway station and that he should go and buy him a ticket to Bombay. Someone said that the monk was not going to Bombay at all. He had said that simply to extract money from Maharajshri. Maharajshri said, "Even if he is a criminal, let him cheat. Cheating is a sin. Being cheated is not. He came here with expectation. What does it matter if I do not get anything to eat for a day?"

When construction activity was going on at the ashram, a carpenter was working there. When the job was finished, he started working at some other place, where he fell and was seriously injured. When Maharajshri heard this, he sent some money to his house to help pay for treatment. He also sent a message that if the man required more money he could send someone for it. He told the milkman who came to the ashram to deliver a liter of milk to the carpenter's house and charge the ashram account. As if this were not enough, Maharajshri went to the carpenter's house to see him. I was growing increasingly amazed at seeing these acts of Maharajshri. Such a delicate and profoundly humane personality in today's illusory, selfish and cruel world!

He used to wear a dhoti [a long loin cloth] above his knees and a pair of slippers on his feet. Once it was winter. I was with Maharajshri on our morning walk. Even I wore a pair of slippers. It was windy and extremely cold. My feet were feeling very cold. The thought came to my mind that if Maharajshri were to start wearing a closed shoe, I, too, might get a pair. Men are so crafty. How they talk in a roundabout way for their selfish motives! Maharajshri was the pretext, but it was my own selfishness. I said, "Maharajji, it is very cold. Your feet must be feeling it. Why not buy a closed shoe?"

But Maharajshri's answer washed away all my hopes. He said, "Why do we need it? It is cold only for a few days. When a cool wind blows here, it becomes cold for couple of days. Generally the weather is pleasant."

My selfish plan was unsuccessful, but it forced me to compare myself with Maharajshri. On one side was renunciation. On the other was selfish intent. I found myself worldly in the presence of Maharajshri's asceticism. There was such a lack of tolerance in me. I couldn't utter another word. Through Maharajshri I came to know my inner self.

During meals Maharajshri would insist that everyone be served everything. It was against the rule to cook good food for one's self and give something else to others. It was also his order that the people who work in the kitchen should be served everything. Once kheer [a sweet dish made from rice and milk] had been prepared. I was serving. People kept on asking for more and I kept on serving. Finally, when Maharajshri heard the sound of the ladle against the vessel, he realized that the kheer was gone. He asked, "Isn't there kheer left for you people?"

I said, "It is okay. The next time it is made, we will have some."

He replied, "This is wrong. The people who work in the kitchen, they themselves do not eat! Is this okay? Serve others after keeping some aside for yourselves. Or else tell people when they are asking for more that you are running out. No one will be offended." Thereafter I became cautious.

Such was Maharajshri and such were his tales.

32. Sadhan and Japa

Once it came to my mind that I must do regular japa [chanting] of the Gayatri mantra. Upon finding a suitable opportunity I asked Maharajshri about this and he said, "I shall think about it."

When I mentioned it again after a couple of days, he said, "Okay, I will think about it."

Now I was reluctant to ask him again and again, but I mustered some courage and asked him one more time. Maharajshri said, "Do one thing. First begin with one round of a rosary. When one round of the rosary is about to end, we shall decide what to do next.

I said, "That is fine."

The next day, after finishing my bath and other things, I sat down on my seat. I had just rolled over a couple of beads when intense kriyas began. The rosary was tossed aside. When the intensity of the kriya subsided I picked up the rosary and had hardly started my chanting when kriyas started. On that day, in spite of many attempts, I couldn't chant. The same thing happened the next day and also the day after that. Helpless, I pleaded to Maharajshri. He laughed and said, "If you are unable to do even one rosary, how will you do it daily?

"After Shaktipat initiation, when kriyas have progressed, regular japa is difficult because kriyas begin to interfere. The moment an aspirant concentrates his mind on performing japa, the kriyas begin. If the intensity of the kriyas is severe, then it becomes still more difficult. So it is best that you give up the thought of regular japa. I did not tell you this earlier because I wanted you to have an experience that would make it easy for you to understand what I am saying. Actually you do not even need japa now. Regular japa and so forth are spiritual practices for the awakening of the Shakti. These rituals can be performed with the desire of attaining something and are not concerned with the awakening of the Shakti. Rituals carried out with a spiritual perspective are the only ones concerned with the awakening of the Shakti. If the ritual of chanting is performed on the basis of prana [the dynamic life-force], then there is a possibility of a quicker awakening. If it is performed on the basis of the mind, intellect and heart, it takes a longer time. But in Shaktipat this same goal is achieved with the grace of a Guru, so there is no need for regular japa. The nature of sadhana is transformed into sadhan. Now why do you want to go back to deliberate egoistic spiritual practice? Do your sadhan. Your mind will continue to be purified by this sadhan."

I said, "Does this mean that after the awakening of Shakti and after it becomes active, worship, recitation, japa and other practices are not needed anymore?"

Maharajshri said, "You certainly do not need them, but if the kriya feels the necessity, then there is a need. That is, after awakening of the Shakti, worship, recitations, japa, and so forth should happen in the form of kriyas. When that type of kriya stops, worship and recitation, too, are left behind. Then even if you sit down to do them, they do not happen, just as you sat down to do the Gayatri japa now but could not do it. This means that your japa was not a form of kriya but simply a desire to do regular japa that arose in you after listening to other people."

I said, "Currently I am reading *Shandilya Bhakti Sutras*. There it is written that japa, kirtans [devotional songs glorifying God] and other practices done after awakening give an impetus to activities of the Shakti."

At this Maharajshri said, "Only so long as the kriyas do not manifest. It is not fixed how long japa, kirtans and other such practices should continue. When the intensity of the kriya is manifested, then all these stop on their own or are transformed into kriyas. In regular japa or a ritual, one has to complete a certain number of chants, which is not possible in sadhan. Hence japa, kirtans, and so forth cannot take place according to rules. If they happen, any number of repetitions might be possible, or none at all. Japa, kirtan and pranayaam [control of breath] are manifested in kriyas, but only as long as the kriya persists."

I said, "The essential point is that the attempt to do regular japa is contrary to the feeling of surrender."

Maharajshri said, "Yes. An aspirant of Shaktipat must prevent himself from becoming an obstacle in the progress of a kriya. When your efforts end, only then will natural kriyas begin to progress."

I asked another question upon hearing this. "Is tolerating the joys and sorrows that come from the world a surrender?"

The answer was, "Joys and sorrows are the results or fruits of the activity of the Shakti on the basis of prarabdha. To accept and bear whatever fruit it gives is surrender. If an aspirant opposes, it means he has not accepted things. Opposition also means that the aspirant has reacted to the effect of the results on his mind, which is a cause of further accumulation of impressions. All these issues deserve serious thinking on the part of the aspirant and are helpful in sadhan."

33. The Problem of Maya

Among Maharajshri's visitors there was a Judge Sahib [a Hindi term of respect; "Sir"]. He had retired from service in Ujjain. One day, when we went for our morning walk, we found him sitting on a bench at the railway station. After mutual greetings Maharajshri asked, "Judge Sahib, what are you doing in your retirement?"

Judge Sahib said, "Earlier I would separate the water from the milk, now I am mixing it. Meaning: earlier I was a judge, now I am a lawyer," and he burst out laughing.

After saying farewell to Judge Sahib, Maharajshri said, "He made such an apt statement. But why just lawyers? The whole world is involved in adding water to milk. The truth is hidden with great skill. Thieves, thugs and cheaters are portrayed as great men. A great man is proved to be dishonest. One has no food to eat at home, his every hair is steeped in debt, but still he shows himself as wealthy to the outside world. This is the era of ostentation. There may be nothing lacking in the house of a beggar, but he will act so miserable, sorrowful and deprived that you feel pity for him. It has become very difficult to find the truth."

I said, "Maya is a criminal. The more a person is influenced by Maya, the more he will cheat."

Maharajshri said, "You are right. That is the job of Maya. To show something that is not there. To restrict something that has no boundaries. If there is no day or night, to show that, too. To even hide the omnipresent. To make one feel happy in a state of sorrow. The hands of Maya are extremely skilled at adding water to milk. But what can be done? Today is the Kali Yuga.

Having gained momentum, Maya roams rapidly in all four directions. She already has under her control the mind of every living being. Everyone is forced to see what she displays. Among worldly people, perhaps, it is understandable, but she hasn't even spared the monks and saints. They, too, are drowning in the desire for heavenly pleasures, attraction and aversion, lust and anger, and other things. They are after physical pleasures, which merely contain a mirage of happiness. Even if an attempt is made to remove someone from the pit of Maya, no one is willing to come out. On the contrary, they try to drag the person who wants to remove them into the pit. Then those who are trying to get the world out of the pit of Maya themselves run away. They take shelter in caves, in solitary places. What an irony."

I asked, "Maharajji, there must definitely be a way to escape from Maya."

He said, "As I observe the mental state of the common masses, it seems that, right now, there is no way of escape. Even if there were, no one is ready to follow it. When some people follow the way, they do not follow the regimen. Abstinence is necessary along with the medicine. Only then can the medicine take effect. As long as sadhana is not accompanied by restraint, sadhana cannot move ahead on the path of progress."

Then he said, "He who is caught in the tide of a flowing river, willingly or unwillingly, is forced to flow with the tide. In the Kali Yuga all beings are in the clutches of Maya. When Maya makes one dance, he must dance — to some extent, at least. Only that being who holds fast to the hem of God's garment can survive, in spite of flowing with the tide and dancing. Sadhana points towards the river bank. As a result the being is aware of his goal and eventually reaches the river bank."

I said, "It is difficult not just for common people, but also for great ones to advance beyond this state."

He said, "It is surely difficult. If you do sadhan, then the pride of sadhan drives you mad. Pride is the work of Maya and all other defects come behind it — lust, anger, jealousy, all of them. An act of love is also Maya's pride. All defects nourish pride [the ego] and pride feeds all defects. Only the grace of God can save a being. But God himself has created Maya. Maya is under his control. She is activated by his inspiration. On one side of God there is Maya and on the other is his grace. What the being experiences is dependent upon what he desires. If he wants God's grace, he must forsake Maya. When God showers his grace on a being, he removes the Maya lying between them. All spiritual practices end at grace. If there is no grace, then the being wanders around swollen with pride. Through sadhana the increase in sattva guna [harmonious qualities] is possible, but the states of all the three gunas [qualities] are subject to change. Again Tamo guna and Rajo guna will increase. The being will fall again. Until Maya allows him passage, a being cannot go across. Removal of Maya is under the control of God."

34. On Nonviolence and Human Birth

Many snakes roamed about the ashram. Now there are walls all around. Many houses have been built below. On one side there is a large slum. But in those days there were no other buildings nearby, and no walls. After Naga Panchami [a festival of snakes] the snake charmers used to release snakes on the hill and thus there would be many in the area. At the ashram one could see all kinds and sizes of them. One was around eight feet long. One day I was washing clothes in the open when suddenly it went past me. I was extremely scared, since there was still an attachment to my body. Cobras apparently lived close by, and they would come into the ashram regularly. Sometimes the snakes would sneak into the kitchen and sometimes into the temple. I used to sleep in the kitchen where there were a lot of rats. The kitchen roof was made of village tiles across which the rats would scamper around at night. If rats are around, snakes will surely come to eat them. The chasing of snakes and rats would continue throughout the night.

One day I told Maharajshri, "Mothers, children, everyone comes to the ashram. In the morning several aspirants come for sadhan in the dark. The presence of snakes is a very frightening thing."

Maharajshri said, "So what if children come here? There is a silent agreement between the snakes and us. We don't say anything to them and they do not say anything to us. Many snakes roam around, but so far we have not killed a snake and they, too, have never troubled us."

I said, "They eat frogs and rats. It can be upsetting to see them eat."

He said affectionately, "Go to the forest and see which animal is eating which. Peek into the depths of the ocean and see how many small fish are being eaten by larger ones. In houses lizards eat so many insects. A living organism is food for another living organism. Who can break this law of nature?"

I said, "Then why has the rule of ahimsa [nonviolence] been established?"

He said, "These rules are laid down for humans, not for animals. Animals do not perform sadhana. They only enjoy. To act violently is the trait of an animal, not a human. A person doing physical, verbal or mental violence does so only after acquiring animal traits. It is necessary for an aspirant to be nonviolent."

I began to wonder to what extent it was possible to practice nonviolence. When we walk, who knows how many living beings are crushed under our feet? When we drink water, who knows how many living beings enter our stomach. Recently a scientist in America discovered that not only are living beings inside our body, they also adhere to various external parts of the body. Living beings are killed when we brush our hand against our face, bathe or change clothes. I asked, "Is it possible for a human to escape from taking lives? Don't innumerable lives perish without our knowing while we eat and drink?"

Maharajshri said, "The issue is not violence; it is the intention of doing violence. People see the act and not the feeling behind it, but it is the sentiment motivating the act that determines whether it is proper or improper. I recognize that there are beings we end up killing unknowingly, but this is without violent intent in the mind. Life is progressing simply according to the laws of nature. God has created most living organisms to provide food for other organisms. Will the huge fish of the ocean come to the land in search of food? Will the tiger satisfy his hunger by eating grass? The way in which these beings kill is unavoidable according to the cycle of nature. One must breathe, eat and drink water. There is also a need to move about, and one cannot commit suicide to prevent the deaths that occur during these actions. That which is inevitably going to happen will happen. God has not made the human body and its sense organs suitable for eating flesh. The animals that have been given permission to eat flesh, their teeth and intestines have a particular kind of structure. They can eat and digest raw flesh. The beaks of some birds are also similarly made.

"A human birth is not for eating flesh, but for attaining moksha [liberation]. However man has lost his way. He has become involved in the pleasures of the palate and has adopted violent tendencies. He is convinced that physical strength can be acquired only by eating meat. Otherwise he can adopt the path of ahimsa, purify his chitta through spiritual practice and derive spiritual benefits. This golden opportunity is not available to snakes. They only have the opportunity to fill their stomach with rats and frogs."

I said, "Maharajshri, what is the basis for regarding snakes as gods and establishing methods to worship them?"

Maharajshri said, "Even though the nature of these prayers has been distorted today, their beginnings were based on a pure, spiritual viewpoint. To show the omnipresence of the divine power, the practice of worshipping some animals, birds, fish, snakes, mountains, rivers, trees, water, fire and other things began. Later idols were made and they were infused with life [prana pratishtha], but prior to that people worshipped those in whom life was already present."

35. The Problem with Academic Knowledge

One day Maharajshri said in his spiritual discourse, "Academic knowledge alone cannot give moksha. In fact there is a higher possibility of it becoming a reason for pride. Until there is a direct experience within, the illusion cannot be destroyed. For this, purity of the mind and sadhan are essential."

The next morning I humbly said that I had doubts whether any one of those speakers who sit on cushions and thoughtfully describe Bramha [the Supreme Being] had actually experienced Bramha; in which case they were overstepping their boundaries.

Maharajshri said, "Look, I, too, have faith in Vedanta. I look upon Adi Shankaracharya with faith and respect, too. If I need to say something about Vedanta, I manage to do so. But just by doing so, one doesn't become an authority on, or an expositor of Vedanta. To become an authority on Vedanta, there is a need for control of the sense organs, control of the mind, detachment from the world based on discretion, a state free from doubt, desire for moksha and tolerance. Without these it is like standing on the earth and trying to touch the moon. All these qualities are not possible without sadhan. Can the mind become pure by mere talk? I cannot comment about all the speakers but, yes, a majority of them are incompetent to lecture on Vedanta."

"But there is a school of spiritual practice based on Vedanta, so why is there a problem in talking about Vedanta?" I asked.

To this Maharajshri replied, "There is no problem if they talk about the nature of the spiritual practice, but they do not even address this subject. They continually analyze Bramha while talking about the principle in an attempt to prove that the living being is Bramha. If this confusion were to take root in beings that are attached to Maya, it is easy to imagine how disastrous it would be. If some thought is given to this aspect of the spiritual practice of Vedanta, one point that will be clear is that a being still lives in dvaita [duality]. He must move from dvaita to advaita [nonduality]. As long as there is confusion, advaita is impossible. Another point that will become clear after serious contemplation is that the Vedanta style of spiritual practice is nothing but devotion and yoga. The purpose of all spiritual practices is to gain authority in Vedanta."

I said, "Academic knowledge and thought must certainly be beneficial in some way."

He answered, "There is a definite benefit. If there is no pride, impressions of knowledge are accumulated. Otherwise more impressions of pride than knowledge are accumulated. But if you continue to accumulate impressions of academic knowledge, then what will happen to the previously accumulated impressions belonging to the three gunas? For their removal, devotion and yoga are necessary. For freedom from prarabdha, tolerant dutiful action [karma yoga] is necessary. The impressions accumulated by academic knowledge and thought will also have to be cleared eventually. Only then can inner knowledge dawn."

Then he said, "A tendency to acquire the fruit of spiritual practice as quickly as possible becomes aroused in a person and thus he wishes to leap directly towards Vedanta. He wishes to become Bramha all at once. He also attempts to adopt an attitude of crude passivity or inaction, and this is very fatal for the advancement of sadhana. If one's patience is forgotten because of over-enthusiasm, then the likelihood of losing the enthusiasm is very high.

"A desire for liberation in the chitta is a prerequisite for becoming an authority on Vedanta. Control over the sense organs, control over the mind, a lack of feeling of passion toward sense objects, a mind free from doubts, and tolerance are essential to desire liberation. For all this, first and foremost, there should be detachment based on discretion. There is also a need for continuous yoga, devotion and service-oriented actions to attain these states. Only then can authority in Vedanta be established. Mental forbearance is a must.

After awakening of the Shakti it becomes simpler for an aspirant. First, a sense of observation arises in place of the ego of doership. Second, accumulated impressions start emerging quickly and are eroded through the medium of kriyas. Third, an aspirant may have merely read about the conscious-self. Now the action of the conscious-self directly manifests within him, and he establishes a healthy dependence on its form. All these together make the path very easy."

36. Householders, Aspirants and Sadhan

One day Maharajshri was saying, "My tendencies have always been inclined towards spiritual practice. Whenever I stayed somewhere for a few days, I would definitely take the support of japa or religious exercises, or plan some study. Due to this, time would be spent properly. Secondly, the mind would not have an opportunity to unnecessarily play mischief. I understood very clearly that by merely memorizing or studying the railway timetable, one doesn't complete the tour of India. For that one has to endure the troubles of the journey. Just by writing and reading, one cannot obtain God. This effort is good for getting information, satisfying doubts and generating interest. Otherwise one must do spiritual practice, develop sentiments, serve and surrender.

"In 1934 when I went on a trip to Uttarkhand for the first time, every day I would start my journey only after doing japa, meditation, and so forth for two or three hours in the morning. Japa would continue even while walking. Before sleeping, too, I would meditate for some time. When I was initiated the nature of my spiritual practice changed. Deliberate effort was replaced by surrender. Then I rented a room in an ashram in Rishikesh and got involved in sadhan. As a result of the sadhana done in the past I had unprecedented experiences there."

A devotee asked, "Maharajji, you are a sanyasi [renunciate], and even before taking vows you were detached. You can do sadhan as you please. You have no worldly responsibilities, no shortage of time, and no dealings with anyone. It is possible for you to do all this. But we worldly folks have many responsibilities and are surrounded by hindrances at every moment. How can we do all this?"

I added, "I have a lot of ashram work. In the evening when everyone sits in the cave, I am busy working. When there is work to be done and, instead, I am doing my sadhan, it doesn't feel good either."

Maharajshri said, "If only renunciation were necessary for the progress of sadhan, then all renunciates would have attained realization. However that is not the case. I know several renunciates who have made no progress in sadhan.

"Sadhan is based on the state of the chitta and not on renunciation. Also, remember that the majority of the saints and great men were householders. They, too, had responsibilities and limitations but they did not let them interfere in their sadhan. "We are householders. We do not have time. We have responsibilities." All these are excuses. Also, think about the amount of time you waste meaninglessly. Then think about what you can do while carrying out your work. Contemplate on how to give your conduct a spiritual form. Don't just neglect your practice by complaining about your helplessness."

Then he turned towards me and said, "Karma [action] never becomes an obstacle in spirituality. It is a supplement, a support to spirituality, but only if it is done in the right way. The suppression of the influence of rajo guna [disturbing qualities] in a being's mind is possible only through karma. Karma is the means to end prarabdha. Nivritti dawns while performing dutiful karma. Karma is also sadhan. If karma is done with a sense of attachment, only then does it become a cause of bondage. Therefore harbor a feeling of service in doing the work of the ashram. Do not expect anything in return, neither respect, nor praise, nor any other special convenience. Now you are progressing with karma yoga [unattached dutiful action] as your focus. At some point in time the opportunity to focus on sadhan will follow."

I was listening silently.

"For an aspirant, the tendencies of an aspirant are a must. If you have the attitude of an aspirant, then talking, walking, conduct — everything becomes a sadhan. The life of an aspirant has an altogether different color from that of others. Many people do sadhan for hours at a time but they do not qualify as aspirants because they lack the proper attitude. If karma is done with the attitude of an aspirant, it is indeed sadhan."

Not only did Maharajshri himself always remain immersed in sadhan, he also maintained the attitude of sadhan. He never let the reins of his mind slacken. He always remained on top of the mind. He kept a tight vigil on the mind. He controlled every mischief of the mind. He attained a high spiritual platform by fighting defects. Thus his life evolved into the kriya form of the Kriya-Shakti. Like a small child, ego did not exist in him.

I continued to think about how maligned my mind was. "There are heaps of defects in the mind. Every corner of the chitta is filled with desires. I cannot see anything except darkness. What will happen to me? Will my life ever be like Maharajshri's? Will I be able to free myself from compulsions?"

37. Miracles, Politics and Selfishness

At the time of the walk today, some devotees who were visiting from outside accompanied us. It was colder than usual. Almost everyone had a shawl around them, but our feet were rather cold. Going to the railway station and back was a two-kilometer walk. We were discussing the subject of miracles, because some people had assumed a particular event to be a miracle and associated it with Maharajshri.

Maharajshri said, "Miracles happen. I do not deny it. But how can I do that? Especially when *Yoga Darshan* has described these siddhis [attainments or psychic powers] in such great detail. It is also mentioned there that they are obstacles in attaining asamprajnat [seedless samadhi]. One thing is clear: that siddhis happen only in the active state of the chitta. All siddhis disappear in asamprajnat. That is, all siddhis are physical. Support of the physical world is essential for miracles. The physical world disappears in asamprajnat. Then there is no support to display miracles. To carry out any action in this world, it is necessary for the chitta to be active. Both these things are absent in asamprajnat. If a person becomes attached to siddhis, feels proud about them, and gets involved in acquiring fame and fortune through them, which is highly possible, he cannot attain asamprajnat. Thus these siddhis are called obstacles.

"On the inner journey of sadhan there are two stages that are very difficult to cross: first, to remove the attention from the visible world and turn it inward; and second, to untie or resolve the knot of jada and chetan [the inert and consciousness], that is, moving from samprajnat to asamprajnat. While crossing this second stage, over and above other things, the siddhis are impediments in the path. Thus an intelligent aspirant should never be attracted to siddhis. This state is the same as going from detachment to supreme detachment, where there is detachment even from the awareness of the difference between jada [the inert] and chetan [consciousness]. In this state the contemplation of supreme detachment is nothing but sadhan.

"In the past there was no tradition of writing the biographies of saints and great men. Several miracles about them would become popular among their devotees and believers, which were often just sentiments of the devotees. On the basis of these rumors, the biography of that particular saint would eventually be written. Devotees used to have complete faith in those miracles, and as a result their faith and trust increased. In this way there evolved a competition among the saints to perform miracles. How a particular saint developed mentally became secondary, as did the consideration of the difficulties he had to face and how he gained control over them — his schedule for sadhana, how he confronted his inner defects, and how he rose above his common condition to achieve a higher state. If people come to know about all these things and think about them a bit, then they also might benefit from them. But the devotee community is content in merely singing praises of a saint's miracles. They do not even remember that a particular saint was troubled by mental defects just like them. "How did he manage to rise so high? If he can achieve so much progress, then why can't I do so by walking on the same path?" But this thought doesn't occur. That is the reason, in India, that we have highly elevated saints and a public shackled in desires. The link between the two is missing.

"As I said, in the state of self-realization there is no miracle or siddhi. Siddhis are only possible in the state prior to samadhi [meditation or trance]. Anyone who becomes involved in the display of siddhis cannot reach the state of asamprajnat samadhi [seedless samadhi]. Thus *Yoga Darshan* advises an aspirant to refrain from the use of siddhis. Even those who have attained self-realization can perform miracles only with the help of the chitta. By doing so, however, they do not accumulate impressions of attachment or pride. A person who has attained siddhis is called a siddha purush [a person who has attainments], but the true siddha purush is one who has attained the siddhi of self-realization. This means that self-realization is the real siddhi. Such a siddha purush does not interfere in the work of God. He does not go against the laws of nature, and even if he does so it is only because he has been ordered to do so by God. A person who has attained siddhis but is not self-realized interferes in the activities and decisions of God if he makes use of them. He does them in the name of public welfare but is feeding his ego within. As a result there comes a day when he is left only with his siddhis, bereft of public welfare. This leads to his downfall.

"The world generally salutes miracles, but those who salute do not understand spirituality. They are inclined towards the world. In addition, those who perform miracles do sadhan in order to master siddhis, which leads to their downfall. It is a waste of time that damages their attitude. Devotees of God never asked God for siddhis, neither did they display siddhis. They always remained engrossed in the love of God. If ever any miracle took place it was done by God and not by the devotee. They endured poverty and carried the burden of insult and failure, but never pleaded to God for any siddhi that could harm their oppressors. They never considered anyone their enemy or opponent. From the perspective of the world, the biggest siddhi is the sentiment of equanimity. All other siddhis come and go. Why try for them?"

Praiseworthy is the Guru Maharaj who gave this understanding. To acquire pure spirituality is extremely difficult in this world. It doesn't take much time for a being to lose his way. He starts walking on the path of God but remains attached to the results.

He considers the Eight Siddhis as a big achievement. A being never understands how difficult the climb is, what kind of slipperiness there is, and how dark it is. He comes to know only when his legs stumble and he falls into a deep chasm, alone, helpless and weak. The poor being can benefit only when God takes care of him or Gurudev saves him. Even if one serves such a Gurudev for many, many births, one still cannot be freed from his obligations.

The subject of another day's discussion was politics. Two or three gentlemen joined us today. One of them initiated the talk. "Maharajji, you too were involved in politics once upon a time. There is such a big difference between today's politicians and Gandhiji."

Maharajshri said, "I met Mahatma Gandhi twice. His simplicity was worth imitating. Such a great leader and no trace of conceit. That was a time of leaders who were replete with simplicity and love for the country: Lala Lajpatrai, Bal Gangadhar Tilak, Gopal Krishna Gokhale, each one better than the other. God-fearing followers of Dharma without fraud or deceit. However at levels below these simple and unselfish leaders the same selfishness, leg-pulling, scrambling and scheming was going on. My interaction was more at the lower level. I was a regional worker and also had an interest in spirituality. Even so, there is no agreement between spirituality and modern politics. I became so fed up that I washed my hands of politics. Even after I severed my relationship with it, it did not leave me alone. People would come again and again and trouble me. I spoke to Guruji and he told me to go far away. I came to Dewas."

One gentleman said, "Politics has become so corrupt that it even makes very honest men selfish. Anyone who enters this arena is painted in its color."

Maharajshri said, "Why do you just blame politics. Is there any field left today that does not have selfishness? Business, industry, arts, literature, education — selfishness has made its way into everything. Selfishness reins supreme in every family, institution and office. Where there is selfishness, there is scheming. That is seen everywhere. Selfishness has entered the human being. Thus it has created damage everywhere."

The other gentleman said, "Mahatma Gandhi held the kingdom of Rama as an ideal for the nation. [Lord Rama's reign was said to be the ideal one. All his subjects were happy in a time of prosperity, peace and justice.] What happened to that, too?"

Maharajshri said, "Mahatma Gandhi's intentions were very good, but the nation was unable to understand them. Some people understood him to mean a certain way of structuring society when he invoked Ram's name. They could not understand that Ram is one of the many names of the Supreme Self. Rather than taking the essence of the kingdom of Rama, they got involved in the words. People assumed that 'the kingdom of Rama' meant that everyone would have good food to eat, a beautiful, comfortable house to live in, money in the bank, television, furniture, a refrigerator; that no one would have to work and life would be full of worldly pleasures. But Gandhiji's kingdom of Rama was not external, in the nation, it was in the mind. The world that is manifest outside is similar to what the mind is inside. He wanted to transform the chitta of every Indian person. That is why he included the last eighteen stanzas of the second chapter of the Gita in his daily prayer. Perhaps Gandhiji forgot that in the past several great men had already tried such an experiment and failed. The chitta of one person can be changed, but it is impossible to improve all of human society. If people did not understand Gandhiji's idea, it wasn't their fault, either, because the state of their chitta was such.

"After all there is no peace in any corner of the world today. Selfishness, pride, jealousy and aversion are everywhere. As I mentioned there is selfishness in every field. The selfishness of politicians is noticed very quickly. Those who call politicians selfish should peek within themselves. There they will see much more selfishness. It is society that supplies the workers to every political party. As society is, so will the parties be, and so will the government that is formed. The layer of selfishness that we see in political leaders is simply a gift of society."

One gentleman said, "Everyone talks about rights, no one talks about duties."

Maharajshri said, "This is a repellent form of selfishness. A right is established only by performing duties. If there is no duty, then what rights are there? But if political parties emphasize duty, they fear they will upset the public because the public only wants rights and conveniences. That is the reason that, in order to procure votes, all parties sing the praises of rights and ignore the issue of duty. How can the government, parties and the political system of a country improve if its people are negligent of their duties towards the nation, society and religion?"

One gentleman said, "Maharajji! What is the remedy for this situation?"

Maharajshri said, "There is none. Man has no remedy to improve human society. God's stick is noiseless. God alone knows when it will fall, how it will fall and what it will do. But it will definitely fall at some time or the other, and then what will happen to which country? What will be the situation of each country? God only knows. Lord Krishna has also said in the Gita that he comes whenever dharma is harmed. He destroys the evil and reestablishes dharma."

38. The Stained Jug

At the upper end of Maharajshri's bedstead, a copper jug filled with water and a glass used to be kept on a small table. He would drink water after his afternoon rest and upon waking up in the morning. Once when, as always, I cleaned the jug, filled it with water and placed it on the table, Maharajshri saw stains on it and said, "If you are unable to remove the stains on the jug, how will you clean the filth of your chitta?"

I stood there stupefied, like a statue. I did not know what to say. Maharajshri had said such a profound thing through the example of the jug. Maharajshri himself broke the silence and said, "Keep a watch on your mind while cleaning utensils, washing clothes or sweeping. The stains on the mind must be removed just as I remove the stains on the jug. Thus cleaning the jug will not merely be cleaning the jug. It will become sadhan. If every conduct and action in the world is done thoughtfully, then it can be given the form of sadhan. If one thinks that the jug is only for holding water and that it does not matter if the stains remain or not, then the jug will surely be filled but the stains will remain. This carelessness will become an obstacle and stand in the way of the purification of your chitta. While doing social activities and sadhan, purification of the mind will be impossible.

"Just as one must scrub a utensil to remove its stains, similarly one must scrub the mind to make it pure. These scrubbings can be either of devotion or of yoga, but actual scrubbings are felt during social interaction. When a common person feels this scrubbing, he starts screaming. Perhaps by screaming he feels the process less but the filth remains. That is the difference between a householder and an aspirant. A householder screams when he feels the scrubbing of the mind. An aspirant endures it with patience and does not place obstacles in the way of the process. He hopes that the mind will continue to be washed and that its shine will increase. Just as a lamp has to burn itself to spread light, similarly a devoted aspirant has to burn the mind in the fire of devotion, yoga and dutiful action for the purification of the mind.

"If the jug is cleaned daily, then it remains clean and it does not take a lot of effort to keep it so. The nature of cleaning daily is called continuous sadhan. The world keeps on influencing the mind. Knowingly or unknowingly, dirt keeps on accumulating. If the mind is cleaned daily with the soap and ashes of devotion, knowledge, yoga, detachment and repentance, then the mind remains pure and one does not have to make too much effort. Beginning all actions with a sense of service is especially helpful. You are initiated in Shaktipat, you have the experience of inner kriyas. The dirt accumulated today is eroded in the morning sadhan. The question remains of the erosion of past accumulations and prarabdha and the impressions that will be accumulated in the future. All your caution, continuous sadhan, sense of surrender and sense of service are essential for that. If you maintain a sense of observation and surrender, then the task of cleaning the mind becomes faster in the kriyas of Shakti. Earlier deep stains would be inflicted on the mind, but they will start to fade slowly if a continuous system of their erosion is maintained.

"All sadhan is for cleaning dirt, be it the dirt of illusion, be it subtle dirt, or dirt of doership and enjoyment. "Dirt" here means the impurities that are accumulated in the chitta. The stains from this dirt become visible on the chitta. Slowly a being forgets that this is dirt. He accepts the dirt as his nature, is inspired by it, and ends up doing grievous wrongs. When the tendencies of an aspirant rise in him and he becomes aware of dirt, he strives for purification. Initially his attempt is halfhearted, just as you filled the jug and replaced it without removing the stains. Slowly seriousness and caution start to come and purity starts to manifest.

"I am cautioning you, not demoralizing you. Your sadhan has just begun. If a temperament of negligence and carelessness is fostered now, then it will be difficult to remove it. Carelessness can be controlled only by carefulness. The continuity of sadhan can be established only by carefulness and only upon being careful will the inner stains become visible to you. Thus the earlier you become aware, the greater will be your welfare. As every second passes one's life span is slightly reduced. The entire life of a being passes away in carelessness. By virtue of being your Guru, I think it is my duty to caution you. The world is full of worldly people. Who cares for the other?"

There was a ten- to twelve-foot deep ditch in front of the ashram. Now it is inside the ashram and, after filling it, a school and a ceremonial hall have been built on top of it. As the ditch was between the town and the ashram, a small bridge had been built over it. It was hardly a bridge. A car chassis had been laid across after laying stones on both the sides, and a tin sheet had been hammered to it.

It rained heavily one night. The hill water drained into the ditch. The flow was very strong and the bridge collapsed. The soil on both the sides had fallen in. As we were leaving for the morning walk, we saw that the bridge had collapsed. Maharajshri laughed very loudly when he saw it. Upon seeing Maharajshri laugh so loudly, I wondered what was so humorous about this incident. The bridge was ruined and one should, I thought, have responded seriously. When I asked him, he said, "The bridge was supposed to fall and so it fell. It cannot rise by itself. You endure it either by laughing or crying. You still have to endure it, so why not do it with laughter?"

I said, "But Maharajshri, it definitely makes one feel bad. Now it will have to be rebuilt on either side. It will definitely involve expense."

Maharajshri said, "The expense is not going to go away if I cry. Whether I accept it with laughter or tears, expenditure must be made. Then why not do it with laughter." And Maharajshri again started laughing loudly.

After remaining silent for a while he said, "These are the times when one comes to know the state of the chitta and an aspirant is tested. When some work is slightly spoiled, the chitta is spoiled even more. Even if something minor happens against the wishes of the mind, it becomes agitated. Even if there is a small altercation with somebody, the mind gets upset. Nothing is achieved by losing the composure of the mind. There is only the loss of composure. That is the difference between a worldly person and an aspirant. An aspirant always remains alert while keeping a watch on his mind. Even if it shakes a little, he composes himself. This is called remaining balanced in loss and profit."

I asked a question. "Does this mean that if some work is spoiled, then one should let it remain so and become negligent towards it."

Maharajshri replied, "It definitely does not mean that we should be negligent. One must definitely try to improve work that encounters difficulties, but without affecting the chitta. That is the duty of a human. A duty must be performed, but the duty is limited to doing the karma. It is not necessary that the work definitely improve after the attempt, thus one should not worry about results at all. If a project is successful, one should also not feel proud about it. Pride is an influence on the mind. In this way, to the extent to which a person prevents his mind from being affected, he will be saved from the accumulation of impressions."

I said, "Is the effect on the chitta a form of attachment and aversion?"

He said, "Attachment and aversion are definitely there. Now

you developed an attachment for this bridge, thus you became worried at its loss. If we have an aversion for something, and if it happens or confronts us, then we become upset. Attachment and aversion arise not just for people, but also for styles of worship, ways of life, ways of thinking, honor and respect, and everything else. We wish that our opinion be accepted, or that a particular person's opinion not be accepted, and otherwise we become sad. If we are doing something, we do not feel like putting it aside. If we are doing nothing, then we feel like doing nothing. All these are attachments and aversions."

I responded to this. "This means that attachment and aversion are very deeply rooted in us. They make us dance in every field and at every moment, sometimes by giving rise to pleasure or pride, sometimes by tormenting the heart."

He said, "That is how it is. We do not even know when, where or how we are playing into the hands of attachment and aversion. In fact, we spend most of our day under the influence of attachment and aversion. That is the reason we feel happy or sorrowful, respected or insulted. Just as when termites infect a piece a wood they eat it from within, similarly attachment and aversion go on eating our insides. Until we are freed from them and reach a natural state, we are obligated to practice dutiful action."

Now I do not remember what I was writing in those days. There was ashram work throughout the day, but I would take time to write out of my periods of rest. Generally, even while working, I would be thinking about the subject on which I was writing. As described earlier, a jug of water and a glass used to be kept at the upper end of Maharajshri's bedstead. One day it so happened that I forgot to clean the jug and fill it with water. I forgot everything. Even in the afternoon at rest time, I remained busy with my writing and forgot about the water entirely. I used to go into Maharajshri's room immediately after he got up from his rest. On that day I was so occupied with my writing that I was late in that, too. When I entered Maharajshri's room, I saw that he was sitting on his cushion, peaceful and silent. On seeing me he said, "Today there was no water in the jug at all. I have been thirsty for a long time, but now that our bramhachariji has become a writer, he does not have time to spare from his writing. Anyway don't worry about me. My time will pass in some way or the other."

Upon hearing this, I was buried in shame. It seemed as if someone had gagged me. What could I say? There was no justification for my error. I said hesitatingly, "Maharajji, I did not remember. I forgot." I speedily went and offered a glass of water.

Now sitting outside the temple, clasping my head, I thought, "It was due to my writing habit that today's undesirable incident took place. If I had not been busy with my writing, I would not have forgotten. My Guruji was sitting thirsty today and I kept on writing. What benefit is there in such writing?"

I cursed my writing again and again as I got up. Meanwhile Maharajshri had come out into the courtyard and was seated on a chair. I bowed to him and humbly told him, "Maharajji, I committed a big mistake today. This happened due to my writing. Henceforth, I have given up writing. There will not be a mistake in the future. I beg your forgiveness."

Maharajshri laughed. "This mistake did not take place due to your writing. It happened due to your attachment to writing. Give up the attachment. There is no need to give up writing. A human considers some work important and other work secondary. The importance of filling the jug with water, of cleaning the cottage or of washing clothes is the same as that of doing sadhan. When it is your duty to do a particular task, at that time that work is important. This demonstrates that the work is not important, duty is. You believed that the work of writing was more important and became attached to it. You considered the task of filling water in the jug unimportant and forgot it. That's where you made a mistake. There is no problem with the work of writing.

"Putting the letter in the envelope, sticking on a postage stamp and dropping it in the mailbox are as important as writing the letter. If all these are not in order, then writing the letter itself is a waste. Negligence towards work, when that work is your duty, spoils the work. Discipline your mind in such a way that it remains focused while doing your dutiful actions and that upon completing them you are mentally free. Now if you think about the subject of writing even while working, that is wrong. In this way the mind goes out of control. Thoughts about work might come to you during writing. That is wrong, too. Concentrating on writing at the time of writing, and on work at the time of work, is the way to control the mind. Now pacify the anger that you are feeling towards writing. It does not matter how harmonious the subject is to which you have an attachment. It is still a cause of bondage."

I asked what could possibly be the relationship between performing one's duty with concentration, and spirituality. Maharajshri answered, "There is a relationship and it is intimate. If the mind cannot focus on karma, it means that the mind does not have the habit of concentration. A mind that can concentrate will concentrate on everything it undertakes. No one can attain one-pointedness in Dhyana [intensified concentration] with a restless mind. It is a question of ending restlessness."

39. The True Nature of Service

A Swamiji came to meet Maharajshri. During their conversation he expressed a pain in his heart. He said, "I served my Guruji greatly, but he ignored that service."

Maharajshri was suddenly taken aback. "Why be upset about that? It is your good fortune that you were saved from the muddle of the ashram. Guruji has done you a great favor by saving you from falling into the chasm of Maya. Another issue is that you never served him. In your mind there was a desire to become the head of the ashram, and for that you were putting on an act of rendering service. Service makes the mind happy, whereas you have become sad. Yet I repeat that Guruji has greatly obliged you, otherwise you would have spent your entire life arranging food and drinks for people. To cover the expenses of the ashram, tendencies of greed would have surfaced. Problems would always have come up. Even if they didn't, when you acquire an ashram through succession there are many difficulties associated with it. Now you may sing bhajans peacefully."

The summary of what Maharajshri explained to him is as follows:

(i) "While serving Guruji, if there is an intention in your mind of acquiring the ashram, then it is selfishness. There are no expectations in service. Service means that there should be no desire for any prize, respect, right, credit or anything else in the mind. Service is important only for its own sake. It is possible that Guruji may have given you shelter to prevent your level of service from diminishing. It is also possible that, although you did not inherit the ashram, you received the blessings of Guruji."

(ii) "It is also possible that you are a good sevak but not a good manager. Every good soldier cannot become a Major or a Colonel in the army. To manage an ashram, apart from being a good manager, it is also necessary to be a good orator, to be well-developed from a spiritual viewpoint, to have good interpersonal skills and tolerance. I do not know to what extent these qualities are present in you."

(iii) "One Guru can have many disciples. But he cannot give the ashram to all his disciples, and if somebody objects to this, then he is interfering in the field of the Guru's authority. A Guru has the same affection for each of his disciples. One must never conclude that the disciple to whom the Guru has given the ashram is his favorite."

(iv) "The ashram can be given to only one disciple, but the Guru maintains his grace on all the disciples and showers it equally. Grace is far more important than the ashram. An ashram is not helpful in crossing the ocean of the world, only grace is. An ashram can become a cause of bondage, whereas grace is the cause of liberation. Why are you making yourself dependent on the ashram?"

(v) "If, even so, it is in you to acquire an ashram, instead of wishing for the Guru's ashram it is more practical to build a new one. I recognize that when you inherit an ashram you also get its wealth and a family of disciples, but along with that some traditional problems are attached, which the new Maharaj has to fight. That is a very difficult task. Additionally, all the old disciples do not accept a new Maharaj in their minds.

"Swamiji, you have been saved. You should be congratulated, not comforted. The possibility of getting tied down is great while running an ashram. Now you are the master of your will. You can come and go anywhere, and do a lot of sadhan. If you take my advice, do not get involved in any ashram. Your welfare lies in that only."

I saw how systematically and minutely Maharajshri thought. The desire to become a Guru is common in disciples. This desire does not make them a Guru and prevents them from remaining a disciple. The desire to become a Guru is also a form of attachment that, while confusing a disciple, makes him dance and run, and pushes him into the deep chasm of tamo guna [inertia or inactivity]. When Maharajshri said, "If there is a desire for an ashram, why does one leave one's home?" the statement directly entered my heart. If you have sacrificed the world by forsaking your attachment towards your children only to get entangled in attachment towards disciples, then what sin have your children committed? There should be a feeling of welfare, not attachment, towards disciples.

40. The Meaning of Sanyas

Maharajshri never succumbed to greed, nor did he worry about the expenses of the ashram. He gave very few initiations, too, which was appropriate from a spiritual point of view. It is incorrect to make initiations a source of livelihood. The sense of welfare towards the disciple becomes secondary if initiations are approached as a source of income. Some people suggested that a couple of shops be built outside the ashram so that the ashram expenses could be met through the income from the shops. It seemed like a good suggestion. I was still ignorant, and thus when I heard it, I liked it, too. When the suggestion reached Maharajshri, he said, "That is not our job. An ascetic's work does not depend on business. It continues according to the wishes of God. If someone wants to trade, then what is the need of becoming an ascetic? The word 'sanyas' means a kind of death from the perspective of family and society. Always remember this before giving any suggestions.

"If you really want to make arrangements, then make arrangements for continuous sadhan, for the singing of devotional songs [bhajans], for spiritual company and singing the praises of the lord [kirtan], for mutual love and a feeling of equanimity. It is appropriate for a business organization or a family to make financial arrangements. As long as sadhan and bhajan continue in the ashram, it will not run into any problems. If there is no sadhan, it is appropriate for the ashram to close. If there is no sadhan, then the attempt to keep the ashram alive with financial oxygen is meaningless. The ashram is not mine, nor yours, it belongs to Shankar. The treasury of Shankar is unlimited. The ashram will run as long as Shankar desires. When he feels otherwise, it will close. Then it does not matter what kind of arrangements you have made for security. There is no organization, society, country or empire in the world that has not had a downfall. In spite of all this, if you still want to build those shops, then surely do so and run the ashram. But then I am not needed here. I can go and live elsewhere."

One gentleman asked a question. "You said sanyas means social death, but nevertheless a relationship with society is still maintained."

In reply to this Maharajshri said, "But this relationship is not social, it is spiritual. From the perspective of social interactions, a sanyasi is dead."

Every one was quiet after listening to Maharajshri. Who could wish for Maharajshri to go away? Thus the thought of building the shops was dismissed.

41. Nature as a Role Model

One day Maharajshri was strolling in the ashram. All around, sky-high eucalyptus trees were standing with their heads raised. Mango, gromia, lime, chickoo, custard apple, neem and peepal trees also graced the surroundings. Marigold, small chrysanthemum, rose, yellow jasmine, xenia and other flowers were blooming. The ashram was looking very attractive. Maharaj stopped and said, "These trees, plants and creepers have a lot to teach an aspirant. Erasing the feeling of friendship or enmity, they give the same uniform cool shade to everyone. For aspirants this quality is worth adapting. They give shade even to the person who cuts them. They offer all their parts for pruning, without grievance, without complaint.

"Such is their tolerance that they endure everything — heat, cold, rain and storms. They themselves stand in the sun and allow a traveler to rest in their shade. They give fruits to others to eat. They themselves do not eat them. They do not have any attachment to their earnings. Neither do they censure anyone, nor backbite. Silently they witness the activity of the world. They please the mind of a pedestrian by their fragrance. Their flowers bloom and make the face of the visitor bloom. People who come to them receive whatever they have hoped for, be it fruits, flowers, leaves, bark or wood. They may become dry in the heat, but will not ask anyone for water. They do not care for their own lives.

"Now, think. How many aspirants have these qualities? Nature has spread these qualities in all the four directions in order to educate us, but which aspirant accepts the education? Everyone is involved in attachment and aversion and selfishness. No one is willing to give up his conveniences for another. No one comes forward to offer peace to anyone else. Hence their own minds have no peace. Everyone's face reflects inner turmoil. Still they consider themselves aspirants. Truly speaking, such aspirants, even after doing sadhan, are far from sadhan."

I was listening to Maharajshri attentively and at the same time churning my heart — contemplating and feeling shame because I, too, was lacking these qualities of the trees. Who knows what Maharajshri was saying, absentmindedly, in his conversation with the trees?

The clouds were roaring in the sky and lightning was flashing and thundering. It seemed that it would fall upon our heads at any moment. I was alone with Maharajshri. Maharajshri said, "Notice how the lightning thunders. No one knows when it will strike or whom it will strike. The same is the case with time. No one knows when it will come or upon whom it will swoop down. Man has become so negligent towards time, yet he moves about with death hanging over his head. Lightning at least flashes and thunders first, but the sound of time cannot even be heard. It pounces like a hawk and takes one away. A living being is so helpless, yet he still has so much pride."

I said, "Maharajji, generally a human falls sick before his death. Isn't this a forewarning?"

Maharajshri said, "Yes, it is, but a living being treats it like an illness, not as a forewarning of death. He doesn't give up the hope of remaining alive until the last moment. This is called abhinivesh [love for life]."

I began to feel rather scared upon hearing about the frightful nature of death. I started feeling, "I don't know when the bed will get rolled." All my plans and aspirations froze in their place. My mind thought it would be better if Maharajshri did not talk about this subject. That is a shortcoming in a human: that he does not wish to listen to, nor understand, nor accept anything about going away from this world. I tried to change the subject by saying, "Maharajji, the thundering of clouds can be heard internally and the flash of lightning can be seen there, too. How are these things related to time?"

Maharajshri said, "They have nothing to do with time. This internal experience is either related to accumulated impressions, or to manifestations based on the tattvas [fundamental cosmic principles]. The experience based on the tattvas comes at a very late stage. Generally an aspirant remains entangled at the level of accumulated impressions and that, too, at an unwanted gross level. Just as the impressions of actions are accumulated, so are the impressions of spiritual practices performed with a sense of pride. These impressions manifest in kriyas and cause such experiences. The basis of the tattvas cannot be understood by you now. As your mind is filled with samskaras, it is incapable of understanding this subject. For now, simply understand that just as tattvas are continually made, one after another, in the same way and in the same order, one after the other, they are absorbed back into the tattvas. The kriya which is manifest when the tattva is made, that same kriya is manifest when it is being absorbed. However, this subject is not to be understood merely on an intellectual plane. To attain a state suitable for that, you will have to do a lot of sadhan."

I asked, "Do sound and light also have a relationship with one another?"

He said, "Yes, both take place due to friction. As of now you only understand gross friction, but the friction of sound and light is between infinitesimal, extremely infinitesimal tattvas. Thunder [sound] takes place due to the friction between clouds and the same friction produces lightning [light]. However, this is gross friction and is manifested in gross space only. Inner space is infinitesimal and the tattva, too, is extremely infinitesimal. To experience them, the valleys of impressions and desires have to be crossed."

I did not understand anything. The only thing I had understood, if indeed there was something, was that I had not understood anything. It seemed as if Maharajshri had read my mind. He said, "I have already told you that, as of now, you do not have any control of this extremely subtle subject. But yes, you definitely understand what I said about the visible gross world, the roaring of the clouds and the flash and thunder of lightning."

42. Shaktipat and Love

There was a lot of activity in the ashram. The Bengali Baba Shri Ramdas Omkarnath was to arrive in a short while. Baba had a large number of devotees and disciples in India and abroad. This great man of Bhakti Marg [the path of devotion] was very simple, straightforward and sensitive. After his arrival there was a conversation between the two great men. Baba was saying, "I know only one love: the love at the feet of God, love for all beings created by him, love for the world considering it to be the manifest form of God. How can attachment and aversion enter a heart that is full of love? Detachment starts rising inside on its own. The mind moves away from sense objects and the mind starts shining with freshness and divinity. Love removes the distinction between a friend and a foe. A devotee full of love is totally dependent on God. God is everything to him. To meet, not to meet, when to meet, how to meet, and in what form to meet, all these are issues for God to decide. A devotee remains covered in the love of God."

Maharajshri said, "You have said such a beautiful thing. The essence of spirituality is detachment towards the world and love for God. First someone moves away from the world, and then love for God is generated. First someone fills his heart with love, and as a result he develops detachment towards the world. Detachment and love complement each other. The more one increases, so will the other. On the reduction of one, the other will reduce. Thus a devotee must remain alert in protecting his detachment in order to maintain his love. Otherwise a lack of detachment can destroy the feeling of love. For this it is important to have a disciplined way of life. Devotion [bhakti], knowledge [jnana], yoga, dutiful action [karma], whatever be the sadhan, love of God is equally important for all of them. Otherwise everything becomes dry. The door of the heart can be opened only with love."

At this Baba asked a question. "You are a preceptor of Shaktipat. In the sadhan of Shaktipat where do you place love?"

Maharajshri said, "Root impressions [samskaras], ripened samskaras [prarabdha] and tendencies of past lives [vasana] are the most important obstacles in progressing on the path of love and detachment. Without removing them, neither can detachment arise in the mind, nor love in the heart. As they are purified, love and detachment will progress accordingly. Shaktipat is the art of attaining freedom from these. If a disciple surrenders to the kriyas of the Shakti with overwhelming love in his heart and with the sense of observation in his mind, love and detachment begin to increase. There is no major difference between surrender and love. There is surrender in love. In other words, you can say that love is incomplete without surrender. Surrender increases with an increase in love and love increases with an increase in surrender. The sadhan of Shaktipat begins with surrender, which, over a period of time, with regular sadhan turns into love. How an aspirant does his sadhan depends on his sentiments. If there is a feeling of attachment and aversion in his mind, that feeling will keep on increasing. If there is a feeling of love and detachment, then it will grow. Basically the goal of sadhan is to promote love and detachment."

Baba said, "The Shakti of some devotees is awakened while singing devotional songs [bhajans]. Then what is the need of Shaktipat?"

Maharajshri replied, "Shaktipat is not important; awakening of the Shakti is important. But in how many people has the Shakti been awakened while singing devotional songs? Only a few. Isn't that true? On the other hand, the Shakti has been awakened in most of my disciples who are initiated in Shaktipat. This is a simple solution by which there is direct experience of the actions of the inner Shakti. The progress of an aspirant is dependent on his sadhan and his feelings, but at least his inner door is opened. That makes it very easy for him."

43. My Bramhacharya Initiation

In the final months of 1960 I suffered from sciatica. It was quite a severe attack. At that time I lived in Maharajshri's cottage in the room opposite to his. I went to Indore for a week for treatment and then to Ahmedabad. On the 20th of January, 1961, I returned to Dewas. On that day the bramhacharya initiation [initiation into celibacy] of a certain gentleman was scheduled. The moment Maharajshri saw me, he said, "Good! He too has arrived."

Along with the other gentleman, Maharajshri initiated me into bramhacharya. After the initiation, he explained the *Maha Vakya* [the Great Pronouncement], "Prajnana Bramha." He said, "This is a sentence from the Rig Veda that states that prajnana [consciousness] is Bramha. But we interpret it from our point of view, which is in accordance with the philosophy of our sadhan. Prajnana is that state of Shakti that gives consciousness to the sense organs. This dynamism, be it extroverted or introverted, is nothing but the power of Bramha, in fact it is Bramha. Generally a living being cannot recognize its divinity and therefore thinks that it is the power of the sense organs. It has two levels, extroverted and introverted. In the extroverted state, it makes one perform worldly activities and acquire knowledge. In spite of being knowledge, it is not knowledge; that is, it is prajnana. Even false knowledge cannot be acquired without the activity of the Shakti. In the introverted state, upon purifying the accumulated impressions and desires, it moves towards the Self. In the terminology of yoga this is called chetana [consciousness] and in the terminology of jnana [the path of knowledge] it is called prajnana.

"Chitta-Shakti, Chaitanya Shakti, Chit Shakti and chetana [prajnana], all these are levels of Chiti Shakti, hence they are Bramha. The first and foremost thing in sadhan is to make prajnana introverted [turned inwards]. Then we experience prajnana through the medium of kriyas. The right understanding of prajnana cannot be obtained by only understanding its literal meaning. It is a subject of experience and not just the intellect, and that is why over a period of time the state of *So Hum* ['What thou art, I am that.'] arises. Without the experience of prajnana and lacking a pure mind, people start chanting 'So Hum.' Before prajnana is directly experienced face-to-face, how can it be said, 'What thou art, I am that"? Lacking experience, mere intellectual exercise is useless. The experience of the awakening of prajnana and its direct knowledge, or the sense of separation from the gross physical body, is the basis of sadhan. Just as a building cannot be constructed without the foundation, in the same way sadhan is not possible without the experience of prajnana. Today scholars have made prajnana a subject of logic, debate and sermons. However, it is a subject of experience. Only after the experience of 'Prajnana Bramha' are the other Maha Vakyas [great pronouncements] experienced."

Question: "Until now you have been saying that the awakening of Kundalini Shakti is the basis of sadhan and its seat is the Mooladhar, whereas today you are saying it is prajnana and its seat is the sense organs."

Answer: "You have asked a very good question. Every religious treatise is supported by a particular vocabulary, style and experience. Often various texts seem to contradict each other. Careful and unbiased observation reveals that all of them say the same thing. The difference is due to country, time, conditions, the author's personal experiences and the presentation method of the subject. Vedanta is a highly advanced philosophy of knowledge [jnana] in which all subjects have been reviewed from the angle of knowledge. Thus chetana has also been called 'prajnana.' Elaboration of the lower levels of sadhan is almost negligible in Vedanta. Generally more stress has been laid on throwing light on Bramha. On the contrary, yoga does the difficult task of lifting up the normal being from lower levels and provides him with an introduction to sadhan. The subject of yoga is not describing the higher states of knowledge, but rather untying or resolving the knot of sadhan.

"The same is the case with devotional texts. Their sadhan is only love for God. They do not break their heads on the very advanced elements of knowledge. In this way, the various texts of knowledge, devotion and yoga each have a vocabulary and a way of sadhan of their own. They have their own levels. It is natural for the sadhan and beliefs of an aspirant of a lower level to be different from those of an aspirant of a higher level. When the lower aspirant attains the higher level, there is a change in the nature of his sadhan and beliefs. The difficulty arises when an aspirant leaps ahead and directly associates with a false understanding of the tenets of Vedanta philosophy. Even though the knowledge imparted by Vedanta is true, he flies and roams in imaginations.

"With this background, we may now approach the main subject. As Vedanta does not address the lower levels of sadhan, it calls the lowest level of chetana 'prajnana,' and positions it there. It is also called Bramha, and the sense organs are considered its basis. The field of sadhan in yoga is from a low level to a specific level. Thus it dissects the various states of the chetana, its various levels, and its activities at various levels. By showing the difference between the dormant and awakened states, it tells us in which direction they are active. It regards the inert Kundalini as awakened towards the world, flowing outwards. The basis of the flow is the sense organs. Yoga might call mooladhar the base of the

Kundalini, but common people recognize the inert Kundalini as the power of the senses organs. In essence, this means that the inert Kundalini of yoga is the prajnana of Vedanta. The inert Kundalini can be experienced through the medium of the sense organs. An awakened Kundalini starts giving up its dependence on the sense organs and, by opening the inner door, starts advancing towards the Self. Such terminology is not used in the context of prajnana, but it can be called 'inert prajnana, and 'awakened prajnana.' The indication of awakened prajnana was given by saying 'Prajnana Bramha.' ['Prajnana is Bramha.'] The reason we can accept this meaning is that all the succeeding Maha Vakyas require the awakening of prajnana.

"If we examine this matter from another point of view, then, in spite of the Kundalini being stable in the mooladhar, the sense organs are the basis of its activity in the inert state. Vedanta does not say anything about the basis of the awakened prajnana. It merely gives an indication about its awakened state and leaves it there because its main topic of research is Bramha. However disagreements arise when yogis lose sight of the goal of Vedanta and the followers of Vedanta neglect yoga in the form of sadhan. By not accepting both schools of thought as sequential links in spiritual progress, they start comparing them."

Question: "The essence is, that prajnana, be it awakened or inert, is the Bramha in every state?"

Answer: "Awakened and inert are only technical terms. Whatever the level of chaitanya, its vibrations and activity never cease. Even in the inert state, it remains active in the world. It is called inert because it is asleep with respect to the soul from which it was born. Indicating this, Lord Krishna has said in the Gita,

> *Yaa nishaa sarvabhutanaam tasyaam jaagarti sayami*
> *yasyaam jagrati bhutani saa nisha pashyato muneh.*

> When it is night for all other beings the disciplined
>   soul is awake.
> When all other beings are awake it is night for the
>   seeing ascetic.
> (II, 69)

When the night is spread all over the world, almost all beings are established in the inert state of prajnana. Neither do they have knowledge of themselves, nor do they have true knowledge of the world. At that time the yogis are awake. In other words, they are established in the awakened state of prajnana. Just as a being has direct knowledge of the world, similarly a yogi has direct knowledge about the awakened prajnana. In that destructible, momentary world where all beings are awake, which indicates their prajnana is active, the sages who know the cosmic principles are asleep. In other words, they are disinterested in it. Their prajnana moves away from this world and flows inward.

Epilogue

Today's era is a very frightening one. It is very difficult for aspirants. The more serious and disciplined an aspirant, the more difficulties he must face. In these days those whom you respect are determined to insult you. Those whom you love will reply with hatred. Those whom you help will betray you at the time of your need. Selfishness is so prevalent that there is no hesitation in slitting a person's throat for personal gain. Those who do not do these things still must endure it. The world has never improved, nor will it improve in the future. Even great aspirants, unable to face the flow of the times, lose patience and grow upset.

A person may go along with the times. If he doesn't do so he may become sad and disturb the chitta, or he may endure with joy and keep the chitta unaffected. Serious aspirants believe that it is beneficial to accept the third option. This secret of sadhan was understood due to the grace of Shri Guru Maharaj. I had heard and read about these things for such a long time, but until now I had never paid full attention to them. But this is the only reality. If an aspirant becomes negligent towards this, he does not remain an aspirant. By focusing on it he receives the fruit of his spiritual practice.

An aspirant has one definite path. Love and respect everyone. Remove the feeling of friendship or enmity, and love everyone equally. Forgive if someone makes a mistake. Do not allow the mind to be affected even while enduring sorrows and difficulties. Do good even to those who do evil. Keep working to improve yourself and leave aside concerns about whether the world is good or bad and be ready to sacrifice anything to attain this goal. The essence of Maharajshri's teachings is as follows:

(i) Sadhan is not merely sitting cross-legged with eyes tightly closed. It is the unceasing process of trying to break the mind away from the world and unite it with consciousness. For this sadhan is necessary. So is keeping a constant watch on the movements of the mind. Stopping the accumulation of impressions is much more difficult than eroding them.

(ii) Many people take initiation but are unable to do proper and well-balanced sadhan. The Guru showers grace but it is the job of the disciple to take advantage of it. One does not become a siddha [one who is liberated] by mere initiation. There is so much dirt inside a being that there is a need for sadhan over a prolonged period of time, for faith in the Guru, for a sense of service while performing an action, and for surrender to the awakened Shakti. All this is not possible without patience and enthusiasm.

(iii) Whether it is time for sadhan or for social interaction, a mental state of surrender and love, devoid of attachment and aversion, should be continuously maintained. For this there is a need to maintain a constant vigil on the mind. If this process is disturbed even for a moment, the mind will create some mischief or the other. The mind, always unstable and restless, is unwilling to stop at any object or place. While doing sadhan or singing devotional songs it is even more active.

(iv) Even before surrender, faith in God and the Guru is essential. If there is no faith, what kind of surrender can there be, and to whom? Surrender and tolerance have a very close relationship. Surrender and love are also dependent upon each other. Only a loving aspirant can surrender and only an aspirant full of surrender can love. Whatever be one's sadhan, love is necessary for all of them.

(v) Love is a principle that can grant continuity to sadhan. Love should be such that one's full heart is for God alone. No division of any sort should be there. Some love for wealth and luxury, some for home, family and others, and some love for God — that is divided love. A divided person can never be a devotee.

(vi) The greater the attachment and aversion within someone, the stronger is the feeling that the world is real. In addition, his mind is more affected by the events of the world. Attachment and aversion is a very acute state of the chitta. The greater the acuity, the greater the sorrow will be in the mind and to that extent life will be more worldly. Attachment and aversion are large obstacles in the path of sadhan. The tendencies of attachment and aversion are suppressed by maintaining a feeling of equanimity.

(vii) The total destruction of attachment and aversion and other defects is possible only when the Shakti, with its play and kriyas, completely erodes the impressions and tendencies and purifies the mind. Then natural equanimity will arise in the chitta. It is the duty of an aspirant to give Shakti an opportunity to perform independent and effortless kriyas. When aspirants become proud and allow their wishes to affect their kriyas, the independent and effortless state of their kriyas is destroyed. Their accumulated impressions are no more the basis for them, their desires are. Kriyas on the basis of accumulated impressions are the cause of the destruction of the impressions, whereas kriyas on the basis of desires are the cause of their accumulation.

(viii) An aspirant performs his sadhan without caring for his life. He is not worried about anything other than sadhan. Whether the world makes fun of him or whether he succeeds or fails in the world, whether the world considers him foolish and cheats him — unaffected by all these questions he remains immersed in sadhan. All great men have had to endure many difficulties. All of them were cheated by friends and strangers. All of them had to pass through the storm of success and failure and all of them had to face deprivation. Spiritual progress is not obtained by mere talk.

(ix) The entire world is filled with consciousness. Inside, outside, above, below, there is only consciousness. What people regard as inert is also a state of consciousness. However this is not something to be understood only mentally. It must be known through experience. By the grace of the Guru, this experience first takes place within us in the form of kriyas of Shakti. As the experience becomes pure, it spreads outward from within. In the world, which seemed inert, now one sees consciousness everywhere.

(x) There is a need for an aspirant to keep churning his heart. Introspection is a tool that brings an aspirant face-to-face with his real inner state. The moment his attention moves away from introspection, different types of confusion raise their head and every temptation to stray from the path comes in front of him. Churning of the heart places the defects and bad qualities of an aspirant before him, makes him aware of his existing state, and provides him with an opportunity to evaluate and improve.

(xi) Continuous efforts to purify social conduct are of great importance on the path of sadhan, because it is social conduct that drives an aspirant towards spirituality. It also pushes him toward the world. The cause of our current pitiable state is our social conduct. The development of detachment in an aspirant is very much dependent on the way he conducts himself. Conduct filled with attachment is the cause of bondage, whereas conduct filled with a sense of service is the cause of love for God.

(xii) Tolerance is another important part of sadhan. It plays a very large role in the purification of conduct, the destruction of prarabdha and the rise of detachment. Some scholars consider tolerance to be a complete sadhan. Tolerance is the means of removing the feelings of attachment and detachment, favorable and unfavorable, and success and failure. Most of the problems of the world are due to the lack of tolerance. Tolerance gives rise to satisfaction in the mind. There can be no progress in sadhan without tolerance.

(xiii) The Shakti that is awakened within an aspirant due to the grace of the Guru should not be considered a common phenomenon. Such awakening is the most important event of one's life and opens up the path of divine experiences, real spirituality and attainment of the Self. However, one must not become complacent after the awakening, thinking that now it is not necessary to do anything. The real test of an aspirant begins only after the awakening. Do not think that sadhan will continue without any obstacles. On the one hand, while the path of success is opened, on the other, a mountain of obstacles, difficulties and problems arise before you.

(xiv) The Guru-tattva [the fundamental cosmic principle in the Guru] has two forms — the external Guru and the inner Guru. The inner Guru is active in the external, physical Guru and lights up the path of progress in the disciple by means of different experiences. The fact is that, in reality, the inner Guru, or the awakened divine Shakti, is the Guru. It acts and manifests through the medium of the bodies of both the Guru and the disciple. An aspirant needs to recognize the Guru-tattva in the body of the Guru and associate with that. But to do so he first must see the Guru-tattva within himself. Only then is he able to recognize the Guru-tattva in the body of the Guru. The union of the Guru and disciple is the union of the Guru-tattva present in both bodies. At that point the Guru-disciple relationship disappears.

(xv) Guru-tattva is an all-pervading power. The beneficial aspect of this power is called "Guru." This power also punishes a person on many occasions for his own benefit. Through the medium of the Guru's body, it showers grace on him by imparting knowledge to him. To establish detachment in the being, this power insults, embarrasses, frightens and arranges for various kinds of sorrows, so that the real nature of the world is manifest.

(xvi) Sadhan is a systematic process that is daily, unceasing, and continuously flowing like a stream of oil in which there is no interruption, not even for a fraction of a moment. If there is an interruption, then the process of sadhan comes to a halt and is no longer sadhan. The division of time between sadhan and activities that are not sadhan-related, is only to explain the subject. In reality, all the time that an aspirant has, belongs to sadhan. Time apart from sadhan is occupied with social conduct. However an aspirant converts this conduct into sadhan, too.

(xvii) Call it a knot in the mind or a fallacy — that is Maya. There is an illusion that the gross [jada] and animate [chetan] are tied together. This is not the case, yet it seems to be so. Stricken with this fallacy, the being has been nurturing pride, accumulating impressions, feeling happy and sad, and has been taking one birth after the other for eons. This fallacy is the basis for the existence of the world. When it ends, the existence of the world comes to an end.

(xviii) A being sees the world according to his state of mind and thus the same world looks different to every being. A sinful mind finds the world full of sins, while a devotee sees God everywhere in the world. Inner feelings, desires, tendencies, qualities, perspectives, impressions — all of them combined together determine the state of mind. If a being moves away from these feelings, impressions, and so forth, then the drama of the world will come to an end.

(xix) Unless one is blessed by God, sadhan is a process that goes on for a long time and in which an aspirant is tested at every step. Therefore an aspirant must maintain the continuity of sadhan with caution and patience. His inner defects incite him again and again and continually rock and corrupt his mind. On the one hand, an aspirant must wage war against his inner defects and, on the other, he must continue to try for spiritual advancement. Only an aspirant can understand this inner struggle. Worldly people laugh at it out of their ignorance. An aspirant has to endure that, too.

(xx) Until lust, anger and greed are destroyed along with their seeds, the incessant cycle of birth and death is not over. All this is the effect of attachment and aversion. They are suppressed for some time through sadhan, but again they raise their heads. Even jnanis, ascetics and yogis bow down before them when they attack. The battle between an aspirant and these defects is called sadhan.

(xxi) Generally aspirants are unable to do the expected amount and type of sadhan that is necessary. The surrender, sentiment of the mind, purity of conduct and continuity in sadhan that is needed is hardly seen in aspirants. There is no control on speech, they cannot stop the waste of time, they have interests in unnecessary acts and they lose their composure in anger. As a result they cannot maintain the sentiment and the surrender that is necessary for sadhan.

(xxii) Seriousness is absolutely necessary for progress in sadhan. It is not necessary to reply to every comment. An aspirant must listen to many things and digest them. His stomach should be huge like that of Lord Ganesha. The world is involved in unnecessary things and actions and would like to drag the aspirant with it. It is dependent upon the state of the chitta of an aspirant whether he is carried away with the worldly flow or, while remaining an aspirant, he engages himself in sadhan. After all, if one has to live in this world one has to move with the world to some extent. But the movement is superficial. An aspirant should not let his mind be influenced. Generally aspirants find a solution to this problem in solitude. This is fine to a certain extent, but it is not possible for everyone.

(xxiii) Never let your mind remain without work. Do sadhan, japa, read, sing devotional songs or do physical work. Otherwise the mind will create mischief. It is said that an empty mind is a devil's workshop. If possible, do japa while doing any physical work. Otherwise, as the hands work the mind will fly.

(xxiv) Fear, anger, lust, shyness, surprise and other feelings are also manifested in kriyas because their impressions are collected in the chitta, and when the Shakti brings them to the surface it affects the chitta accordingly. An aspirant must endure these negative influences with utmost caution. Remember that even when it is Shakti that brings them to the surface, these are the influences of the impressions. It is the duty of an aspirant to endure them, and thereby neutralize their intensity. This inner tolerance at the time of sadhan is extremely important because it is through tolerance that impressions become active and erode. If an aspirant is carried away in their flow, then the impressions become stronger.

(xxv) While sitting in sadhan, an aspirant must not sit with any worldly desire in his mind. As the Shakti is knowledgeable, she is very well aware of all your needs and wishes. Shakti will give you only that which is beneficial. An aspirant lacks knowledge and thus is incapable of deciding what is good or bad for him. Perhaps one of the aspirant's desires is very strong, but its fulfillment may not be beneficial for him. Also destiny plays a big role in the fulfillment of desires. A being makes lofty wishes, however he only gets what is in his destiny. The path of spirituality is a path of sacrifices, not wishes. One should be satisfied with what one gets. Whatever kriyas one has, one should recognize them as the grace of the Guru. One should not get attached to harmonious [sattvic] kriyas and one should not hate inertial [tamasic] or disturbing [rajasic] kriyas. All kriyas are beneficial. A kriya happens and goes away. It is not one's duty to wish for any specific type of kriya. That is why an aspirant is advised to maintain a sense of surrender. By making a mental wish, the kriya of the wish takes place, not the kriya of the Shakti.

(xxvi) There is no benefit in starting your sadhan with an unenthusiastic mind. It raises the possibility of sadhan being disturbed. Only on entering the spiritual battle like a brave warrior, with enthusiasm and great patience, can one wish for success. This internal battle is no ordinary battle. In fact it is a difficult battle march that can be won only on the strength of unshakable faith in God, surrender, incessant sadhan, patience and service.

(xxvii) Do not underestimate the strength of your inner foes. Well-versed in the demonic arts, these enemies have always been successful in cheating you, through many births. They have deceptive weapons such as temptation, fear, attraction, confusion, and so forth. If need arises, they also use discretion as a weapon. They say one thing and do another. They are skillful in disguising themselves as duty. You are faced with deceptive enemies who shoot arrows while remaining invisible. Thus there is a need for the aspirant to remain very alert. He has the great weapon of the Guru's grace with him, but there is a fear of getting lost in kriyas. Even if one has a powerful weapon it is necessary to use it appropriately at the proper time. Enemies can be confronted by arming oneself with weapons like surrender, tolerance, generosity, a lack of anger, compassion, and so forth. In the Gita, *"asangha shastra,*" that is, remaining aloof from the world in spite of living in it, is a great weapon of the aspirant. See the kriyas happening within as separate from oneself and stay detached from them, that is, do not be affected by them. The active Shakti will destroy the inner enemies by giving them an opportunity to use their weapons.

(xxviii) Also, do not underestimate the kriyas of Shakti. Shakti is activated on the basis of the samskaras, but always remains unaffected by them. In the form of kriyas, an aspirant has a weapon that cannot be destroyed, neither does its sharpness ever get blunted, nor does it ever rust. The weapon of kriya will definitely complete its task. The only questions are: To what extent does an aspirant use it? How much does he use it? To what extent does he seek its protection? And to what use does he put it during times other than sadhan? If an aspirant uses the weapon of kriya properly, then he progresses at an intense speed. Just as the leaves fall during autumn, in the same manner samskaras, too, are eroded one after the other.

(xxix) Do not be afraid of difficulties, obstacles and problems. Failure comes in order to give you new energy and strength. There is a possibility that pride may arise in an aspirant as he continues to do sadhan, and so these obstacles are presented to shake the aspirant violently and awaken him. The occurrence of obstacles is natural and also necessary, because sadhan is improved only through obstacles, difficulties and failures. The one who is frightened by them and turns away from sadhan finds himself in the middle of nowhere. The one who confronts them and gets up again when he falls, his inner-self is imbued with the fragrance of sadhan.

Another point is that facing obstacles and difficulties is a process of inner purification only. It is the samskaras of the aspirant that manifest as obstacles. An aspirant should be happy that negative samskaras are being absorbed in the form of obstacles. A serious aspirant welcomes sorrows, hardships, failures and difficulties so that his chitta can be purified as early as possible. For those who have as their only goals the purification of the mind and the experience of the conscious-self, all other things are inconsequential. Sorrows come and go. But the inner journey of an aspirant continues uninterrupted. Climbing difficult slopes, facing storms, without worrying about heat and cold, he keeps forging ahead.

(xxx) When the Shakti rises upwards it often feels as if one is going to die at any moment. There is still attachment to the body in the mind of the aspirant. He is afraid of dying and wishes to live, yet he begins to see that death is close to him. At such a time he opens his eyes out of fear and gets up from his sadhan. An aspirant must definitely understand that the kriyas of the Shakti are for his welfare and not for his misfortune. So far no on has seen or heard of a person dying during kriyas. On the other hand, many aspirants get the feeling that they are losing their lives.

(xxxi) The path of spirituality is the way to end our ego, a way to die while being alive. Therefore the defenders of ego, that is, lust, anger, greed, and so forth are ended first. The more these defects exist in a person, the stronger is his ego. Do not think that if your ego is dead, then your life will become meaningless. What a common man believes to be life, that is not life. Death is always running behind such a life and one day it takes it away from this world. Real life will begin when you have no fear of death. That life will be obtained only when the ego has been vanquished.

Whatever divine words spoken by Shri Guru Maharaj in 1960 I can remember I have written down. Maharajshri was an ocean of knowledge. The Ganges of knowledge would keep on flowing through his divine lips in every statement, but my cup was very small, and thus I could grasp only a little. From that, too, much has been forgotten over a period of time. It is also difficult to remember when he said a particular thing. In spite of this, I have attempted to compile only the events of 1960. As I have already stated in the introduction, it is extremely difficult to remember every word used by Maharajshri after an interval of forty years. However the sentiments described in this book are those of Maharajshri's, and an attempt has been made to express them in the most appropriate words. If any impurity is noticed in that, then it is the fault of my limited intelligence, for which I pray forgiveness.

❁   ❁   ❁

Glossary of Terms

Aarti — A short prayer or eulogy sung in reverence of a deity or a Guru; a short religious ceremony in which a prayer is sung and lighted lamps are used to worship a God or a saint.

Adi Shankaracharya — Adi ("first") Shankaracharya (686 A.D. - 718 A.D.) coordinated the vedic spiritual tradition in India at a time of turmoil and dispersion. He gave enormous inspiration, insight and understanding of the underlying truth of life and living, relevant to this day. He is considered the greatest spiritual saint India has ever produced

Advaita — The theory of nonduality. The exponents of this theory believe that God is present in each person.

Amba — Also known as Parvati. The wife (consort) of Lord Shiva, she exists in various divine (both friendly and fearful) forms. Two of her fierce but very powerful forms are Durga (goddess beyond reach) and Kali (goddess of destruction).

Anvopaaya — That expedient which is concerned with "anu," a limited being, signifying his mental effort to end ignorance of his true nature.

Asamprajnat samadhi — Seedless meditation.

Ashram — Monastery.

Asmita — The identification of a subject with his limiting adjuncts.

Bhagwati — A goddess who is the form of divine energy — Shakti — created by the confluence of all the powers of all other gods and goddesses. An epithet of Parvati, the consort of Lord Shiva.

Bhairav — A manifestation of Lord Shiva.

Bhajan — Devotional hymns which describe the glory of the Lord.

Bhakta — A devotee.

Bhakti marg — Path of Devotion.

Bramha — The one, self-existent, impersonal spirit; the one universal soul; the divine essence and source from which all created things emanate, with which they are identified, and to which they return; the self-existent; the Absolute; the Eternal. Not generally an object of worship, but rather of meditation and knowledge.

Also: the one, impersonal, universal Spirit manifested as a personal Creator and as the first of the triad of personal gods in the Hindu religion.

Bramhachari — A spiritual aspirant who has taken a vow of celibacy and devoted his life to the practice of spiritual discipline.

Bramhacharya — The practice of celibacy.

Chaitanya — The conscious-self.

Chamunda — A Hindu goddess, a form of Durga. The name Chamunda is apparently derived from the names of the two demons, Chanda and Munda, whom she is said to have killed.

Chetan — Animate; conscious.

Chetana — Consciousness.

Chitta — Mind-stuff.

Dakshina — Offerings made at the time of obtaining knowledge, usually presented at the feet of the Guru.

Devatma Shakti — Divine power.

Devi Anusuya — Anusuya is quoted as the model of chastity. She was the wife of Atri Maharishi, a great sage and one of the seven foremost seers and sages.

Dewas — A city in central India. Swami Vishnu Tirth Maharaj established his ashram here in Narayan Kuti.

Dhyana — Meditation.

Dhyana Yogi — One who practices the science of meditation.

Diksha — A ceremony of initiation. It is, in fact, a procedure of bestowing the divine powers of a Guru upon the disciple, by which he progresses continuously on the path of divinity.

Garwhal — An Indian region in the middle of the Himalayas.

Gayatri Mantra — Gayatri is a Mantra (Vedic Hymn) that inspires righteous wisdom. It is a prayer that the almighty God may illuminate our intellect, which may lead us on a righteous path.

Gaziabad — A town in the state of Uttar Pradesh in Northern India. It is close to New Delhi.

Gita — The Bhagavad Gita, also called Shreemad Bhagwat Gita. This is one of the holy texts of the Hindus, which contains the divine discourse given to Arjun by Lord Krishna at the battle of Kurukshetra.

Jnana — Knowledge.

Jnana Yoga — The science of knowledge for attaining self-realization.

Jnana Yogi — One who practices Jnana Yoga.

Jnaneshvar — Jnaneshvar was a great siddha, mystic and poetic genius of Maharashtra, India who gave up his mortal form at the age of 21. His spiritual roots were in both the nath and bhakti traditions, and his lineage is listed as: Shiva, Shakti, Matsyendra, Gorakhnath, Gahini and Nivritti. At the age of fifteen (1290 C.E.) he is said to have delivered *ex tempore* the nine-thousand verses of his poetic commentary on the Bhagavad Gita; *Jnaneshvari*.

Gopal Krishna Gokhale — (1866-1915) Indian nationalist leader.

Guru — A spiritual teacher or mentor. According to ancient Indian Philosophy, one cannot attain success in the spiritual field without the help of a Guru or Sadguru (true Guru).

Gurudev — A reverential form of the word Guru.

Guru Purnima — The day of full moon, Purnima, in the month of Ashadh (June/July) is traditionally celebrated as Guru Purnima by Hindus. Also known as Vyas Purnima, the day is celebrated in remembrance and veneration of the sage, Ved Vyas.

Guru-Shakti — Power of the Guru; Power of God.

Guru-tattva — The elemental power of the Guru.

Hanuman — The ever-living (Chiranjeevi) son of Lord Vayu (the wind god) and a devotee of Lord Rama. He is a symbol of devotion and love.

Haridwar — A city situated on the banks of the holy Ganges river in the northern plains of India. Associated with both Lord Shiva and Lord Vishnu, Haridwar is one of the seven sacred cities of India.

Harishchandra — An emperor of India who was renowned for his charitable nature, devotion and virtue. He symbolizes truth.

Himachal Pradesh — A state in Northern India at the foothills of the Himalayas. It is referred to as the land of eternal snow peaks.

Indore — A city near Dewas, in Madhya Pradesh in Central India.

Japa — Chanting a Mantra.

Kabir — Kabir was a great musician saint of fifteenth century India, a weaver by profession. The hallmark of Kabir's poetry is that he conveys in his two line poems (doha) what others could not do in many pages.

Kali Yuga — The Dark Age. In this era there is an abundance of strife, ignorance, vice and irreligion, true virtue being practically nonexistent.

Karma — Action in progress.

Karma Yoga — The science of dutiful action.

Karma Yogi — One who practices karma yoga.

Kashi — Also known as Varanasi, Kashi or Banares; one of the oldest living cities in the world and the ultimate pilgrimage for Hindus, who believe that to die in the city is to attain instant salvation. It is located on the left bank of the Ganges River.

Kirtan — Singing of devotional hymns.

Kriyas — Automatic movements that are observed by an individual after his Kundalini has been awakened.

Kriya-Sadhana — Spiritual practices involving kriyas.

Lahore — Present-day city in Pakistan, it was a part of India before the partition.

Lala Lajpatrai — (1865-1928) A great national leader who fought against the British for Indian independence; came to be called "The Lion of Punjab."

Lokmanya Bal Gangadhar Tilak — (1856-1920) He was described by the British as "The Father of Indian Unrest."

Lord Rama — An incarnation of Lord Vishnu; one of the most commonly adored gods of Hindus, known as an ideal man and hero of the epic poem Ramayana.

Madhya Pradesh — A state in the central part of India.

Mahakaleshwar — Lord Shiva.

Mahamandaleshwar — Lord Shiva.

Maharajshri — Term of highest respect. In this work it refers to Swami Vishnu Tirth Maharaj.

Maharshi Atri — The great sage, Atri, was one of the sons of Bramha who helped him with the creation of this world. His wife, Devi Anususya, is also revered as a model devotee.

Mahatma — A Great Soul.

Mantra — Sacred words or sounds invested with power.

Marathi — A language spoken in the state of Maharastra in Western India.

Maya — Illusion.

Meerabai — (1504-1550) Meerabai was a princess from Rajasthan, India who is known for her steadfast devotion to Lord Krishna.

Moksha — Liberation.

Mooladhar — First chakra, which corresponds with the pelvic plexus of the sympathetic nervous system.

Namdev — (1270-1350) A famous saint of Maharashtra. He is regarded as one the pioneers of the Bhakti movement in India, along with Jnaneshwar and Tukaram

Nangal — A town in Punjab state, a Northwestern Province of India.

Narada Bhakti Sutras — An exposition of the path of Bhakti Marg by the great Saint Narada.

Narayan Kuti — Narayan Kuti was the place at the foothills of the mountain in Dewas where Swami Vishnu Tirth Maharaj settled.

Narsi Mehta — (1414-1481) A great poet-saint from Gujarat, India. He was a devotee of Lord Krishna.

Nivritti — Inward path by abstention from all acts. The path of sanyas is known as "Nivritti Marg."

Prajnana — Supreme Knowledge.

Pranayaam — Exercises involving breath control whose primary aim is the awakening of the Kundalini.

Prarabdha — Destiny.

Prasad — During any form of worship, ritual or ceremony, Hindus offer some items of food to the Lord. After the ceremony, this sacred food is distributed to worshipers as the offering of the Lord.

Pravritti — Active participation in life and due discharge of one's duties and obligations to society.

Punjab — A State in Northwestern India.

Puranas — The Puranas are a class of literary texts, all written in Sanskrit verse, whose composition dates from the 4th century B.C.E. to about 1000 C.E.

Puri — A holy place in the state of Orissa in India. Swami Gangadhar Tirth Maharaj lived there.

Rajas (Rajo Guna) — Guna (quality) of activity.

Ramayana — One of the Great Indian epics. The story of Lord Rama.

Rig Veda — The Rig-Veda is a collection of over 1,000 hymns, which contain the mythology of the Hindu gods, and is considered to be one of the foundations of the Hindu religion. The Rig is the oldest of the Vedas.

Rishi — Sage. Literally, it means "the seer."

Rishikesh — A spiritual center on the banks of the Ganges in Uttar Pradesh in Northern India. Rishikesh is one of the most popular pilgrimage centers and there are many ashrams there.

Rudraksha — "Asian wonder beads." These beads are supposed to have a lot of miraculous healing powers.

Sadhak — Spiritual aspirant.

Sadhan — Automatic spiritual practices, as in the case of Shaktipat.

Sadhan Dairy — A diary written by Swami Vishnu Tirth Maharaj describing his experiences in Sadhan after his initiation in Rishikesh from Swami Yoganand Maharaj.

Sadhana — Spiritual practices involving effort.

Samadhi — Super-consciousness; when individual consciousness merges with the universal consciousness.

Samprajnat samadhi — Samadhi with intellectual consciousness; Samadhi with seed.

Samskaras — Accumulated impressions.

Sanchit samskaras — Accumulated impressions from past lives.

Sanyas Diksha — Initiation into the monastic order.

Satsang — The company of good men.

Sattva Guna — Harmonious quality.

Sattvic — Harmonious.

Seva-Dharma — The Dharma of serving or the rules for servants.

Sevak — A servant dedicated to serving his master.

Shakti — Spiritual energy; spiritual power.

Shaktipat — Descent of Spiritual energy. Literally defined as "the fall" of spiritual energy.

Shaktopaaya — A yogic practice of thought only. In this the seeker has to develop concentration upon God-consciousness by means of a special initiating thought unfolded by the master. He does not have to practice pranayaam or any other practice on his own.

Shandilya Bhakti Sutras — A treatise written by Rishi Shandilya with the objective of understanding the Bhagwat Gita and other Shrutis. It propounds the path of devotion.

Shankar — Another name for Lord Shiva; the lord of destruction and one god of the Hindu trinity.

Shishya — Disciple.

Shiva — Lord Shiva or Maheshwara. One god of the trinity in Hindu spirituality. He is the God of Destruction.

Shloka — A short Sanskrit verse or stanza.

Siddha — A perfected, realized or enlightened being. One who possesses siddhis.

Sita — Consort of Lord Rama.

Sutlej — A river that flows through Punjab and other Northwestern states of India and Pakistan.

Swami Gangadhar Tirth Maharaj — Founder of the Shaktipat system of Yoga, he lived in Puri, a town in eastern India.

Swami Narayan Tirth Dev Maharaj — The only disciple of Swami Gangadhar Tirth Maharaj, the founder of Shivom Tirth's spiritual lineage, who was given the power to initiate other disciples and spread Shaktipat.

Swami Ramtirth — A great saint from Northern India.

Swami Shankar Purushottam Tirth Maharaj — Purushottam Tirth Maharaj was the Sanyas Guru of Swami Vishnu Tirth Maharaj, and a disciple of Swami Narayan Dev Tirth Maharaj.

Swami Vishnu Tirth Maharaj — A preceptor in the Shaktipat order, he was initiated into Shaktipat by Swami Yoganandji Maharaj and was the Guru of the author.

Swami Yoganand Maharaj — He was the Shaktipat Guru of Swami Vishnu Tirth Maharaj and a disciple of Swami Narayan Dev Tirth Maharaj.

Tamas (Tamo Guna) — Guna of rest, passivity, inertia.

Tantra — Tantra, or more properly Tantrika, is a diverse and rich spiritual tradition of the Indian subcontinent. A system of spiritual beliefs and practices said to be derived from Sanskrit roots signifying: "body" because of its emphasis on bodily activities; "stretch" because it extends the faculties of humans; "rope" because it secures the devotee to the deity; "harp" for the music and beauty of its philosophy; "interiorness" for the secrecy of its doctrine; "loom" suggesting the two cosmic principles, male and female, that make up the warp and woof of the woven fabric of the universe.

Titiksha — Tolerance. Adi Shankaracharya stressed heavily tolerance and forbearance.

Tratak — Concentration techniques discussed in the tantrik texts.

Tukaram — (1608-1649) Great seventeenth century saint from Maharashtra. Spread the bhakti movement in India. Tukaram was a Vaishnava bhakta, a true man of God.

Ujjain — A historic capital of central India in Madhya Pradesh. A venerated pilgrimage center enshrining Mahakaleshwara, one of the Jyotirlinga manifestations of Shiva.

Urdu — Official language of Pakistan and also the local language that is prevalent in the towns along the India-Pakistan border. It was developed in

Punjab. Its writing style has been adopted from Persian and Arabic where as there are a lot of words from Hindi. Some scholars say it originated from Sanskrit.

Uttarkhand — The north Indian towns of Nainital, Almora, Pauri, Tehri and Dehradun make up this land of Uttarkhand. It is full of temples.

Vedanta — The word Vedanta is normally read as a combination of two words: *veda* and *anta*, end. The Upanishads are sometimes called Vedanta since they are seen as the end and the fulfillment of the Veda. The Vedanta viewpoint is a family of philosophical schools which take up the issues discussed in the Upanishads: the nature of the self, the relation of the Ultimate Self to Ultimate Reality, Atman to Bramhan, the status of the world given inexperience, the relation of the world we experience to Bramhan.

Vishwamitra — A great Hindu sage and scholar who is referred to as the Bramharshi; Incidentally, he was born a king and, due to penances, he acquired the status of a Bramharshi.

Vrindavan — A town in Northern India that is another major place of pilgrimage. It was the sacred abode of Lord Krishna.

Yoga Darshan — Written by Patanjali, this is the basic treatise of the philosophy of Yoga. Considered the most authoritative text on the school of Yoga.

Index

1933, initiation in Rishikesh 38
1959, came to Narayan Kuti, Dewas 11
1960, first book 13
1961, initiated into Bramhacharya 11
1965, Sanyas Diksha 13
1969, Maharajshri's union with the divine 13
abhinivesh 227
accumulated impressions. *See* samskaras
action
    essence of 91
advaita 54, 94, 203
afflictions, five 61
ahimsa 200, 201
akarma 63
anvopaaya 40, 41
asamprajnat 70, 169, 208, 209
ashram 24, 26, 27, 28, 29, 31, 38, 39, 69, 92, 94, 95, 97, 102, 103, 105, 106, 107, 109, 110, 111, 112, 113, 115, 117, 120, 123, 125, 126, 128, 129, 130, 131, 132, 136, 139, 145, 146, 149, 150, 152, 170, 171, 175, 177, 180, 181, 183, 190, 191, 199, 205, 206, 216, 221, 222, 223, 224, 226, 230
    burden on the 95
    concerns of 176
    leaving the 135
    my first lesson in the 25
    relationship with the 176
    residents of, ashramites 24
    returned to the 29, 142
    to run an 36
    visitors to the 31
asmita 71
astrologers 62
atheists 58
attachment 139, 140, 157, 240
attachments 106, 113, 114, 121, 145, 157
    destroying our 15
    freedom from 11
    root cause of 14
    sacrificing our 14
attachments and aversions 28, 57, 71, 72, 97, 113, 132, 218
    conduct involving 120
    invariably arise 27
    rise above 115
    swamp of 27
austerities 16
aversions 106, 114, 163
awakened state 15, 16
awakening
    of Shakti 51, 194, 231
Bhairav 65
bhajans 26, 137, 138, 221, 224, 231
Bhishma 101
Bible 18

Bramha
    light on 235
    power of 233
    Prajnana 233
bramhachari 111, 117, 139, 146, 157, 219
    from Garwhal 26, 31, 32
Bramhacharya
    initiation in January 1961 11
breath control. *See* See pranayaam
chaitanya 15, 169
    direct knowledge of 170
    level of 236
    plane of the 44
    rope of 19
    the mind and the senses 15
chetan 169, 208, 243
chetana 233, 234, 235
    state of 235
chitta 45, 92
    activity of 70
    basis of 45
    images in the 56
    is impure 94
    of the saints 37
    purification of 63, 214
    state of 49, 72
conscious-self. *See also* chaitanya 15, 17, 41, 45, 72, 204
    activity of 45
    agitations of the 52
    separateness 16
    state of 21, 71
consciousness 93, 169, 208, 233, 239, 241
cosmos
    infinite 22
dakshina 32

defects, root cause of 45
delusion
    principle of 94
desire-patterns 13
desires
    ocean of 35
    surrendering to 46
desires and defects 14, 131
detachment 36, 58, 62, 91, 114, 157, 158, 202, 204, 209, 215, 230, 231
    development of 241
    feeling of 241
    lack of 230
    love and 231
    rise of 241
    supreme 209
        study of 209
    to acquire 58
    to establish 243
Devatma Shakti 56
devotion
    path of 57
Dewas 26, 28, 146, 177, 178, 179, 183, 211, 233
    Before coming to 46, 95
    coming to 31, 47, 132
    in Madhya Pradesh 24
    September 1959 11
    state of 31
dharma 103, 117, 118, 151, 156, 157, 213
    and Shaktipat 157
    essence of 157
    followers of 211
    Sevak 117
    what is 156
Dhritrashtra 101

disciple
   disrespectful behavior 30
   surrender 30
dissolution 93
   of knowledge 52
   of the ego 16
   state of 53
divine power 24, 36, 43, 173, 178, 201
dormant power, to awaken the 37
Draupadi 102
duality. *See* dvaita
Duryodhana 101
dvaita 94
effort
   conscious 40, 44, 49
ego
   and attachments 14
   and Sadhana 42
   destructon of our 40
   dissolution of the 16
expectations 91, 221
   different kinds of 14
experience 20, 51, 52, 97, 109, 193, 234
   direct 37, 48, 53
      spiritual 35
   reflection of your emotion 21
experiential knowledge
   direct 17
   of the consciousness 17
false pride 15, 87, 147
fate 17, 34, 177
Gandhi, Mahatma 212
Gangadhar Tirth Maharaj 13, 35, 96
   a great soul 36
   an absolute renunciate 36
   divine grace of 35
Garwhal, bramhachari from 31

Gaziabad, Maharajshri in 28
Gita 124, 138, 155, 188, 213, 236, 246
   and karma 156
   commentary on 18
   indian spirituality 123
   second chapter of 212
   sermon of 140
   shlokas of the 168
God, craftiness with 149
Goddess Amba 11
Guru 21, 22, 25, 69, 87, 88, 95, 96, 97, 102, 103, 105, 106, 114, 115, 119, 121, 122, 132, 135, 139, 150, 159, 162, 177, 216, 222, 223, 238, 239, 246, 248
   and God 239
   blesses the disciple 36
   blessings of 34, 44, 120
   by the grace of 160
   command of the 100
   desire to become a 88
   forms, external and internal 34
   grace of the 22, 97, 101, 194, 241, 242
   in previous births 56
   incarnate of Shankar 20
   losing some power 36
   need of 55
   praises of the 34
   psychic power of 37
   seek refuge with the 109
   service of the 120
   shelter of 72
   talk ill about 162
   task of 38, 91
   torture by the 159
   true nature of 34
Guru Purnima 126, 128, 152

Guru-Shakti 37, 73, 121
Guru-Shishya
    delicate but beneficial 30
    relationship 30, 90
Guru-tattva 105, 242
    On manifestation 22
Hanumandasji 181
happiness and sorrow, cause of 13
Harishchandra
    emperor 58
Himachal Pradesh 33, 95, 96, 135
    Bilaspur, district of 64
    jungle in 26
    living in 31
    Mandi district of 24
    people of 25
ignorance 14
impurities 100, 105, 106, 118, 215
    sparks of 34
inert 208, 236, 237, 241
    division of inert and conscious 21
initiation 12, 27, 31, 44, 69, 88, 95, 130, 131, 139, 152, 153, 161, 162, 193, 239
    about my 25
    Bramhacharya 233
    give 36
    immediately after my 132
    in Rishikesh 38
    inquisitiveness for 163
    tomorrow is the 32
japa 156, 157, 193, 194, 195, 205, 245
jnanis 48
Kabir 56
karma 61, 91, 93, 94, 156, 160, 173, 190, 203, 206, 207, 217, 220, 231
    a delusion 93
    cycle of 61

evil 92
fruit of his 165
mystery of 92
performing 63
ripened 62
rules of 94
knowledge
    academic 202
    elemental 17
    experiential, direct 17
    seekers of 47
kriyas 18, 33, 34, 38, 41, 49, 69, 71, 86, 87, 88, 89, 137, 152, 159, 160, 165, 172, 173, 194, 195, 207, 228, 231, 234, 240, 245, 246, 247, 248
    after Shaktipat initiation 193
    bout of madness 37
    defective, fruit of 86
    do not start 44
    ego in 71
    experiencing a unique bliss 33
    inner 215
    intense 19, 38, 39, 193
    intensity of 33, 193
    job of 172
    joy in 27
    meaning of 173
        crying and laughing 159
    medium of 43, 165, 204
    natural 105, 195
    nature of 41
    not progressing 18
    of devotion 50
    of kriya-Shakti 173
    of the Shakti 173
    rapid 33
    role of 159
    sense of observation in 166

similarity in 37
sounds of 27
state of intoxication 33
stay away from 86
to control 39
Kundalini
 and Sri Yantra 178
 awakening of 234, 236
 inert 235
liberation 45, 61, 201, 203
 cause of 222
madness
 act of 38
 and Sadhan 37
 bout of 37
 intellect is agitated in 37
Maha Vakya 233, 234
Maharajshri
 and me 12
 commentary on the Gita 18
 grace of 11
 hand-written diary 18
 morning walk 12, 29
  discourses 12
 sermons of 11
 style of thinking 15
 voice of 11
mantra
 chanting of 19
 Gayatri 193
Marathi
 official language of 31
Maya 151, 183, 185, 196, 198, 203, 243
 chasm of 221
 circle of 16
 clutches of 197
 complication of 14
 escape from 197

inticements of 184
misconception of 183
tactics and doings of 185
mind
 defective, flirtatious and desirous 46
 defects of the 45
 devil's workshop 98
 impressions 61
 inhibited state 70
 moksha 45
 plays mischief 65
 the main problem 45
 weakness of the 46
miraculous powers 16
Moksha 201, 202
monotheism. *See* advaita
Mooladhar 234, 235, 236
Nangal 24, 28, 55, 64
 babaji from 33
 I came from 24
 past memories 55
Narada Bhakti Sutras 169
Narayan Kuti 24, 178
 came to 11
 cottage 24
Swami Narayananand Saraswati 177
Narayan Tirth Dev Maharaj 35, 103
Nivritti 94, 96, 135, 136, 140, 206
 and Pravritti 136
 natural state of 135
non-duality 54
observer, sense of an 17
One-pointedness 69, 70, 71, 220
passion 20, 57
 destruction of 72
 form of 16
 waves of 34
past lives 164
penance 16

prajnana
  awakened 236
  awakened state of 237
  inert 236
  inert state of 237
  yoga 236
pranayaam 34
prarabdha 62, 63, 72, 90, 121, 136, 165, 173, 177, 195, 203, 206, 215, 231, 241
  creation 61
  of Swami Gangadhar Tirth 36
Pravritti 94, 96, 136, 140
pride 15, 25, 30, 35, 36, 51, 71, 88, 90, 97, 100, 103, 105, 106, 107, 115, 117, 118, 121, 122, 126, 132, 134, 142, 143, 144, 145, 146, 151, 172, 189, 190, 198, 202, 203, 210, 212, 218, 227, 228, 243, 247
  awakened 34
  human has 33
  lack of 72, 189
  stay away from 165
pride and false pride
  difference between 15
puja 153
  After the 32
  material for 32
Puranas 158, 188
Rama, kingdom of 212
Ramayana 17, 180
Ramtirth, Swami 33
renunciates
  different levels of 36
restlessness 16, 96, 220
Rudraashtadhyayi 123
Rudraksha, broken rosary of 28
sadhak 13, 17, 27, 34, 38

first difficulty in front of 13
  novice 25
  only true 33
  stopped the kriyas of 18
sadhaks 22, 42
  fake 33
  problem for 38
  sounds of kriyas from 27
sadhan 5, 18, 19, 37, 38, 49, 51, 61, 63, 66, 70, 72, 86, 87, 88, 90, 91, 95, 97, 100, 104, 105, 122, 123, 135, 137, 138, 142, 151, 153, 155, 156, 159, 160, 166, 172, 174, 175, 176, 178, 179, 186, 187, 189, 194, 195, 197, 199, 202, 205, 206, 207, 208, 210, 214, 215, 216, 219, 222, 224, 227, 228, 231, 232, 234, 235, 236, 238, 239, 240, 241, 242, 243, 244, 245, 246, 247, 248
  an intoxication 40
  and japa 193
  basis of 234
  beneficial for my 39
  continuous 67
  cycle of 61
  destroys ego 42
  difference between Sadhana and 40
  different kind of 48
  doctrine of 20
  Householders, aspirants 205
  in Shaktipat 40
  instruments for 43
  internal 43
  intricacies in 55
  introduction to 235
  and kriyas 37
  misconceptions about 41

path of 240
philosophy of 233
problems in 38
purpose of 69
requirements 43
role of 15
self-realization 50
sense of an observer 41
Shaktopaaya 41
shame in 159
social conduct 90
state of 190
turning point in 16
ultimate goal of 21
Sadhan Diary 18
sadhana 21, 33, 69, 102, 106, 122, 137, 155, 158, 185, 187, 194, 197, 198, 200, 205, 209
advancement of 203
becomes sadhan 40, 51
ego 42
outcome of effort 41
pride 42
study of mind control 40
sadhana and sadhan
difference between 43, 49
salvation 23
samadhi 66, 70, 208, 209
asamprajnat 70
samprajnat 169, 208
samskaras 13, 20, 46, 72, 86, 128, 130, 164, 168, 172, 173, 182, 186, 231, 247
desires 14
destruction of 17, 172
mind filled with 228
of the internal world 14
reservoir of 16
sanchit 41, 62, 173

Sanatana Dharma Association 33
sanyas 13, 36, 69, 224
meaning of 224
social death 225
sanyasi 146, 205
satchitanand 157
satsang
time for 139
Sattva guna 148
sattvic 36, 246
scriptures 20, 52, 53, 58, 93, 138, 139, 146, 157
According to the 20
on the basis of 17
praises of the Guru 34
study of 41
the knowledge of 18
Self-inspection 241
Self-Knowledge 61
self-realization
siddhi of 210
selfishness 21, 35, 97, 105, 107, 136, 146, 191, 211, 212, 213, 221, 226
sense of an observer 15, 158
sense of doership 15
sense organs 51, 169, 201, 203, 233, 234, 235, 236
control of the 164, 202
work through the 16
worldly pleasures 16
sevak 103, 107, 108, 117, 119, 120, 121
a good 222
mental state of 146
Shakti 22, 36, 41, 53, 71, 86, 88, 165, 171, 173, 231, 242, 245, 246, 247, 248
a benefactor 87
active 165

activity of the 13, 194, 195
after the awakeing of 50
agitation in 52
awakened 87, 148
   surrender to 239
awakening of 13, 18, 34, 47, 49, 50, 51, 63, 71, 194, 204
   after 59
   inner 35
before the awakening of 41
Chaitanya- 234
charged with 19
Chit- 234
Chitta- 234
free from agitation 52
Goddess 178
introverted 33
Kriya- 172, 173
kriyas of 160, 173, 215, 241
   lack of control 87
Kundalini- 234
not awakened 34
play of 240
Shaktipat 13, 18, 35, 139, 158, 179, 193, 195, 230
   and dharma 157
   aspirants of 172
   conducted by a Guru 37
   and Guru Purnima 153
   initiated in 215
   initiation 40, 44
   need of 231
   preceptor of 231
   science of 31
   This is 37
   This is not 37
Shaktopaaya 41
Shankar 19, 20, 126, 129, 176, 224

Shankar Purushottam Tirth Maharaj 103
Shankaracharya 109, 164, 202
   Vivek Chudamani 164
Shiva 19, 24, 123, 176
Shiva Sutras 189
Siddha Purush 210
siddhis 208, 209, 210, 211
spirituality 14, 43, 62, 123, 149, 151, 210, 220, 241
   abstruse aspects of 154
   advanced state of 70
   biggest problem in 61
   branch of 58
   essence of 230
   field of 25
   goal of 61
   help in 178
   obstacle in 206
   reality of 242
   social conduct and close relationship with 135
   state of 57
   interest in 211
   life full of 36
   path of 46, 62, 186, 245
      difficulties on the 13
   practice of 162
   pure 210
   turns away from 90
Sri Yantra 178
Sufism 47
Supreme Being 202
   can see the 20
   qualities of the 157
Supreme Lord 20, 21
supreme self 20
Suthra, cult of 137

Sutlej, River 25, 27, 33, 55, 135
Tantra
   Saundaryalahiri 189
   tratak yogi 41
tantriks 62, 158
tattva
   atma- 165
   Guru- 242
tattvas
   basis of 228
   infinitesimal 228
temple 27, 43, 139, 151, 159, 175, 178, 183, 199, 219
   evening prayer 29
   Hanuman 149
   of Mahakaleshwar, Ujjain 19
   of Shiva 24
   priest of a 143
titiksha. *See* tolerance
tolerance 59, 72, 145, 148, 164, 165, 166, 241
universe, creation and dissolution 53
untouchability 181
Uttarkhand, trip to 205
Veda, Rig 233
Vedanta 46, 62, 202, 203, 234, 235, 236
   doctrines of 54
   philosophy 235
Vishwamitra, Maharshi 58
world
   external 13
      knowledge of 43
   Giving up this 14
   gross 45
   internal 13
Yoga
   Jnana 58
   Karma 91
Yoga Darshan 70, 139, 208, 210
Yoganandji Maharaj 177
Yogi
   Bhakta 41
   Dhyana 41
   Jnana 41
   Hatha 41
   tratak 41
Yuga
   Kali 151, 196
   Krita 151
   Satya 151

About the Author

Swami Shivom Tirth was born in 1924, in a village in Punjab, with the name Om Prakash. He pursued university studies in Lahore, but was compelled by the partition of India to return to Punjab with his family. There, as a householder, he aspired to an ideal way of life, devoted to the pursuit of higher objectives. After coming to know about the spiritual attainments of Swami Vishnu Tirthji Maharaj, he sought permission to join him. He bid farewell to his family and was initiated in 1959.

Swami Vishnu Tirthji arranged for his disciple to be in the company of many distinguished spiritual personalities and to visit important religious centers. After receiving initiation into the order of renunciation (Sanyas), which he took in 1965, he was given the name of Swami Shivom Tirth. Swami Vishnu Tirthji afterwards authorized Swami Shivom Tirth to succeed him and propagate the system of Shaktipat for the welfare of all people. Since then, Swami Shivom Tirth has traveled to many countries of the world, including the United States. His works published in English are: *A Guide to Shaktipat; Rays of Ancient Wisdom; Sadhan Path, A Guide to Meditation; Shivom Vani, The Songs of Shivom*; and the three-volume *Churning of the Heart.*

For more information about Swami Shivom Tirth and Shaktipat, readers are invited to contact:

Sadhana Books
P. O. Box 9877
Berkeley, California 94709

Or email: sstirth@hotmail.com